D1571176

One Holy
—and—
Happy Society

One Holy
—and—
Happy Society

The Public Theology of Jonathan Edwards

Gerald R. McDermott

The Pennsylvania State University Press
University Park, Pennsylvania

Library of Congress Cataloging-in-Publication Data

McDermott, Gerald R.
   One holy and happy society : the public theology of Jonathan
Edwards / Gerald Robert McDermott.
        p.   cm.

   Includes bibliographical references and index.
   ISBN 0-271-00850-4 (alk. paper)
   1. Edwards, Jonathan,—1703–1758. 2. Civil religion—United
States—History—18th century. I. Title.
BX7260.E3M33   1992
261.8'092—dc20   91-42492
                                                                              CIP

It is the policy of The Pennsylvania State University Press to use
acid-free paper for the first printing of all clothbound books.
Publications on uncoated stock satisfy the minimum requirements of
American National Standard for Information Sciences—Permanence of
Paper for Printed Library Materials, ANSI Z39.48–1984.

Contents

To Jack McSherry, S.J.,
who gave me a love for writing

Preface

This book began with my interest in the two things one is not supposed to discuss in public: religion and politics. During the course of my graduate studies in American religious history, I became intrigued by the phenomenon of civil religion—that species of thinking that baptizes the political community in the waters of religious approbation. How did it start in American history? I wondered. My questioning led me to the antebellum period, when civil religion was in full bloom. But the more I rummaged around in texts from that period, the more evident it became that a towering figure stood behind much of the religion of that period. I quickly discovered that this same figure, whose mantle so many in the antebellum period claimed to inherit, was blamed by some historians for catalyzing American civil religion. I soon became convinced that I could understand neither American civil religion nor the wider religious scene in early America without coming to terms with this American icon, Jonathan Edwards.

So to Edwards I went. And I have been there ever since. For, as

William Morris put it, "genius must always fascinate; that is its character."[1] Not only did I become increasingly absorbed by the genius of this early American thinker, but I discovered that no book-length study of his socio-political theory had ever been published.

As I settled down for a systematic study of his thinking on the civil community, I began to conclude that this was not the same man described by a host of scholarly interpreters. Most of them had sketched the portrait of an ivory-tower recluse who was happy to let the world go to hell (in both senses). But I found a theologian who was also a concerned citizen, deeply interested in the social and political currents swirling about him, and brimming with ideas about Christian citizens and civil community. In fact, his thinking on these matters was at least as fully developed as that of his better-known contemporaries, and more progressive in its attitude toward citizen rights.

I was also surprised to discover that Edwards was not the provincial chauvinist he has been made out to be. Rather than teaching that the millennium would begin in America, and imminently, for example, he spoke of the coming of the Kingdom of God in international terms, and pushed back its inauguration until after the beginning of the twenty-first century. America for Edwards usually deserved condemnation, not celebration. The further he progressed in his career, the more distance he put between his country and the Kingdom of God.

The upshot of all these discoveries was my realization that the sum total of this Massachusetts theologian's deliberations on American and civil polity constitute an integrated and intriguing public theology. Thus the book.

Insofar as this book has any merit, it is the work of many. I am very aware that I stand upon the shoulders of many other scholars, and have tried to credit them in the footnotes. But some deserve special mention. Harry Stout, for instance, went out of his way to introduce me to Edwards's thinking on the national covenant, even loaning me his notes on the subject. When I came up with an interpretation that challenged his, Harry displayed his magnanimity by affirming it and encouraging its

---

1. William Sparkes Morris, *The Young Jonathan Edwards: A Reconstruction* (Brooklyn, N.Y.: Carlson, 1991), 2.

development. Both he and Mark Noll provided important critical feedback at a late stage in this project to save me from much embarrassment. Through his critique of an early version of the first chapter, Michael McGiffert showed me how to reinterpret the significance of Edwards's national covenant. Sydney James helped make this book more accessible to scholars outside religion, but I am sure he will wish I had gone further with his suggestions. William Schweiker gave encouragement and direction at times when I felt particular need of them. James Spalding's comments and letter from Istanbul were much appreciated. James Kennedy showed me the "Dutch connection." Tom Johnson, Al Pieratt, Art Thomas, John and Jenny Wiers, Joan Childress, Ken Kuntz, Cary Covington, Michael Heller, and James Smylie helped sharpen the prose and argument of several chapters.

But my greatest debt as a scholar is to T. Dwight Bozeman, my dissertation adviser at the University of Iowa. By his example Dwight taught me what it means to do historiography, though I cannot claim to have reached the standard he set. I learned from him the importance of a thorough ransacking of the sources, a healthy skepticism for "traditional" interpretations, and careful interpretation. I will always admire, but never be able to approach, his elegance of style. His warmth, congeniality, and personal support were indispensable to the completion of this project.

This book could never have been written without the support of the institutions where I have studied and taught. I am grateful to the University of Iowa for an Ada-Louise Ballard Dissertation Year Fellowship, the National Endowment for the Humanities for a Summer Stipend, and Roanoke College for a Faculty Starter Grant. The librarians at the University of Iowa Main Library, Yale's Beinecke Rare Book and Manuscript Library, Roanoke College Library (Pat Scott has chased down scores of books for me with unflagging cheerfulness), Boston's Congregational Library, and the Franklin Trask Library at the Andover-Newton Theological School were always helpful and cordial. Don and Joanie Westblade provided me with accommodations and introductions on my first visit to New Haven, the mecca for Edwards scholars. Ken and Lori Minkema have also housed and hosted me, and Ken has been a continuing encouragement and help in this work. Tom Schafer was always prompt and forthcoming when I asked him to draw from his encyclopedic knowledge of Edwardseana. Alex Ferrate lent his interest and time to help me update several chapters. I wish also to express appreciation to *American Presbyterians: Journal of Presbyterian History*, which published an adaptation of Chapter 1 in volume 69:1 (Spring 1991). Used by permission.

Finally, words of thanks are due to several communities of friends. Robert Benne and my other colleagues at Roanoke College have been unfailingly supportive of my efforts to get this manuscript finished. Salem Evangelical Free Church in Fargo, North Dakota, and Parker's Grove Church, in Shellsburg, Iowa, helped me keep the McDermott body and soul together while I researched and wrote the first draft of this book. But Jean, Ryan, Ross, and Sean Edwards are owed the greatest debt of gratitude for their patience while husband and Daddy was obsessed with Jonathan Edwards.

List of Abbreviations

AW   *Apocalyptic Writings,* ed. Stephen J. Stein, vol. 5 of *The Works of Jonathan Edwards.*

CF   *Charity and Its Fruits,* by Jonathan Edwards, in *Ethical Writings,* ed. Paul Ramsey, vol. 8 of *The Works of Jonathan Edwards.*

DM   *The Distinguishing Marks,* by Jonathan Edwards, in *The Great Awakening,* ed. C. C. Goen, vol. 4 of *The Works of Jonathan Edwards.*

FN   *A Faithful Narrative,* by Jonathan Edwards, in *The Great Awakening,* ed. C. C. Goen, vol. 4 of *The Works of Jonathan Edwards.*

GA   *The Great Awakening,* ed. C. C. Goen, vol. 4 of *The Works of Jonathan Edwards.*

HA   *An Humble Attempt,* by Jonathan Edwards, in *Apocalyptic Writings,* ed. Stephen J. Stein, vol. 5 of *The Works of Jonathan Edwards.*

HWR   *History of the Work of Redemption*, ed. John F. Wilson, vol. 9 of
      The Works of Jonathan Edwards.

OS   *Original Sin*, ed. Clyde A. Holbrook, vol. 3 of *The Works of
      Jonathan Edwards.*

"PN" "Personal Narrative," in *Jonathan Edwards: Representative Selec-
      tions*, ed. Clarence H. Faust and Thomas H. Johnson.

RA   *Religious Affections*, ed. John E. Smith, vol. 2 of *The Works of
      Jonathan Edwards.*

ST   *Some Thoughts Concerning the Revival*, by Jonathan Edwards, in
      The Great Awakening, ed. C. C. Goen, vol. 4 of *The Works of
      Jonathan Edwards.*

TV   *The Nature of True Virtue*, by Jonathan Edwards, in *Ethical Writ-
      ings*, ed. Paul Ramsey, vol. 8 of *The Works of Jonathan Edwards.*

Introduction

Since at least the medieval period, Western history has been full of claims that particular peoples were specially chosen by God. In the fourteenth century, French lawyer Pierre Dubois argued that Christ had elected the French king, who was successor to Moses and David, to a higher place of honor than any other ruler in Christendom because the Christian faith, as the pope himself had asserted, had a more reliable base in France than anywhere else.[1] In his (1598) book on the Spanish monarchy, Tommaso Campanella called the king of Spain the Catholic king of

---

1. Percy E. Schramm, *Der König von Frankreich* (1939; 2d ed., Darmstadt, 1960), cited in Wolfhart Pannenberg, *Human Nature, Election, and History* (Philadelphia, 1977), 75.

Though not a Western people in origin or national organization, the Jewish people's sense of divine calling has been singularly vivid and uniquely influential in the history of Western development of the concept. See Bernard J. Bamberger, *The Story of Judaism* (New York, 1957), 290–93, and passim, and Ernest Lee Tuveson, *Redeemer Nation: The Idea of America's Millennial Role* (Chicago, 1968), vii, 1–25.

the world, commissioned to unify all humanity under the pope.[2] After
the fall of Byzantium in 1453, Russia adopted Constantinople's heritage
and styled Moscow the Third Rome, the center for the completion of
history. In his *Acts and Monuments,* England's John Foxe told his
sixteenth-century countrymen that England had a special role in God's
providence because Constantine was an Englishman, Henry VIII the first
to renounce the pope, and the English the first people to embrace the
gospel and establish it throughout the world.[3]

More recent examples of this sense of national chosenness are South
Africa and Poland. Because the Boers succeeded against overwhelming
odds in their trek from the Cape Colony into what became the Transvaal
and the Orange Free State (1836–40), they were convinced that God
had specially elected their new nation.[4] At the end of the twentieth
century many Poles believe that their land holds "a kind of heavenly
nuptial covenant" with the Virgin Mary. This belief goes back to Polish
victory over the invading Swedes in 1655, which they credit to the
miraculous intercession of the Virgin of Czestochowa.[5]

Belief in a national God-given destiny is alive and well in contemporary America. Ronald Reagan often referred to America as a "city upon a
hill," recalling the biblical passage that refers to the city on a hill as "the
light of the world." In his address to the 1988 Republican National
Convention, Reagan proclaimed: "I believe that God put this land between the two great oceans to be found by the special people . . . from
every corner of the world who had that extra love of freedom that
prompted them to leave their homeland and come to this land to make it

---

2. Hans Kohn, *Die Idee der Nationalismus: Ursprung und Geschichte bis zur französischen
Revolution* (Heidelberg, 1950), cited in Pannenberg, *Human Nature,* 75.

3. *An Abridgement of the Book of Acts and Monuments of the Church Written by that
Reverend Father, Master John Foxe, and now abridged by Timothy Bright* (London, 1589),
cited in Winthrop S. Hudson, ed., *Nationalism and Religion in America: Concepts of
American Identity and Mission* (New York, 1970), 159.

4. J. Alton Templin, *Ideology on a Frontier: The Theological Foundations of Afrikaner
Nationalism, 1652–1910* (Westport, Conn., 1984), cited in Mark Noll, *One Nation Under
God: Christian Faith and Political Action in America* (San Francisco, 1988), 190.

5. Many Poles today believe that God is using them to bring his light to the whole world.
George H. Williams, *The Mind of John Paul II* (New York, 1981), cited in Noll, *One Nation
Under God,* 191–92.

a brilliant light beam of freedom to the world." His successor George Bush told the nation that America is "the last best hope of man on earth."[6]

Scholarly interest in American religious nationalism exploded in the late 1960s and early 1970s. Disturbed by American military involvement in Southeast Asia, sociologists and historians began a search for what Robert Jewett has called the "Captain America Complex."[7] By this Jewett meant the belief that America has a mission to redeem the world from its political and/or spiritual failings. Some of these scholars uncovered what they call an American "civil religion," that is, a set of symbols, beliefs, and practices, alongside traditional religion, that in various ways relates the nation, culture, or political system to ultimate reality (in Christian parlance, "the Kingdom of God").[8] In Fourth of July ceremonies, presidential inauguration addresses, political campaign speeches, and elsewhere, scholars discovered countless references to America as a chosen nation destined to bestow her blessings on the rest of the planet.

---

6. Matthew 5:14; Ronald Reagan, last televised address to the American people, 11 January 1989, *New York Times* (12 January 1989); Reagan, speech to the Republican National Convention, 15 August 1988, *New York Times* (16 August 1988); George Bush, second debate with Michael Dukakis, 13 October 1988, *New York Times* (14 October 1988).

7. Robert Jewett, *The Captain America Complex: The Dilemma of Zealous Nationalism* (Philadelphia, 1973).

8. Definitions of civil religion vary, but mine is elastic enough to subsume most of them. For an introduction to the literature on civil religion, see Robert Bellah, "Civil Religion in America," *Daedalus* 96, no. 1 (1967): 1–21; *The Broken Covenant: American Civil Religion in Time of Trial* (New York, 1975); and "The Revolution and the Civil Religion," in *Religion and the American Revolution*, ed. Jerald Brauer (Philadelphia, 1976), 55–73; Robert Bellah and Philip Hammond, *Varieties of Civil Religion* (New York, 1975); Robert Bellah, "Public Philosophy and Public Theology in America Today," in *Civil Religion and Political Theology*, ed. Leroy S. Rouner (Notre Dame, 1986), 79–97; Catherine Albanese, *Sons of the Fathers: The Civil Religion of the American Revolution* (Philadelphia, 1976), and "Civil Religion," in *America: Religions and Religion* (Belmont, Calif., 1981), 283–308; Sidney Mead, *The Old Religion in the Brave New World: Reflections on the Relations between Christendom and the Republic* (Berkeley and Los Angeles, 1977); Elwyn Smith, ed., *The Religion of the Republic* (Philadelphia, 1971); John Wilson, *Public Religion in American Culture* (Philadelphia, 1979); and Michael W. Hughey, *Civil Religion and Moral Order: Theoretical and Historical Dimensions* (Westport, Conn., 1983).

The blessings were usually freedom, democracy, Christianity, capitalism, or simply "the American Way of Life."[9]

Historians of the phenomenon generally agree that nineteenth- and twentieth-century American civil religion is based on the American Revolutionary experience, which for many Americans functions as a "hierophany collectively manifested and received."[10] The Declaration of Independence and the Constitution hold the status of sacred scriptures, George Washington becomes (often explicitly) the American Messiah, and divine intervention on behalf of the New (American) Israel is found in the Continental army's remarkable victories over the British.[11]

Many students of American culture have sought the genesis of this American Revolutionary civil religion. Some trace it back to the Puritan Fathers.[12] Others contend that although the seventeenth-century Puritans gathered the conceptual materials for such an interpretation of America, Jonathan Edwards (1703–58) laid the foundation. For Edwards, America's greatest theologian before the Revolution, was a prominent leader of the revival (the "Great Awakening") that united thirteen previously disparate colonies,[13] and at one point Edwards associated that

---

9. The last phrase comes from Will Herberg, who wrote a seminal study of civil religion in post–World War II America: *Protestant, Catholic, Jew: An Essay in American Religious Sociology* (Garden City, N.Y., 1955). For varying interpretations of these references to America's transcendent meaning found in the political arena, see Bellah, "Civil Religion in America," and Wilson, *Public Religion in American Culture.*

10. Albanese, *Sons of the Fathers,* 6. For a sampling of the scholarly consensus that the mythical drama of the Revolution was "the fundamental basis for American civil religion as we know it" (Albanese), see Sidney Mead, "Christendom, Enlightenment, and the Revolution," in *Religion and the American Revolution,* ed. Brauer, 30–52; Martin Marty, preface to Albanese, *Sons of the Fathers,* ix; Bellah, *Broken Covenant,* 1–35, and "Civil Religion in America," 9; Albanese, *Sons of the Fathers,* 6; Mark Noll, *Christians in the American Revolution* (Washington, D.C., 1977), 168; and Nathan Hatch, *The Sacred Cause of Liberty: Republican Thought and the Millennium in Revolutionary New England* (New Haven, 1977), 92–96.

11. Albanese, *Sons of the Fathers,* 6, 9, 143–81, 182–220.

12. See, for example, Sacvan Bercovitch, *The American Jeremiad* (Cambridge, Mass., 1978), and Harry S. Stout, *The New England Soul: Preaching and Religious Culture in Colonial New England* (New York, 1986). Bercovitch also sees Edwards as a progenitor of American nationalism.

13. Jerald Brauer, "Puritanism, Revivalism, and the Revolution," in *Religion and the American Revolution,* ed. Brauer, 18–27. See also Edmund Morgan, "The Puritan Ethic

revival with God's plan to begin a final, golden age (the "millennium") in America.

I intend here to assess Edwards's view of America by examining what I call his "public theology," that is, his understanding of civil community and the Christian's responsibility to it. It is beyond the scope of this work to assess the relation of Edwards's public theology to later versions of American civil religion. But it will become clear from the following chapters that his social and political views could not have directly fathered the Revolutionary civil religion just described.

Several earlier studies of Edwards's social and political views have used his published works, few of which were directed to civil or political concerns, to portray the Massachusetts theologian as a tribalist provincial and optimistic nationalist. But Edwards's unpublished "occasional" sermons, given on fast, election, or thanksgiving days for the purpose of commenting on social and political matters, reveal a public theology quite different from the sort usually attributed to him.[14] When the published works are read in conjunction with the unpublished corpus, it becomes apparent that no straight line can be drawn from the Edwardsean public theology to the self-congratulation of the Revolutionary period.[15] Edwards emerges as the prophet not of America's manifest

---

and the American Revolution," *William and Mary Quarterly,* 3d ser., 24 (1967): 3–43. To say that the revival lent a degree of unity to the American colonies is not to pronounce on the vexed question of the relation between religion and the causes of the Revolution. For an introduction to that debate, see the opposing interpretations of Alan Heimert, in his *Religion and the American Mind: From the Great Awakening to the Revolution* (Cambridge, Mass., 1966), and Bernard Bailyn, in his "Religion and Revolution: Three Biographical Studies," *Perspectives in American History* 4 (1970): 11–24. See also Bailyn, *The Ideological Origins of the American Revolution* (Cambridge, Mass., 1967).

14. Harry S. Stout was the first to point out the importance of these occasional sermons. See Stout, "The Puritans and Edwards," in *Jonathan Edwards and the American Experience,* ed. Nathan Hatch and Harry S. Stout (New York, 1988), 142–59.

15. See Gerald R. McDermott, "Civil Religion in the American Revolutionary Period: An Historiographic Analysis," *Christian Scholar's Review* 18, no. 4 (June 1989): 346–62. Several scholars have recently argued that a significant minority of colonials were not "self-congratulatory." Mark Noll has pointed out that pacifists, loyalists, Edwardsean reformist ministers (the New Divinity), and blacks dissented from the prevailing civil religion. So "self-congratulation" describes a limited number of persons in the period. Noll, "The Image of the United States as a Biblical Nation, 1776–1865," in *The Bible in America: Essays in*

destiny but of the traditional New England jeremiad. Forever castigating
his people for their moral failures, he never congratulated them for moral
progress. He believed that God had shown special favor to New England;
yet he complained tirelessly that the colony had abused her privileges and
should expect nothing but annihilation. In fact, he thundered, it was a
wonder that his people had not been exterminated already. New England
a redeemer nation? Only by default. Its failure might cause God to
transfer his favors to another people.

Edwards's millennial doctrine poses comparable problems for recent
interpretations of his attitude toward America. Edwards prophesied that
the millennium would be global; hence every form of tribalist nationalism
was inherently misconceived. He did not forecast an American millennium, as commonly held, but only that the two and a half centuries that
would eventually bring on the millennium would begin in America. Even
that prediction was cast in ironic terms: the great age of the Spirit would
begin in America because God likes to begin his works in the "meanest"
and "weakest" of places.

Others have argued that Edwards's theories of citizenship and magistracy are characteristic of "medieval feudalism." I shall show that these
scholars, too, are incorrect. Edwards's political theory was similar to New
England "Country" ideology; he mistrusted the magistrate's use of power
and took care to guard religious and civil liberties. Yet Edwards went
beyond Country thought by adding a religious urgency to its political
appeals. In addition, he ennobled the Christian citizen and relegated
politics to a second-order concern, which combined to undermine the
deferential hierarchicalism so prevalent in his day. In this regard he was
more progressive than Boston's leading "liberal" ministers.

A word is needed to explain my use of the term "public theology" for
Edwards's conception of the civil community and the Christian's relation

---

Cultural History, ed. Mark Noll and Nathan Hatch (New York, 1982), 48–51; and Noll,
Christians in the American Revolution, 103–22. Melvin B. Endy, Jr., argues that most
sermons in the period did not relate the Revolution to a coming millennium but conceived
of the war as essentially political rather than religious. Yet he concedes that "the clergy
believed that the struggle of liberty against tyranny was God's cause and that their conflict
was center stage in God's providential rule." Endy, "Just War, Holy War, and Millennialism
in Revolutionary America," William and Mary Quarterly, 3d ser., 42 (1985): 15.

to it. Although such a conception has often been referred to as "political theology," I avoid that term for a number of reasons. First, it is ambiguous. Sometimes it simply refers to a theological understanding of political community, and at other times it means the politicization of religion.[16] To many it is identified with the Hegelian-Marxist tradition of social thought. Second, the method used today by those called political theologians differs drastically from Edwards's. Some of these thinkers, particularly those sympathetic to liberation theology, believe that theological truth arises from a given historical situation through personal participation in class struggle.[17] Edwards, on the other hand, believed that truth is to be found in revealed scripture and then applied to historical situations. Finally, the term "political theology" is sometimes associated with projects like liberation, black and feminist theologies that have agendas narrower than Edwards's "public theology."[18]

I have chosen not to refer to Edwards's deliberations on the public square simply as his "social" or "political theory."[19] These terms obscure

---

16. There is a long tradition of Western political theology going back to the Greeks and Romans, encompassing both uses of the term. For a concise analytical survey of this tradition, see Jürgen Moltmann, "The Cross and Civil Religion," in *Religion and Political Society,* ed. Jürgen Moltmann et al. (New York, 1974), 21–41.

17. See, for example, Gustavo Gutierrez, *A Theology of Liberation: History, Politics, and Salvation* (Maryknoll, N.Y., 1973), 6–13; José Miguez Bonino, *Doing Theology in a Revolutionary Situation* (Philadelphia, 1975); James H. Cone, *God of the Oppressed* (New York, 1975); and Rosemary R. Ruether, *Liberation Theology: Human Hope Confronts Christian History and American Power* (New York, 1972).

18. Edwards was sensitive to discrimination against blacks and women, but nevertheless kept black slaves and was a patriarchalist. See Chapter 5 for more on his attitude toward blacks and women. My point, however, is that Edwards's public theology encompassed far more than just the social and political rights of certain classes. So the term "political theology," because of its programmatic connotations, is too restrictive. Even the political theologies of German theologians such as Moltmann and Metz are narrower in scope than Edwards's public theology.

Bellah has recently used the term "public theology," but without defining it. See Bellah, "Public Philosophy and Public Theology." His use of the term implies a public theology that explains the common basis for life under God in a pluralistic society. As far as I know, however, Bellah nowhere delineates the particulars in anywhere near the complexity and detail that Edwards did.

19. When I refer to Edwards's "social theory" or "political theory," I use the terms in a strict and narrow sense, that is, abstracted from his theological and other views.

the intimate link between ethics and theology in Edwards's thought. As Paul Ramsey writes, "It is a mistake to treat Edwards' moral philosophy apart from his moral theology, his theological ethics. That would be to separate the merely distinguishable."[20] For Edwards, ethical consideration depends on theological understanding. Unaided reason, he believed, can teach us our ethical duties, but only because it also teaches us that there is a God to whom we are obligated. Edwards's *Nature of True Virtue* comes closest of all his works to pure moral philosophy. Scripture is never quoted. Yet God as the "Being of beings" stands in the background of the text, which, as Ramsey points out, was written as a companion to *Concerning the End for Which God Created the World,* more than half of which is titled "What Is to Be Learned from Holy Scriptures Concerning God's Last End in the Creation of the World."[21]

For the purposes of this work, I distinguish between "civil religion" and "public theology." Both refer to understandings of society and culture within an ultimate order. "Civil religion" refers to how a *society* relates itself or its culture to ultimate reality. Public theology, on the other hand, refers to how an *individual* reflects critically on the meaning of civil community and the role of the religious community within it. My focus is on the public theology of Jonathan Edwards, not the civil religion of his society.

I have organized this book around the topics of a national covenant, the millennium, citizenship, and the magistracy, for these are the categories in which Edwards thought when he considered the relationship between God and public life. When Edwards reflected on God's relations to society, he looked first to the past, when his society's national covenant was established. For him, New England's status with God could be assessed only by reference to the original agreement forged with the Founding Fathers. When he imagined the ideal society, he looked to the future millennium. He used the contours of that future society both to judge and to challenge eighteenth-century New England. When he deliberated on political life in his own day, he considered first the nature of ethics,

---

20. Paul Ramsey, introduction to *Ethical Writings,* vol. 8 of *The Works of Jonathan Edwards* (New Haven, 1989), 33.

21. Ibid., 5, 117–19, viii.

then he looked at the two political actors most familiar to the colonial mind—the magistrate and the citizen. Although he viewed each of these through the prism of his general ethical principles, his construal of each was deeply indebted to eighteenth-century historical conditions. It is here, in his consideration of contemporary political and social life, that Edwards's application of theological ethics to social reality can be seen most clearly.

1 God's Manner with a Covenant People: The National Covenant

In July 1736, when Northampton, Massachusetts, was suffering drought, Jonathan Edwards informed the anxious farmers in his congregation that rain had not come because "God is displeased," for He had seen the "corruption in our hearts." Repentance and reformation were therefore in order. Seven years later, when worms devoured the crops, Edwards again knew why: God was judging Northampton's stinginess to its poor. "If a people would but run the venture of giving their temporal good things" to God through the poor, "it would be a sure way to . . . [have]

The chapter title is an adaptation of Edwards's language in the doctrine of his sermon on 2 Chronicles 36:15–17, 27 March 1740, Edwards Papers, Beinecke Rare Book and Manuscript Library, Yale University: "Tis not Gods manner to destroy a Covenant People for their backslidings till . . ." The phrases "Gods manner" and "a Covenant People" are very common in Edwards's fast and thanksgiving day sermons. All subsequent references to sermons are taken from the Beinecke collection of Edwards's unpublished sermons unless otherwise noted.

those Judgments Removed that would destroy them & to have a plenty of them bestowed."[1]

Edwards's claim to understand the ways of God surprised no one, for this was standard fare in New England's Reformed orthodoxy. In a tradition stretching back to the Reformation and before, God was conceived as entering into covenant with a people or nation, and blessing or punishing that people in proportion to their fidelity to the terms of the covenant. As John Winthrop had told the New England founders, the Lord would "expect a strict performance of the articles contained in" his covenant with them. "If we shall neglect the observation of these articles . . . the Lord will surely break out in wrath against us, be revenged of such a perjured people, and make us know the price of the breach of such a covenant."[2]

New England's religious leaders found the national covenant useful for interpreting the colonies' troubles. Indian attacks, crop failures, and a diversity of other natural disasters were attributed to failure to keep the national covenant with God. The eighteenth century brought little abatement of covenantal rhetoric.[3] Nearly all religious leaders

1. Sermon on Deuteronomy 28:12, July 1736; sermon on Malachi 3:10–11, July 1743, 2.

2. John Winthrop, "A Model of Christian Charity," in *The Puritans in America: A Narrative Anthology*, ed. Alan Heimert and Andrew Delbanco (Cambridge, Mass., 1985), 90–91. For other examples of use of the national covenant among the first generation, see Thomas Hooker, "The Danger of Desertion," in *Thomas Hooker: Writings in England and Holland, 1626–1633*, ed. George H. Williams et al. (Cambridge, Mass., 1975), esp. 230–32; George William Hooke, "New Englands Teares for Old Englands Feares" (London, 1641), 15, 18–19; John Norton, "Sion the Outcast Healed of Her Wounds" (Cambridge, 1664), 3–5, 11–12; John Higginson, "The Cause of God" (Cambridge, Mass., 1663), 8; and Edward Johnson, *The Wonder-Working Providence of Sion's Saviour in New England* (London, 1654; reprint, New York, 1910), 60–121, 238.

3. Until somewhat recently, scholars had assumed that the national covenant disappeared with the rise of "secularism" at the end of the seventeenth century. Perry Miller, *The New England Mind: From Colony to Province* (Cambridge, Mass., 1953), 447–63; Timothy H. Breen, *The Character of a Good Ruler: A Study of Puritan Political Ideas in New England, 1630–1730* (New Haven, 1970), 150ff., 204ff. Sacvan Bercovitch and Harry S. Stout, however, have refuted this claim. Bercovitch, *The American Jeremiad*, 93–154; Stout, *The New England Soul*, 166–79. Stout argues that scholars have focused exclusively on the sections of eighteenth-century election sermons that are addressed to royal audiences and have overlooked the "sacred portions" that use the national covenant. Stout, *The New England Soul*, 140–41.

seem to have believed that "in all Ages since their [the Jews'] national Rejection, God has had, in some Country or other, a peculiar people owning his revelation and their Covenant Engagement to him." Since New England was the latest peculiar people, its calamities were "Signs of his Displeasure." Evangelicals and liberals alike preached that God would "favor a righteous nation" and punish nations "for every act of unrighteousness."[4]

Therefore, when Jonathan Edwards interpreted agricultural crisis in terms of the national covenant, he was using a familiar paradigm. Yet until recently students of Edwards overlooked this component of his thought. Perry Miller concluded that Edwards rejected covenant theology altogether. Conrad Cherry and others demonstrated that Edwards was as Puritan in his covenant theology as in his view of human nature, but they found only the covenant of grace, not the national covenant, in his writings.[5] They found, in other words, God's unconditional commitment to give eternal life to individuals but not his conditional ministration of temporal rewards to nations on the basis of obedience to divine law. The first covenant concerns individuals, is based on faith, and pertains primarily to the life to come; the second concerns nations, is based on works, and pertains to this life only.

More recently, Sacvan Bercovitch and Harry S. Stout have demonstrated that, as Stout puts it, Edwards "was every bit the federal theologian

4. See, e.g., Solomon Stoddard, "An Appeal to the Learned" (Boston, 1709), 55; Thomas Prince, "The Salvation of God in 1746" (Boston, 1746), 8; and "The Natural and Moral Government" (Boston, 1749), 34; John Barnard, "The Throne Established by Righteousness" (Boston, 1734), in The Wall and the Garden: Selected Massachusetts Election Sermons 1670–1775, ed. A. W. Plumstead, (Minneapolis, 1978), 273, 275, 288; Joseph Sewall, "Repentance" (Boston, 1727); and Nathanael Eels, "Religion is the Life of God's People" (Boston, 1743), 38–43.

5. Perry Miller, Jonathan Edwards, 2d ed. (New York, 1959), 76, 116; Conrad Cherry, The Theology of Jonathan Edwards: A Reappraisal (Garden City, N.Y., 1966), 107–23; Heimert, Religion and the American Mind, 126; Carl W. Bogue, Jonathan Edwards and the Covenant of Grace (Cherry Hill, N.J., 1975); Harold P. Simonson, Jonathan Edwards: Theologian of the Heart (Grand Rapids, Mich., 1974), 140–52; M. Darrol Bryant, "America as God's Kingdom," in Religion and Political Society, ed. Moltmann et al., 63; Robert W. Jenson, America's Theologian: A Recommendation of Jonathan Edwards (New York, 1988), passim.

that his Puritan predecessors were."[6] Bercovitch has shown that there are traces of the national covenant in Edwards's published works, and Stout argues persuasively that the national covenant is displayed most prominently in Edwards's weekday "occasional" sermons, most of which remain in manuscript.[7] Like his Puritan predecessors, Edwards reserved most of his political and social commentary for special occasions, usually fast and thanksgiving days, held during the week rather than on Sundays. Since most of these occasional sermons have never been published, Edwards's use of the national covenant has only recently come to attention.

Edwards's use of the national covenant in occasional sermons was hardly novel. He was simply continuing the tradition of the American jeremiad, which, as Perry Miller first described it, was the homiletic employment of the national covenant to bewail a people's transgressions and threaten punishment—sometimes even revocation of the covenant itself—should reform not be forthcoming. "For the second generation" in New England it became "the dominant literary form," and by the end of the seventeenth century a "ritualistic incantation." Preachers routinely invoked the national covenant on fast, thanksgiving, and election days to remind congregations of the privileges they had been given and berate them for their ever-renewed capacity to abuse those privileges.[8]

For some time scholars have claimed to find an underlying optimism in the American Puritan jeremiad. Miller identified in seventeenth-century New England sermons a "paradoxical" blend of condemnation and en-

---

6. Stout, "The Puritans and Edwards," in *Jonathan Edwards and the American Experience*, ed. Hatch and Stout, 143.

7. Sacvan Bercovitch, "Horologicals to Chronometricals: The Rhetoric of the Jeremiad," in *Literary Monographs*, vol. 3, ed. Eric Rothstein (Madison, Wis., 1970), 82–87, and *The American Jeremiad*, 98–109. Stout's argument is in Stout, "The Puritans and Edwards." Fifty-four of these occasional sermons are housed at Beinecke Library; of these fifty-four, forty-five contain material relevant to the national covenant. Twenty-nine were delivered on fast days, and eleven on thanksgiving days; one was a quarterly lecture, one was given at a "private meeting," and four are unspecified. Of the forty-five, seven date from the 1720s, twelve from the 1730s, twenty-five from the 1740s, and three from the 1750s. On occasional sermons and their importance, see Stout, *The New England Soul*, 27–31. I am indebted to Stout for discovering the connection between Edwards's national covenant and his occasional sermons.

8. Perry Miller, *The New England Mind: From Colony to Province*, 29, and *Errand into the Wilderness* (New York, 1956), 8.

couragement. Preachers threatened divine wrath, yet "the total effect, curiously enough, is not at all depressing." Through introspection and contrition both preacher and flock were freed from guilt by a "purgation of soul." Following Miller's lead, Bercovitch suggests that the jeremiad was a calculated "strategy." Puritan jeremiahs, Bercovitch asserts, "mixed self-congratulation and self-abasement" in order to revitalize New England's "errand."[9] To tell New Englanders that God judged them for violating the covenant actually reaffirmed God's concern for them. Divine wrath could be "a sign of election" because it assured the community of its place within the covenant. Revocation of the covenant might be threatened, but the threat was only "rhetorical," for, as preachers often reassured their flocks, "God would ultimately *not* forsake his people." Such assurances "all but submerge[d] the prognostications of disaster." The result was, as Miller had sensed and Bercovitch reaffirms, an underlying tone of "unshakable optimism."[10]

Some scholars are now contesting this interpretation of the jeremiad.[11]

---

9. Miller, *Errand*, 8–9; Bercovitch, *The American Jeremiad*, xiv, and "Horologicals," 88. Bercovitch interprets the New England errand as a mission to redeem the world.

10. Bercovitch, "Horologicals," 34; *The American Jeremiad*, 89–90; "Horologicals," 29, 6, 6. Stout and James Holstun observe a similar optimism in the Puritan jeremiad; Stout, *The New England Soul*, 217; James Holstun, *A Rational Millennium: Puritan Utopias of Seventeeth-Century England and America* (New York, 1987), 256. There is evidence for this claim of "deep stubborn optimism." Bercovitch, "Horologicals," 29. Urian Oakes is fairly typical: "If it should come to pass that New England should yet be more sinful & more miserable than now it is . . . yet there is Scripture ground to hope, that after God had vindicated his Holiness by sore punishment on us, God would again restore reform and bless New England." Oakes, "New England Pleaded With" (Cambridge, Mass., 1673), 15, 63. See also Johnson, *Wonder-Working Providence*, 60–61, 238; Increase Mather, "The Day of Trouble is Near" (Cambridge, Mass., 1674), 27–28, and "A Discourse Concerning the Danger of Apostacy" (Boston, 1685), 77–78; Samuel Willard, "Israel's True Safety" (Boston, 1704), 32; Cotton Mather, *Magnalia Christi Americana, Books I and II*, ed. Kenneth B. Murdock (Cambridge, Mass., 1977), 93; and Thomas Prince, "The People of New-England," in *The Wall and the Garden*, ed. Plumstead, 208. The apotheosis of such optimism is Jonathan Mayhew, "An Election Sermon," also in *The Wall and the Garden*, ed. Plumstead, 302.

11. T. Dwight Bozeman, for instance, argues that seventeenth-century jeremiahs were not convinced of the inevitability of an American future that would reform the world. See Bozeman, *To Live Ancient Lives: The Primitivist Dimension in Puritanism* (Chapel Hill, N.C., 1988), 333–35. Andrew Delbanco makes a similar case in *The Puritan Ordeal* (Cambridge, Mass., 1989).

This debate on the character of early New England jeremiads is beyond the scope of this study, but the optimistic interpretation is important to note for its application to Edwards. Some of these same scholars who insist that the jeremiad, despite its apparent pessimism, was consistently used to affirm New England as specially favored by God, claim that Edwards shared his predecessors' confidence that New England would undoubtedly succeed and might by its positive example even help redeem the rest of the world.

Bercovitch, for example, maintains that Edwards perpetuated the "exultation" and "celebration " of his Puritan predecessors and shared with them a hearty confidence that New England's covenant would eventually prosper.[12] Stout asserts that Edwards's national covenant contained the seeds of American messianism. The Northampton pastor was "dazzled" by "the vision of a redeemer nation," and subscribed to the "quintessentially Puritan notion of a *righteous* city set high upon a hill for all the world to see."[13] This interpretation tends to support the thesis of C. C. Goen and others that Edwards developed a tribalist public theology.[14] His occasional sermons would thus suggest that the parochial nationalism hinted at in *Some Thoughts Concerning the Revival* (1742) was not a passing aberration in his thought, as some have argued,[15] but a perspective sustained throughout his career.

---

12. Sacvan Bercovitch, *The American Jeremiad,* 99–100, 105–10, and *The Puritan Origins of the American Self* (New Haven, 1975), 153–57.

13. Stout, "The Puritans and Edwards," 157 (my emphasis).

14. C. C. Goen, "Jonathan Edwards: A New Departure in Eschatology," *Church History* 28 (March 1959): 25–46, esp. 26–27, 37–38; C. C. Goen, ed., *The Great Awakening,* vol. 4 of *The Work of Jonathan Edwards* (New Haven, 1972), 71–72 [henceforth cited as GA in notes and text]; Lawrence Cremin, *American Education: The National Experience 1783–1876* (New York, 1980), 57; James F. Maclear, "The Republic and the Millennium," *The Religion of the Republic,* ed. Smith, 189; Mason I. Lowance, Jr., *The Language of Canaan: Metaphor and Symbol in New England from the Puritans to the Transcendentalists* (Cambridge, Mass., 1980), 179, 183–84, 190.

15. Stephen J. Stein, ed., *Apocalyptic Writings,* vol. 5 of *The Works of Jonathan Edwards* (New Haven, 1977), 26–29 [henceforth cited as AW in notes and text]; M. Darrol Bryant, "From Edwards to Hopkins: A Millennialist Critique of Political Culture," in *The Coming Kingdom,* ed. M. Darrol Bryant and Donald W. Dayton (Barrytown, N.Y., 1983), 45–70; Bryant, "America as God's Kingdom," 49–94. Edwards speculated that the Great Awakening "may prove the dawn of that glorious day [which] . . . shall renew the world of mankind." GA, 358, 353.

Further study of Edwards's occasional sermons, however, reveals that pessimism about New England's status and destiny dominated the North-ampton divine's deliberations on the colony. He never considered New England or Northampton to be basically righteous. Northampton was a city on a hill for all to see, but only as a *negative* example of behavior to be *avoided.* Rather than forecasting eventual and certain prosperity for the region, he seemed obsessed by the possibility of its permanent destruc-tion. Instead of seeing Northampton or New England as a redeemer nation, he speculated that God would transfer the covenant from a stubbornly wicked New England to another, worthier people. In other words, he threatened that God might do what his hearers so greatly feared—revoke New England's covenant.

It is my burden here to demonstrate that Edwards's use of the national covenant was predominantly pessimistic in its treatment of Northampton and New England. The underlying optimism that scholars have found in other early American jeremiads is relatively rare in Edwards and, at best, muted. It is important to note, however, that Edwards did not look to the horizon of *human* history with pessimism. He may have been cynical about New England's future, but he was bullish about the future of God's work of redemption. Human societies might fail to fulfill the terms of their covenants, but even their failures were under God's control. Every human step, whether for good or evil, was ordered to serve the divine plan, which Edwards called God's great "work of redemption." This was the establishment of the Church as a kingdom dedicated to Jesus. So despite what he considered to be nearly uninterrupted violations of New England's covenant, he could nevertheless be optimistic about the *ulti-mate* direction of the present. For Providence was ordering every histori-cal contingency, even New England's faithlessness, toward a final happy conclusion—a cosmic order transcending race and nation.[16]

In this chapter I will illustrate Edwards's pessimistic application of the national covenant by examining his consideration of Northampton's sta-tus before God and New England's destiny under God. That is, I will first

---

16. John Wilson, ed., *A History of the Work of Redemption*, vol. 9 of *The Works of Jonathan Edwards* (New Haven, 1989), 493, 513, 518–20, 525 [henceforth cited as *HWR* in notes and text]; *An Humble Attempt*, by Jonathan Edwards [henceforth cited as *HA* in notes and text], in *AW*, 346.

discuss his sermons on the "city on a hill" biblical text to determine whether he thought of his town and colony as righteous societies that were positive influences on the world. Then I will examine his deliberations on New England's present and future status in the covenant to test the thesis that he thought of New England as a redeemer nation that would bring salvation to the world. But even before I can open these discussions, I find it necessary to address a certain ambiguity. Scholars have spoken to Edwards's thinking on *both* Northampton *and* New England.[17] With which society was Edwards's national covenant concerned? And what of America in general?

In his occasional sermons Edwards applied the national covenant model to four societies: New England, Northampton, England and England's American colonies, and America in general. New England was the most common referent. On fourteen separate occasions he singled out New England as a subject of address, referring to it as "this land" or "this country."[18] Like his contemporaries, he viewed New England as a single "colony" or "American plantation."[19] Northampton was the next most common referent (nine times). Once he referred to "this church," but every other time he spoke of "this town."[20] On three occasions he directed attention to "our nation's" covenant. By "our nation" he meant England and its American colonies.[21] Finally, in the 1755 sermon after

---

17. Stout, for instance, speaks of Edwards's use of both the "city on a hill" motif (pointing to Northampton) and the "redeemer nation" motif (pointing to New England in general). Stout, "The Puritans and Edwards," 157.

18. Sermon on Proverbs 14:34, 1729, 24–25, 30; sermon on Ezekiel 7:16, part 1, 1724, 16, part 2, 1724, 7, 10; "Fragment Three" [the last ten pages of what may have been an election sermon from early 1728], 8; sermon on 2 Chronicles 23:16, March 1737, 23, 31; sermon on Jeremiah 51:5, 5 December 1745, 23; sermon on Jeremiah 2:5, April 1738, 29. See also *Some Thoughts*, by Jonathan Edwards [henceforth cited as *ST* in notes and text], in *GA*, 330, 343–44. Dates of the sermons before 1733, when Edwards began dating his sermons, have been determined by Thomas A. Schafer.

19. "Fragment Three," 8; see also *ST*, 345, 358.

20. Sermon on Numbers 12:9, 12 March 1748, 18; sermon on Acts 19:19, 1 April 1736; sermon on Deuteronomy 28:12, July 1736; sermon on Ezekiel 20:21–22, 1737; sermon on Jeremiah 2:5, April 1738, 38ff.

21. "Fragment Three," 1–7; sermon on Proverbs 14:34, 1729, 19; sermon on Jeremiah 51:5, 5 December 1745, 15; see also Paul Ramsey, ed., *Freedom of the Will*, vol. 1 of *The Works of Jonathan Edwards* (New Haven, 1957), 407.

General Edward Braddock and his British regulars were defeated by a combined force of French and Indian allies, he addressed "the British Plantations in America."[22]

The variation in referents was a function of the historical or homiletical occasion. In a fast-day sermon on 21 December 1727, he addressed "this land" because New England had suffered an earthquake two months before.[23] In one 1737 sermon he appealed only to Northampton because the message of the sermon was an interpretation of why the church's galleries had recently collapsed. But in 1738, when Edwards thought both Northampton and New England had declined in fervor, Edwards appealed to the covenant for "this Land *and* this Town." In occasional sermons in 1728, 1729, and 1745 he emphasized similarities of covenant status between New England and old England: they shared blessings (1728 and 1729) and unfaithfulness (1745). In all three sermons, Edwards's referent was thus "our nation," England and New England as one unit. Finally, in the 1755 sermon interpreting Braddock's defeat, Edwards addressed all the "British Plantations in America" because all would be affected by the military fortunes of Braddock and his successors.[24]

His message was the same for all four societies: Because you have shown ingratitude for your blessings by failure to keep the covenant, you are under God's judgment and face possible destruction. What applied to Northampton applied as well to New England, the other American colonies, and England itself. So when Edwards thought of a national covenant, he thought primarily of God's covenant with New England. Northampton was a subset of New England, and tended to behave the way New England behaved. Hence Northampton's relationship with God mirrored the dynamics and the status of New England's covenant.

The closer to home his focus, the greater the intensity of this message. New England and Northampton, he believed, enjoyed more covenantal privileges than other societies, and hence were more accountable. New

---

22. Sermon on Psalms 60:9–12, 28 August 1755, 21.

23. Sermon on Jonah 3:10, 21 December 1727. On the earthquake, see Stout, *The New England Soul*, 177–79.

24. Sermon on Ezekiel 20:21–22, 1737; sermon on Jeremiah 2:5, April 1738, 37–38, and passim; "Fragment Three"; and sermons on Proverbs 14:34, 1729, Jeremiah 51:5, 5 December 1745, and Psalms 60:9–12, 28 August 1755.

England's abundance of favors distinguished that colony from every other people and land in history—from pagan peoples "that have not knowledge of the true God," from Jews and Muslims who "don't own Jesus Christ," and from Roman Catholics "that are yet under the power of strong delusions & gross darkness." New Englanders were more fortunate than Protestants in France, Germany, and Poland, whose children were forced to take Catholic instruction and who could practice their faith openly only under threat of "prison, slavery and death." New Englanders should be grateful that the English constitution prohibits the rule of a "papish king" and the sort of "despotick power" that oppressed their Protestant brethren in "the Turkish domains, Muscovy and France."[25]

Yet New England surpassed even England in covenantal favor. New England was a "land of light," whereas England was "more of a mixture of darkness with light." Nonconformists in England had to support Anglican ministers as well as their own and could not hold office unless they conformed to Anglican worship. Finally, God had blessed New England with "greater plenty of the means of grace than any of the American Plantations from one End of America to the other." The other American colonies had received gospel light, but New England had been "glutted with" the gospel, besides having greater "Civil liberties."[26] Of all the New England towns, Northampton had been given the greatest share of covenantal "mercies." The degree of distinction, in fact, between Northampton and the rest of New England was as great as the distinction between New England and the rest of Christendom.[27]

The City on a Hill

Did Edwards therefore think of New England or Northampton as more righteous than other towns and lands? In the two sermons in which

---

25. "Fragment Three," 1, 2, 3, 6, 7, 8.
26. Sermon on 2 Chronicles 23:16, March 1737, 23–24; "Fragment Three," 9; Henry Abelove, "Jonathan Edwards's Letter of Invitation [12 Feb. 1740] to George Whitefield," *William and Mary Quarterly*, 3d ser., 29 (July 1972): 488; "Fragment Three," 9.
27. Sermon on 2 Chronicles 23:16, March 1737, 31.

Edwards commented on the "city upon a hill" (Matthew 5:14), he did not portray Northampton as either righteous or as any sort of positive example for the rest of the world. On each occasion he addressed what he considered to be a backsliding people. In a July 1736 sermon, Edwards referred to recent offenses that had damaged Northampton's reputation since the Awakening of 1734–35. "People abroad" had heard of "these things that have happened amongst us" that have been a "blemish to our Profession & take great notice of them." Northampton's sins had been gleefully "Rehearsed over" by the awakening's detractors, "to our dishonour as well as the dishonour of Relig[ion]." But this should come as no surprise, Edwards admonished, "for we are a City that is set on an hill & such a City Cant be hid." The lesson to be learned was that "if you dont behave your selves well[,] you Cant hide it."[28]

Edwards did indeed entertain an exalted conception of Northampton's importance to the progress of true religion. Not only their own reputation and that of the revival, "but the Credit of all vital Relig[ion] & the Power of Godliness in this Land depends very much on the behaviour of the People in this Town." Yet when he reminded his auditors that people in "the Jerseys," Long Island, "the Highlands on Hudson's River," England, and "Eminent divines in London," had "taken notice of" Northampton's revival, he was impressed not with the blessings Northampton would convey, but with the "dishonour" the town would bring on itself and the awakening: "How much to be Lamented is it that they [foreign observers] Cant be Informed that the work of G. still Continues Gloriously to be Carried on amongst us."[29] That Northampton was a city on a hill—by virtue of the great works God had done in the town and its consequent influence on America and England—was cause for complaint and warning, not congratulation. Northampton had perforce been thrust into the limelight. Now that all eyes were upon it, the town was all the more obligated to honor religion. But its failure to do so threatened the forfei-

28. Sermon on Matthew 5:14, July 1736, 34, 16. Edwards did not in this sermon identify the "blemishes" beyond alluding to "Enthusiastical Impressions and Imaginations" (25), but in a sermon three months earlier chastised members of his congregation for their contentiousness, "licentiousness," neglect of family discipline, and negligence in paying debts. Sermon on Acts 19:19, 1 April 1736, 21.
29. Sermon on Matthew 5:14, July 1736, 39, 35–36, 36–37.

ture of all future blessings and had already begun to turn its newfound
fame into a curse.

Almost two years later (April 1738), Edwards delivered another jeremiad lamenting the town's retreat from its earlier fervor. Once more,
Northampton's status as "a city on a hill" was a dubious distinction. The
doctrine that Edwards attempted to "prove" was that "when a Covenant
People that have formerly seemed to Cleave to God & manifests an high
Esteem of him[,] do after it depart from him[,] it carries in it a Reflection
on God as tho they had found some iniquity in him." This was a people,
then, that had "greatly departed from God." Rather than showing the
world the way to corporate salvation, their departure would only "bring
shame & disgrace on ourselves." Indeed, "we are as a city set on a hill,"
and "the eyes of the [world] are upon us to observe." But what would they
see? Northampton's shepherd spoke only of failure and sin. The outcome
was cast in terms not of what the world would miss, but of the shame that
Northampton would have to bear: "If we lose what we found to gain &
depart from what we had an appearance of . . . it will be more abundantly to our reproach . . . our backsliding . . . [is] exceeding disgraceful
towards ourselves[.] by dishonouring G[od] we disgrace ourselves & expose ourselves to contempt."[30]

Edwards, then, sometimes referred to Northampton as a city on a hill,
but not to indicate its capacity to redeem other towns, colonies, or
nations. He used the image instead as a reminder that her infidelity
would not be hidden, but exposed to the world and thus become a source
of public disgrace. Northampton was truly a city set upon a hill, but a
righteous, exemplary city it was not.

Both the occasional sermons and the formal treatises reveal that Edwards's denial of Northampton's (and, by implication, New England's)
righteousness was even more fundamental. No polity, he indicated, can
be righteous in the sense that the majority of its citizens are Christian or
even relatively free from sin. There never has existed a whole nation
outwardly moral or even with a majority of its people in the visible

---

30. Sermon on Jeremiah 2:5, April 1738, 5, 29, 44–45. The same use of the "city on a
hill" text as a *negative* example can be found in the sermons on 2 Samuel 20:19, May
1737, 59–60, and 2 Chronicles 23:16, March 1737, 34.

Christian church. When Edwards referred to "Christian countries," he meant no more than polities whose formal adherence was to Christianity. The majority of people in all "Christian" lands were not regenerate, he believed, and even the "godly" had an abundance of sin in their hearts. New England, for example, was a Christian land only in the sense that Christianity was the established religion. There were some virtuous Christians in New England, of course; in the occasional sermons Edwards praised New England's Founding Fathers, and in revival treatises he lauded the piety of his wife Sarah, a four-year-old girl, and a dying woman.[31] But most New Englanders were not true Christians.

No people, therefore, and New England least of all, is righteous. Edwards condemned New Englanders for a host of sins. He railed against their impiety and cold formalism in religion. Preachers taught "morality" and "natural religion" rather than "vital and experimental religion," while their parishioners were more concerned with the world and its pleasures than God and his excellencies. The cause of such a lamentable condition was not ignorance or inability but "obstinacy." At times people were pressed by their consciences toward true piety, but more often they ignored such calls. As a result, as Edwards consistently declaimed at fast-day services, they were hypocrites. "We draw nigh unto him with our lips, while our hearts are far from him."[32]

After impiety Edwards was most concerned with social "contention" and injustice. He noted that Northampton had been plagued by "strife"

---

31. Sermon on Proverbs 14:34, 1729, 2; *The Distinguishing Marks of a Work of the Spirit of God*, by Jonathan Edwards [henceforth cited as *DM* in notes and text], in *GA*, 246; sermon on Proverbs 14:34, 1729, 2. See also Clyde A. Holbrook, ed., *Original Sin*, vol. 3 of *The Works of Jonathan Edwards* (New Haven, 1970), 161 [henceforth cited as *OS* in text and notes], sermon on Jeremiah 2:5, April 1738, 25–26, *A Faithful Narrative*, by Jonathan Edwards [henceforth cited as *FN* in notes and text], in *GA*, 191–205, and *ST*, 331–47. Of course, Edwards also esteemed the piety of David Brainerd; see Norman Pettit's introduction to *The Life of David Brainerd*, vol. 7 of *The Works of Jonathan Edwards* (New Haven, 1985) [henceforth cited as *David Brainerd* in notes and text].

32. Sermon on Jeremiah 2:5, April 1738, 32, 27, 31; sermon on Proverbs 14:34, 1729, 25, 4, 3. Other religious sins censured by Edwards were "false doctrine" (mentioned four times), "profanity" and "profane oaths" (three times), "worldliness" (twice), "extravagance in fashions" (twice), "hypocrisy" (twice), "pride and vanity" (twice), "declension of family education and government" (twice), "covetousness" (once), "infidelity" and "apostacy" (once).

during Solomon Stoddard's pastorate, and continued to lament its presence throughout his own tenure there.[33] In addition, the prosperous
citizens of the town failed to care properly for the poor. When worms
devoured crops in 1743, Edwards declared that God was judging townspeople for their failure to do "deeds of justice" toward the poor. Many
Christians, he said, failed to understand their duty to the indigent. "Christian people are to give to others not only so as to lift him above extremity
but liberally to furnish him." Injustice toward one another was mirrored
by New England's exploitation of Native Americans. Instead of "Chris-
tianizing" them, which was part of the Founders' covenant when they first
came to New England, "we have debauched em with strong drink . . .
which [does harm] to—their souls & bodies & continues to do so."[34]

The venality of corrupt politicians and their cynical use of religion also
angered Edwards. In 1743 the Massachusetts governor had ordered a day
of thanksgiving for the "king's preservation and victory at the Maine
River in Germany." In what was probably an oblique indictment of the
patronage system in George II's court, Edwards sobered the occasion by
assailing rulers who were "governed by their Private Interest," buying and
selling "places of publick trust" for private gain. Such men, he pronounced, have "little reason . . . to expect any *continued* success in
war."[35] God would not overlook moral turpitude no matter how earnest a
magistrate's public piety.

---

33. Letter to Thomas Gillespie, 1 July 1751, in GA, 563. Strife was condemned in all
of the following sermons: on Acts 19:19, 1 April 1736, 21; on 2 Chronicles 23:16, March
1737, 29; on Jeremiah 2:5, April 1738, 32; and on Joshua 7:12, 28 June 1744, 25. All of
these sermons were delivered between 1736 and 1744. Three were given in the three
years immediately following the first revival, and one in the aftermath of the second.
Strife and contention were particularly vexing to Edwards after a revival.

34. Sermon on Malachi 3:10–11, July 1743, 31; sermon on Jeremiah 2:5, April 1738,
35. Edwards's empathy for the plight of Native Americans demonstrates that he was at
least partly successful in attaining "disinterested love" for others. Some Native Americans
had murdered one of his aunts and two cousins, and had carried into captivity an uncle
and four more cousins. Ola Elizabeth Winslow, *Jonathan Edwards 1703–1758: A Biography*
(New York, 1940), 29.

35. Sermon on Isaiah 47:4, 13 October 1743, 29, 28, 29. On royal patronage in the
early eighteenth century, see John A. Schutz, "Succession Politics in Massachusetts,
1730–1741," in *Essays in Colonial History*, ed. Paul Goodman (New York, 1967), 497–
510, and J. R. Pole, *Political Representation in England and the Origins of the American
Revolution* (New York, 1966).

Edwards also condemned sins of the flesh, such as excessive drinking and fornication.[36] But these and all other sins were subsumed by the fundamental sin of ingratitude. That is, sins of impiety, contention, injustice, venality, and sensuality are simply various manifestations of an underlying ingratitude to God for the unparalleled mercies showered upon New England. Ultimately, it was this attitude that caused God's anger. New England had been given the greatest of civil and religious privileges, yet its people had arrogantly abused them. They were more guilty than Sodom and Gomorrah, for if those towns had received the same blessings they certainly would have "awakened . . . and reformed." Indeed, because of its unprecedented blessings, New England was more guilty than any other people in history. Those blessings made the colony more nearly parallel to Israel than any other people on earth, but this was cause for alarm, not congratulations. For Israel was a "whore" and a "witch," and her children were "bastards." In 1747 Edwards told his Northampton parishioners—three years before they ejected him—that New England was on the verge of committing "the unpardonable sin against the Holy Ghost." Two years later he declared that New England was worse than Pharaoh, who responded in part to some of God's judg-ments despite having fewer means of grace. Since New England's means were greater, its guilt would be greater. And, as with Pharaoh, New England's obstinacy would result in "utter destruction."[37]

---

36. Sermon on Proverbs 14:34, 1729, 10, 27; sermon on Jeremiah 51:5, 5 December 1745, 28; see also sermon on Matthew 18:7, May 1734, 47–48, sermon on Jeremiah 2:5, April 1738, 32, sermon on Acts 19:19, 1 April 1736, 21, and sermon on Proverbs 14:34, 1729, 25. Outside of the context of the national covenant, Edwards said that the greatest sins were the sins of the spirit, not the sins of the flesh. Of all the sins of the spirit, pride was the worst. Of all kinds of pride, spiritual pride was the most dangerous. John E. Smith, ed., *Religious Affections*, vol. 2 of *The Works of Jonathan Edwards* (New Haven, 1959), 181 [henceforth cited as *RA* in notes and text]; *ST*, 415–16, 467.

37. Sermon on Jonah 3:10, 21 December 1727, 20; sermon on Exodus 8:15, 15 June 1749, 11; sermon on Jonah 3:10, 21 December 1727, 20; sermon on Jeremiah 51:5, 5 December 1745, 10; Jonathan Edwards, *Misrepresentations Corrected, and Truth Vindicated in a Reply to the Rev. Mr. Solomon Williams's Book, Entitled, The True State of the Question Concerning the Qualifications Necessary to Lawful Communion in the Christian Sacraments*, vol. 4 of *The Works of President Edwards: With a Memoir of His Life, In Ten Volumes*, ed. Sereno E. Dwight (New York, 1829–30, 568; Jonathan Edwards, letter to William McCulloch, 21 January 1747, in *The Life of President Edwards*, vol. 1 of *Works*, ed. Dwight, 231–32; sermon on Exodus 8:15, 15 June 1749, 11–12.

New England as Redeemer Nation?

Were Edwards's threats of destruction any different from those of his predecessors in the jeremiad tradition? Bercovitch and others have argued that seventeenth-century prophecies of doom were often little more than rhetoric. The jeremiahs were less certain that New England *would* be destroyed than that New England *deserved* to be destroyed, and so predicted destruction in the hope of inducing repentance.[38]

Did Edwards predict New England's destruction with similar rhetorical purpose? As any pastor, he undoubtedly hoped that his warnings of imminent judgment would produce repentance. Perhaps he too was never certain that destruction would come. But unlike Bercovitch's jeremiahs, he never promised in the years after the Great Awakening that the covenant would persist regardless of New England's behavior. Edwards was obsessed not with New England's future glory but the possibility of its obliteration as a people of God. As the years progressed, his warnings of coming catastrophe grew increasingly shrill, and he more frequently threatened that the covenant might be revoked altogether. For Edwards New England would never be "the unconquerable people of God."[39] Military success could be assured only if New England kept the terms of its covenant, and the colony's recent history of infidelity offered little hope of that.

Edwards's deliberations on New England's destiny varied over the course of his career. Changing historical conditions altered the tone and sometimes, slightly, the message from period to period. But through them all Edwards steadily solidified his conviction that New England deserved, and could be on the verge of experiencing, destruction.

From 1724 to 1737 Edwards asserted New England's massive guilt, but stopped short of saying that the colony would certainly be destroyed. He charged New England with sin deserving of judgment, but chose to focus on conditions that would allow for reprieve. In a 1724 fast-day sermon, for instance, Edwards declared, "It is only worthy of wonder that God has

---

38. Bercovitch, "Horologicals," 6, 29, 34; *The American Jeremiad*, 89–90; Stout, *The New England Soul*, 217; Holstun, *A Rational Millennium*, 256.

39. Stout, "The Puritans and Edwards," 157.

not yet had us to drink more deeply of the cup of his wrath," but allowed
that the penitent would be delivered from "common calamities" by being
spared from them entirely or from their negative effects. "He will either
keep them out of the fire or if they are cast in will cause that they shall
not be burnt." Besides being spared from judgment, however, the penitent could also look forward to the prospect of a divine "design of mercy
upon the Land in general."[40]

In a sermon following the 1727 earthquake Edwards focused on God's
distaste for punishment. Comparing the New England tremor to that
before the destruction of Jerusalem, and warning that God may be "weary
of repenting" his threats of destruction, the Northampton pastor reassured his auditors that reformation and repentance would avert that
judgment. For God does not enjoy judgment. "He has no pleasure in the
Destruction or Calamity of persons or people . . . he is a God that
delights in mercy & judgement is his strange work." In what may have
been an election sermon the following year, Edwards admonished his
auditors that God might withdraw New England's civil and religious
freedoms if citizens were ungrateful for those freedoms. But this remark
was a parenthetical flourish at the end of a long recitation of the colony's
covenant privileges that was appreciative, not threatening, in tone.[41]

A similar pattern can be seen in an occasional sermon from the following year. Edwards was preaching on the text, "Righteousness exalteth a
nation but sin is a reproach to any people" (Proverbs 14:34). In the
beginning of the sermon he lamented the moral degeneration of both the
world and the Anglo-American peoples, and suggested that God might
soon look upon them all as ripe for destruction. That judgment, he
explained, would consist of the withdrawal of God's "Gracious Presence,"
after which "a People will be their own destroyers." Yet Edwards qualified
his threat. Through most of the sermon he predicted destruction restricted to England and the rest of the world. He also turned abruptly
from a discussion of looming judgment to the eschatological hope that
"Glorious times" were near. "We may hope that G[od] wont suffer this
[world] to decline much more[,] that the darkest time of night is Come

---

40. Sermon on Ezekiel 7:16, part 2, 1724, 7, 10–11, 10.
41. Sermon on Jonah 3:10, 21 December 1727, 8, 12, 11; "Fragment Three," 10.

and that it will not be Long before break of day." And, when at the close of the sermon Edwards accused New England of betraying its covenant, he contended that all deserved punishment because all had sinned in some way, but acknowledged that there were "many" who did not partake of the colony's "Publick Crimes."[42]

Eight years later (1737), on a day of prayer after the collapse of the church galleries at Northampton, Edwards warned of approaching judgment but stopped short of threatening utter destruction. The near-catastrophe (Edwards noted that it was only by God's mercy that no one was killed) was a judgment upon the congregation's contentiousness and profanation of the Sabbath, and a warning of greater judgments to come. The doctrine and argument of the sermon, however, centered not in a prophecy of coming judgment but a recognition of God's wondrous "compassion."[43]

In another sermon delivered the same year (1737) Edwards demonstrated that he was still choosing to hope for the best despite signs of the worst. New England, he declared, had departed from God. Its fasts and thanksgivings were good for nothing at all in God's sight because New Englanders were still hankering after the onions and leeks of Egypt. "We make a pretense of humility and yet go on with our corruptions and wickedness." Yet God would prove faithful regardless of what his covenant people did: "However a covenant people may be unfaithful to God & not fulfill their obligations G[od] never fails of fulfilling his Covenant promises."[44] Either this conviction of God's faithfulness or his own confidence that only a minority of his own town were still unregenerate encouraged Edwards to dream of "what an honor it will be to us to be the Lord's People."[45]

As the War of the Austrian Succession (1739–49) threatened to engulf the American colonies, Edwards reflected on New England's failure to maintain the revival spirit of 1734–35 and turned pessimistic. The coming war, he surmised, might be God's instrument to destroy New En-

42. Sermon on Proverbs 14:34, 1729, 2, 19, 22, 24, 30.
43. Sermon on Ezekiel 20:21–22, 1737, 37, 1, 15.
44. Sermon on 2 Chronicles 23:16, March 1737, 29, ibid., 30, 47, 49, 7.
45. Ibid., 47, 34.

gland.[46] In a 1738 fast-day sermon he castigated the inhabitants of New England and Northampton for departing from the revival piety of three years before. They had departed from God, he thundered. Pastors were preaching moralism and natural religion, while their people were "cold" in things of religion, cheating, contentious, uttering profane oaths, and debauching the Indians with strong drink. The region could expect only shame and disgrace. God had designed "long ago" to utterly destroy it and take away all its privileges, but had shown mercy in the 1734–35 revival.[47]

By early 1740 Edwards thought he knew how destruction might come. A fast day had been called for March 27 because of a "strange distemper" that had killed an unprecedented number of people in New England.[48] Edwards mounted the pulpit that day to interpret the recent tragedy. God uses a progression of steps, he proclaimed, to try to reclaim a "covenant people" from their backslidings. First, he sends faithful messengers to point out their sins and threaten destruction if they do not repent and reform. If that fails, he then sends "corrections" and "various Publick Calamities." In the process he will "mingle mercies with affliction . . . as a Prudent Father would deal with a Rebellious perverse child." If "moderate chastisements" do not bring repentance, God will "Chasten them severely." After giving a people "hints of the destruction they expose themselves to," God will finally grant, as a last resort, "times of special pouring out of his spirit."[49]

Since God had sent such a time in 1734–35 and they had shown ingratitude for it, New Englanders had "great reason to fear destruction." The Jews had been blessed with a similar revival some years before their destruction. Just as God had used that revival to bless the rest of the world while at the same time destroying the Jewish nation, New England might be destroyed while their covenant mercies were transferred to

---

46. The War of the Austrian Succession eventually came to the North American continent as King George's War (1744–49). See Douglas Leach, *Arms for Empire: A Military History of the British Colonies in North America, 1607–1763* (New York, 1973), 206–61.

47. Sermon on Jeremiah 2:5, April 1738, 38, 29, 31–35, 44–45, 37.

48. "Many more have probably been slain with it than have ever died in the Land." Sermon on 2 Chronicles 36:15–17, 27 March 1740, 35.

49. Ibid., 5–16.

another people. God "may give other Countreys much of this mercy & give us no more of it. he [sic] may take away the Kingdom of God from us & give it to other People bringing forth the fruit of it."[50] Thus, in a subtle twist usually missed by interpreters of Edwards's national covenant, revivals did not "[ensure] God's continued presence in New England" but were seen by the Massachusetts seer as moments of divine patience, which may only increase New England's guilt and could precede an act of divine vengeance. Religious awakenings were ambivalent signs that could augur divine desertion and temporal destruction.[51]

Removal of the covenant would come by either physical or religious removal from the sources of revelation, the means of the covenant. That is, a people may be carried off into captivity and separated from the means of the covenant and thus lose their religious heritage, or they may "be destroyed as to their religious state" by being given over to "gross darkness & delusion" such as the "darkness of popery." In each case, there are still two more possibilities. Each deprivation may be either total or partial. That is, all the people may be lost from the covenant—as were Sodom and Gomorrah, or a small remnant may remain within the covenant—as Benjamin and Judah remained after the destruction of the ten northern tribes of Israel.[52]

At the end of this frightening sermon Edwards reminded his hearers that "the calamity of war is near," and speculated that their destruction could come through its devastations. Just as God used Assyrian and Babylonian kings to punish ancient Israel, he might use the king of France to destroy an irredeemable New England.[53]

During the years of tension and war with France and their Native American allies, Edwards did his part to support the colonial cause. In a

---

50. Ibid., 39, 40.

51. Scholars who have discussed Edwards's national covenant without noting its overriding pessimism have not treated occasional sermons in 1728 and 1740 that threatened the transferral of New England's covenant to other countries, and sermons in 1746, 1748, and 1749 that warned of New England's destruction. See "Fragment Three"; see also the sermon on 2 Chronicles 36:15–17, 27 March 1740; and sermons on Exodus 33:19, August 1746, Numbers 12:9, 17 March 1748, and Exodus 8:15, 15 June 1749.

52. Sermon on 2 Chronicles 36:15–17, 27 March 1740, 26–27.

53. Ibid., 46.

1741 "Fast for Success in the War" he assured his congregation that God would preserve his servants in battle. They might suffer, but only in ways that would lead to their eventual happiness. In a sermon before the Cape Breton expedition four years later[54] he exhorted the men in his church to do their "duty," and warned that cowardice would offend their God. The expedition would give them great benefits, he promised. The sea journey north to Nova Scotia would show them "gods wonders in the great deep," and the difficulties experienced along the way would be good for their souls. In three other sermons during this period he defended colonial participation in the war as a just means of preserving religious and civil liberties.[55]

But in nearly all of his occasional sermons before and during the war Edwards was doubtful about its outcome. His hearers were assured that God would be with them, but only if they obeyed him. Because New England's history was so stained by ingratitude and infidelity, the divine presence could not be presumed. Even in the 1741 sermon promising only suffering conducive to future happiness, suffering was said to include death. In the 1745 sermon before the Cape Breton expedition Edwards warned that if New England continued to stray from God it could not count on God's help. A year earlier, during a "fast on occasion of the war with France," Edwards had told his congregation that New England was in a state of rebellion against God that—if unrepented—would lead to "destruction by the sword of the enemy." At the time Massachusetts was protected by an admirable line of fortifications on the frontier. But they could not be trusted, because "sin above all things weakens a people in war." The colony had rebelled against God by degenerating from the piety it had shown during its awakenings in 1734–35 and 1740–42. And

---

54. On 17 June 1745 a colonial army joined an English naval squadron in a successful assault on the French fortress at Louisburg on Cape Breton Island in the mouth of the St. Lawrence River. This protected—for a time at least—New England fisheries and trade. See Leach, *Arms for Empire*, 80–164, and Howard H. Peckham, *The Colonial Wars 1689–1762* (Chicago, 1964), 25–76.

55. Sermon on Revelation 7:1–3, 26 February 1741, 19–20; sermon on Leviticus 26:3–13, 28 February 1745, 97, 98; sermon on 1 Kings 8:44–45, 4 April 1745; sermon on Nehemiah 4:14, June 1746. On 10 July 1746 he preached a sermon teaching that Christians should engage in war with "anti[christ]ian forces" when so called by Providence; sermon on Revelation 17:11, 10 July 1746, 14.

history had shown that destruction often comes to such a people, particularly after "extraordinary calls and warnings," such as the awakenings, fail to bring reformation. Despite the fortifications, therefore, "if our sin remains . . . we shall lie open & shall be like a city without walls."[56] By 1744, then, Edwards was interpreting both New England awakenings as forerunners of future glory not for America but for the world, and as possible preludes to New England's destruction. New England would then be a redeemer nation only by default. Her betrayal of the covenant would lead to the blessing of other nations, just as Israel's unbelief caused God to give the gospel to the Gentiles. New England's role in future blessings to the world therefore would be a cause for shame, not pride.

Immediately after the success at Cape Breton, Edwards was euphoric. In August he called the victory a mercy unparalleled in history. In September he predicted eventual French defeat because France belonged to the kingdoms of the Antichrist, which "are appointed to destruction." By December, however, Edwards warned that New England had enjoyed temporary success only because of God's consideration of the righteous Founding Fathers, the few righteous ones who still remained in the land, and his own mercy. The mercy at Cape Breton was only a warning that "some terrible destruction" was around the corner. Without repentance God would forsake New England, just as he forsook Israel's ten lost tribes, the ancient Eastern churches, and the Protestant churches in France. Once again Edwards reflected on New England's religious decline after its awakenings, and concluded that because of Northampton's abundance of light, its guilt was greater: "We are a small part of the Land but a great part of the Provocation of the Lord."[57]

After the end of the war Edwards continued to see a dark future for New England. He grudgingly accepted George II's deliverance from an attempted coup d'état in 1745 as a "temporal mercy on a very wicked people." Unless followed by repentance, he reminded his audience, these

---

56. Sermon on Revelation 7:1–3, 26 February 1741, 21; sermon on Leviticus 26:3–13, 28 February 1745, 1; sermon on Joshua 7:12, 28 June 1744, 13, 2, 23–24, 37.

57. Sermon on 2 Chronicles 20:27–29, 17 August 1745, 18; sermon on Isaiah 8:9–10, September 1745, 28–29, 26; sermon on Jeremiah 51:5, 5 December 1745, 6–8, 40, 37–38, 25, 38.

mercies would not be continued.[58] In 1748—two years before his dismissal—he admonished his church that it may be "utterly broken in pieces." Some of them, he predicted, would reside "in hell where there is no token of his Favourable Presence." At a public fast for rain in 1749 Edwards charged the same audience with phony repentance and warned that the drought might be only the beginning of judgments, with their end being destruction.[59]

After 1750 it is difficult to determine, from his occasional sermons, Edwards's attitude to New England. He preached to a Native American audience, for whom such considerations were somewhat irrelevant. More-over, nearly all the occasional sermons from the Stockbridge period were repetitions of sermons from earlier decades.[60] But in *The Nature of True Virtue* (1755) he displayed a cynical view of patriotism. Most patriotism, Edwards argued, is rooted in self-love, not genuine benevolence. Unless it is subordinated to love for universal being—which is true only for the regenerate—patriotism is generally a mélange of subtle calculations cali-brated ultimately, and often unwittingly, to serve the self. In addition, he averred, patriotism is peculiarly susceptible to self-deception. Because it is a commitment to a large number of persons, it is easily mistaken for true virtue. But Roman patriotism was employed "for the destruction of the rest of the world of mankind," as are all patriotisms that are not committed to the good of being in general.[61]

---

58. Sermon on Exodus 33:19, August 1746, 15, 20. On Prince Charles Edward's attempt to retake the throne of England for his father James (III) from the ruling Hanove-rian dynasty, see Charles Petrie, *The Jacobite Movement* (London, 1932), 177–217.

59. Sermon on Numbers 12:9, 12 March 1748, 18–19; sermon on Exodus 8:15, 15 June 1749, 8–10, 12.

60. Edwards's sermon after General Edward Braddock's defeat in 1755 offered some consolation to the frightened colonists—God might help them if they would deeply humble themselves—but conceded "dark appearances in this defeat." Sermon on Psalms 60:9–12, 28 August 1755, 29, 24. On Braddock's defeat, see Leach, *Arms for Empire*, 368.

61. *The Nature of True Virtue*, by Jonathan Edwards, in *Ethical Writings*, ed. Paul Ramsey, vol. 8 of *The Works of Jonathan Edwards*, 609–13, 611 [henceforth cited as *TV* in notes and text]. Despite Edwards's cynical view of most patriotism, he nevertheless considered it necessary and valuable to the civil community; for that and other reasons, he believed self-love to have limited but positive value. See the discussion of love in Chapter 4 and the analysis of patriotism in Chapter 5.

Edwards's treatises from the 1740s indicate that his view of America darkened after the Great Awakening. In *Some Thoughts Concerning the Revival* (1742) he predicted that the premillennial "glorious work of God" might begin in America (*ST*, 353). He did not specify the length of this work of the Spirit. But in *An Humble Attempt* (1747), written after the tumult and dissension of the Great Awakening, Edwards described the same premillennial age of the Spirit in strictly international terms. America was mentioned only to be condemned for its profligacy, and the premillennial age was said to be two hundred fifty years long. In other words, the premillennial work of the Spirit no longer had any connection with America, and the millennium itself was thought to be centuries in the future.[62]

Final Assessment

Edwards's doctrine of the national covenant was neither tribalist nor provincial. The Massachusetts pastor was a prophet in the tradition of the New England jeremiad who never consistently embraced the optimistic nationalism often attributed to him. God's judgment on a sinful people was the predominant message of his sermons on public and civil concerns. As his career progressed he became more convinced that since New England was the most blessed of all peoples, it was the most guilty. Hence the two early eighteenth-century awakenings were signs not of God's pleasure but of his anger, and perhaps omens of coming destruction. For neither awakening had brought reformation. If New England was to be a redeemer nation, it would be by default. Its unfaithfulness might cause God to transfer his covenant blessings to another people. If Northampton was a light on a hill, the light it radiated to the world only exposed its own corruption, thus inviting contempt.

Therefore, Edwards, if he had lived that long, would *not* have turned his pen in the Revolutionary period to "promises of national success."[63]

---

62. *HA*, 320, 329, 333, 357–58, 411.
63. Stout, "The Puritans and Edwards," 156.

He probably would have supported the "sacred cause of liberty," since he believed that civil liberties were inextricably linked with religious liberties, and that the preservation of liberties was worth fighting for.[64] But, as in the French and Indian War, he would have warned that moral and religious corruption could cripple the prosecution of political ends. So he would have been convinced of the eventual fall of the Antichrist, as he was in the earlier wars, but unsure of America's success in its battles against a tyrannical England.

This reading of Edwards's national covenant has several implications for American religious history. First, it sheds new light on one of the most puzzling episodes in the history of New England Congregationalism— Edwards's dismissal from the Northampton pulpit. That he was so relentless and ferocious in denouncing his countrymen's sins makes it more comprehensible, though perhaps no less defensible, why they should have banished him to a lonely frontier outpost for most of his last decade.

Second, theological responsibility for self-congratulatory civil religion in the Revolutionary and early national periods cannot be placed at Edwards's feet. Later religious thinkers who claimed his mantle may have danced jingoistic jigs,[65] but in so doing they compromised his covenantal principles. Of course, the extravagance of Edwards's accusations against Northampton and New England may have, ironically, encouraged a sense of American exceptionalism. For only a people under a special covenant could warrant such divine severity. But Edwards reminded his auditors that their covenant was only the most recent in a series of such divine contracts with nations, and that it might terminate shortly. For their sins might cause God to transfer his covenantal favors to a more faithful people. Hence American exceptionalism—in the Edwardsean dispensation— could not forestall American destruction.

64. Sermon on 1 Kings 8:44–45, 4 April 1745; sermon on Nehemiah 4:14, June 1746. On the New England clergy's understanding of the Revolution as a defense of their religious and political rights, see Hatch, *The Sacred Cause of Liberty*.

65. See, e.g., Timothy Dwight's epic poems celebrating America's millennial greatness "Greenfield Hill" and "The Conquest of Canaan" in *The Major Poems of Timothy Dwight*, ed. William J. McTaggart and William K. Bottorf (Gainesville, Fla., 1969). On New Divinity ministers who subscribed, at least in part, to Revolutionary civil religion, see Donald Weber, *Rhetoric and History in Revolutionary New England* (New York, 1988).

Finally, Edwards must now be added to the distinguished list of American cultural leaders who rejected triumphalist interpretations of the American experience. Martin Marty has distinguished two types of civil religion—that is, two sorts of religious interpretations of nationhood. The *priestly* type is "celebrative" and "affirmative" of culture; the *prophetic* takes a "dialectical" approach, with a "predisposition toward the judgmental." Priests "comfort the afflicted," whereas prophets "afflict the comfortable."[66] This reading of the Edwardsean national covenant places the beleaguered theologian from Northampton within the small band of influential cultural leaders whose reflections on America's religious meaning were prophetic afflictions of the comfortable.

---

66. Martin Marty, "Two Kinds of Two Kinds of Civil Religion," in *American Civil Religion*, ed. Russell R. Richey and Donald G. Jones (New York, 1974), 145.

2 That Glorious Work of God and the Beautiful Society: The Premillennial Age and the Millennium

Although Edwards's doctrine of the national covenant, long buried in unpublished sermons, has come to attention only recently, Edwardsean millennialism has been open to public view for more than two centuries. Significant portions of some of his most important published works were devoted to its explication. As a result, it has received considerable critical attention. Some scholars have noted how Edwards's millennial doctrine implicitly challenged contemporary social mores,[1] but others have held that Edwards's vision of future glory constituted an idolatrous civil reli-

---

The first phrase is Edwards's description of the 250-year process leading up to the millennium, and the second is a term he used to describe the millennium itself. See *ST*, 353, and *HWR*, 484.

1. Miller, *Jonathan Edwards*, 327; Heimert, *Religion and the American Mind*, 99, 102; Robert B. Westbrook, "Social Criticism and the Heavenly City of Jonathan Edwards," *Soundings* 59 (1976): 397–409; Ruth H. Bloch, *Visionary Republic: Millennial Themes in American Thought, 1756–1800* (Cambridge, Mass. 1985), 18–19.

gion. Sacvan Bercovitch, for example, wonders at Edwards's "astonishing arrogance, both on his own behalf and on behalf of his region and continent." The Northampton pastor, Bercovitch claims, was a case study in religious and nationalistic "provincialism"; his exaggerated sense of New England's role in the eschatological drama of redemption "drew out the proto-nationalistic tendencies of the New England Way."[2]

That Edwards's millennialism characterized America or New England as a redeemer nation with a mission to save other peoples is a familiar theme. C. C. Goen's 1959 article opened the discussion by suggesting that Edwards began to "entertain the idea that God might have purposed to realize the biblical prophecies in America as a land to accomplish the renovation of the world."[3] Subsequent commentaries on Edwards's eschatology have elaborated on the theme. New England for Edwards was the "city on a hill" that would knit together "all of Protestant America"[4] and then, on behalf of the world, inaugurate the final stage of earthly history, the millennium.[5] America was to be the center of future glory, "a locus for the building of the earthly Jerusalem, that 'New heavens and new earth' prophesied by Isaiah."[6] The religious imagination should focus on the New World as the scene of God's future glorious acts, for "the wilderness-to-become-paradise is America."[7] Even before the advent of the eschaton, America had things

---

2. Bercovitch, *The American Jeremiad*, 105.

3. Goen, "Jonathan Edwards: A New Departure in Eschatology," 29; see also his introduction to GA, 71–72.

4. Bercovitch, *The American Jeremiad*, 106.

5. Heimert, *Religion and the American Mind*, chap. 2; Goen, "Jonathan Edwards: A New Departure in Eschatology," 29, 40; Cushing Strout, *The New Heavens and New Earth: Political Religion in America* (New York, 1974), 29; Conrad Cherry, ed., *God's New Israel: Religious Interpretations of American Destiny* (Englewood Cliffs, N.J., 1971), 55–59; Lowance, *The Language of Canaan*, 179, 187, 190; Bercovitch, *The American Jeremiad*, 106, 124, and *The Puritan Origins*, 154–56; AW, 26.

6. Lowance, *The Language of Canaan*, 187. See also Jay Fliegelman, *Prodigals and Pilgrims: The American Revolution against Patriarchal Authority, 1750–1800* (Cambridge, 1982), 191.

7. Bercovitch, *The Puritan Origins*, 154. Both Bercovitch and Lowance wrongly identify the "new heavens and new earth" as the millennium. For Edwards the new heavens and new earth are to come *after* the millennium, when the kingdom of the Son is finally and fully consummated, far from this earth in another part of the universe: "The everlasting residence and reign of Christ & his church will be heaven, & not this lower [earth]

to teach the world, for America, in Edwards's view, was "a brighter type of heaven."[8] Bercovitch claims for Edwards the thesis that perception of America's importance in the history of redemption is the key to Christian epistemology: one can understand nature in general only if one perceives "Christ's *magnalia Americana.*"[9] The most recent illustration of the redeemer-nation interpretation is John Wilson's conclusion that Edwards invested the American experience "with preeminent significance for concluding the drama of Christian redemption."[10]

Some scholars have proposed a link between Edwards's millennialism and various incarnations of "self-interest" in later American culture. Thus, for example, Edwards "and his postmillennial disciples" are said to have provided Calvinists "with a radical justification for early nationalism" that served to baptize the status quo in the waters of divine approbation. In the words of James Maclear, "they tended to accept and sanctify American institutions and social values."[11] Among those values was laissez-faire economics, which Edwards's millennialism is said to have stimulated by using American commerce as a type of the millennium and by equating "conversion, national commerce, and the treasures of a renovated earth."[12]

A second value recently associated with Edwards's eschatology is the idea of American progress. Associated with the millennium, American economic and social progress became part of the deity's plan for world redemption. Thus the American political and social orders, which during the Great Awakening were regarded with suspicion by Edwardsean New

---

purified and refined." *Miscellanies*, Beinecke Rare Book and Manuscript Library, Yale University, New Haven, Connecticut, nos. 743, 946. All citations from the *Miscellanies* will refer only to Edwards's numbering—not page numbers of various modern editions—since there are various editions available. Unless otherwise indicated the Yale edition is being cited.

8. Heimert, *Religion and the American Mind*, 236.

9 Bercovitch, *The Puritan Origins*, 155–56.

10. John Wilson, introduction to HWR, 82. See also his "Religion at the Core of American Culture," in *Altered Landscapes: Christianity in America, 1935–1985*, ed. David W. Lotz et al. (Grand Rapids, Mich., 1989), 373.

11. Bercovitch, *The American Jeremiad*, 108; Lowance, *The Language of Canaan*, 179; Maclear, "The Republic and the Millennium," 196.

12. Bercovitch, *The American Jeremiad*, 109, 157, 185.

Lights, came to be seen through the diffracting lens of Edwardsean eschatology as divinely appointed custodians of the work of redemption.[13]

Although many students of Edwards's eschatology have found it to be
self-indulgently nationalistic—at least at certain points in Edwards's
career[14]—and some have connected Edwards's millennialism and later
American egoism, a minority of critics have argued that Edwards's eschatology was apolitical. James West Davidson maintains that Edwards's
millennium is privatistic in the sense that it describes an inner, spiritual
world that transcends existing political institutions. Liberty reigns but
existing civil governments are not overthrown. So the "liberty" therein
described need not be political. Furthermore, the millennial vision requires regeneration, but many—perhaps most—members of society are
unregenerate. Therefore, one cannot speak of a wholesale political
change.[15] Nathan Hatch reaches the same conclusion but by a different
route. He argues that Edwards was too pessimistic in his forecasts of the
historical future to hitch his eschatology to the chariots of secular parties.
Whereas Calvinists during and after the Revolution linked the advent of
the millennium to the new American republic, Edwards insisted that the
millennium would come by spiritual means such as the preaching of the
gospel.[16]

What *were* the social and political implications of Edwards's millennialism? Did his eschatology really exalt America to a position of spiritual
and political preeminence in cosmic history? Was America to be both the

---

13. Ibid., 108; Goen, "Jonathan Edwards: A New Departure in Eschatology," 26, 39–
40. Other scholars have been more hesitant to connect Edwards with later nationalism
and self-interest. Wilson, for instance, says only that Edwards's *History of the Work of
Redemption* "legitimated the social experiment that was the new American culture."
Introduction to *HWR*, 82. Alan Heimert was more positive, finding the source for the
Revolutionary era's "ideal of continental union" in Edwards's focus on the union of
Americans to pray for the millennium. Heimert, *Religion and the American Mind*, 100, 95.

14. Even Ernest Lee Tuveson and Bercovitch, both of whom read Edwards as promoting America as a redeemer nation, concede that Edwards seems to have reversed himself
midway through his career. Tuveson, *Redeemer Nation*, 101; Bercovitch, *The American
Jeremiad*, 99.

15. James West Davidson, *The Logic of Millennial Thought: Eighteenth-Century New
England* (New Haven, 1977), 220–21, 226–32, 258–59.

16. Hatch, *The Sacred Cause of Liberty*, 1–2, 32–36, 167.

catalyst to inaugurate the millennium and the center of that final, glorious stage of history? If New England and America were central to Edwards's eschatology, both as agents to bring on history's culmination and as most favored nations during that reign of glory, then Edwards's eschatology was inconsistent with his (national) covenantal theology. For in the last chapter we saw that in Edwards's view of the national covenant, New England was not a redeemer nation, but a bad example that the world would be wise to avoid. New England had sinned so grievously that, as Edwards stopped to contemplate its eschatology, he foresaw not future glory but the possibility of imminent destruction.[17] He wondered only why it had not already come. If in Edwards's eschatology New England was to be the locus of the earthly reign of Christ, then his public theology was full of inner contradictions.

It is my thesis in this chapter that on the point at hand Edwards's thought is consistent. There is no conflict between his doctrine of the national covenant and his millennialism. If the former casts a dark cloud of judgment over the colonies, the latter relegates them to obscurity by its overwhelming emphasis on the international dimensions of the millennium. Edwards's eschatology is dominated by an unyielding concentration on the coming global community that implicitly relativizes all merely national concerns and condemns all egoistic nationalism. Before the majestic dimensions of the "one holy and happy society"[18] that is to come, New England and America fade into insignificance.

Scholars have properly concentrated on Edwards's millennialism for clues to his thinking on other issues. The work of redemption within

---

17. In the Christian tradition judgment does not necessarily forfeit future participation in the work of redemption. For, as the biblical author put it, "The time has come for judgment to *begin* with the household of God." (1 Peter 4:17 RSV) The judgment that Edwards saw looming for New England, however, would bring New England's usefulness to an end. It would result in New England's "destruction," and the transference of her covenant to a people more worthy of it: "God may give other countreys much of this mercy & us no more of it."

18. Edwards uses this phrase in a letter to a Scottish correspondent to describe the transnational community of the millennial age. It is not clear from the context whether he was referring to the time of worldwide revival preceding the millennium, or to the millennium itself. But in either case, his vision is of the global society to come that will transcend all national boundaries. AW, 446.

human history was an obsession for Edwards, and the union of nations and peoples in the millennium was the next and last earthly phase of that work of redemption. His vision of the millennium's realities and his anticipation of the "glorious work of God's Spirit"[19] that would bring it to fruition so pervaded his thinking that nearly every one of his central doctrines is illuminated by an unfolding of the millennial vision. It is sometimes remarked, for instance, that Edwards's doctrine of divine sovereignty was as exalted as any in the history of Christian thought.[20] Yet Edwards's doctrine cannot be appreciated fully unless it is understood that every event in history is divinely orchestrated to prepare for the millennium.

Divine typology in history and nature is another characteristic feature of Edwards's theology. For Edwards, typology pointed not only to past redemption and present spiritual realities, but to future events in history as well.[21] Yet the most exciting future events were the millennium and "that glorious work of God's Spirit" leading up to it. Every sunrise, for instance, was for Edwards a type of the bright glory to come in the millennium.[22]

An understanding of Edwards's millennialism will, similarly, shed much light on his public theology. For we shall see that it was in the "one amiable society" (HWR, 483) of the millennium, not his own, that Edwards was absorbed. It was the "one holy city, one heavenly family" (HA, 339) that looms in the background of nearly every treatise and

---

19. This is Edwards's phrase for the worldwide series of revivals that would precede and bring on the millennium. It will be discussed in the last section of this chapter. HWR, 391; see also ST, 353.

20. See, for instance, Douglas J. Elwood, The Philosophical Theology of Jonathan Edwards (New York, 1960), 155–60; Norman Fiering, "The Rationalist Foundations of Jonathan Edwards's Metaphysics," in Jonathan Edwards and the American Experience, ed. Hatch and Stout, 79; and Wallace E. Anderson, ed., Scientific and Philosophical Writings, vol. 6 in The Works of Jonathan Edwards (New Haven, 1980), 26–27.

21. The best survey of Edwards's typology—despite his misunderstanding of Edwards on America and the millennium—is Lowance, The Language of Canaan, 178–207, 249–95.

22. Jonathan Edwards, Images or Shadows of Divine Things, ed. Perry Miller (New Haven, 1948), 92. [All references to this work are to page number of this edition, not to item number. Also, this work will be cited as Images, both in notes, and parenthetically in the text.]

many of his sermons, and that fills many pages of his private notebooks. In short, in his religious imagination Jonathan Edwards was a world citizen. The parochialism and egoistic nationalism ascribed to him would have struck him as myopic and characteristic only of unregenerate, natural virtue.[23] I shall demonstrate this thesis first by describing the intensity of Edwards's absorption with the millennium and its antecedent events, then by delineating in detail the contours of each of those periods—the millennium and the "glorious work of God's Spirit" preceding it—and drawing out the implications of each for Edwards's public theology.

Edwards's Entertainment and Delight

Jonathan Edwards was not the first New Englander to be interested in the millennium. Religious leaders since the Founding had spoken and written of it. In 1710 Increase Mather wrote that belief in the millennium "has ever been received as a Truth in the Churches of *New-England.*" Yet from the first generation eschatology was seldom a central concern for religious leaders. John Winthrop wrote very little about the millennium in his voluminous writings, and "[Thomas] Shepard and [Thomas] Hooker, after John Cotton the two most prolific writers in New England of the 1640s, had far less than he to say upon millennial topics." The focus of Shepard's *Ten Virgins* is Christ's Second Coming, not a final earthly age of glory. John Norton refers to the fullness of the Gentiles in *The Answer,* but this notion plays no significant role in the book.[24]

Religious leaders of New England's later generations "rarely preached specifically on millennial prophecies pointing to the end of time, and when they did it was generally in the most undogmatic and speculative of

---

23. As indeed he argued; see *TV,* 554–56, 609–12.

24. Increase Mather, *A Discourse Concerning Faith and Fervency in Prayer, and the Glorious Kingdom of the Lord Jesus Christ, on Earth, Now Approaching* (Boston, 1710), 1; cited in Bloch, *Visionary Republic,* 11; Robert Middlekauf, *The Mathers: Three Generations of Puritan Intellectuals, 1596–1728* (New York, 1971), 322; Bozeman, *To Live Ancient Lives,* 234; John Norton, *The Answer to the Whole Set of Questions of . . . William Apollonius,* trans. Douglas Horton (1648; Cambridge, Mass., 1958), 7.

terms."[25] Michael Wigglesworth's *Day of Doom* (1662), the most popular eschatological statement of the seventeenth century, pointed its readers to hell, not the millennium.[26] The jeremiahs in mid and late century found little or no use for millennial eschatology.[27] Eighteenth-century election sermons show a similar pattern. The millennium is either absent or merely a rhetorical flourish.[28] Even those who celebrated the millennial import of Cape Breton and other events in the French and Indian War were nevertheless unwilling to say that the war was the climactic battle against the Antichrist.[29] In sum, millennialism was a paradigm used more for comprehending the meaning of occasional crises than for understanding everyday life.[30]

For Jonathan Edwards, however, the millennium was a continual obsession. What William Ellery Channing once said of Samuel Hopkins, Edwards's closest disciple, could be said with equal accuracy of Edwards, "The millennium was more than a belief to him. It had the freshness of visible things. He was at home in it. His book on the subject has an air of

---

25. Stout, *The New England Soul*, 8.

26. Michael Wigglesworth, *Day of Doom*, in *The American Puritans: Their Prose and Poetry*, ed. Perry Miller (Garden City, N.Y., 1956), 282.

27. Mitchell, Stoughton, Oakes, and Torrey turned to it only briefly; it did not play any significant role in their jeremiads. Bozeman, *To Live Ancient Lives*, 338; Davidson, *The Logic of Millennial Thought*, 54, 60–61, 67.

28. In Samuel Danforth's "Repentance" (Boston, 1727), for instance, there is no mention of the millennium. For examples of sermons where mention of the millennium was merely a rhetorical flourish, see Charles Chauncy, "Marvellous Things" (Boston, 1745), and Thomas Prince, "The Natural and Moral Government" (Boston, 1749). Millennialism was even less prominent in eighteenth-century England. Because of the lingering public associations of millennialism with the radicalism of the Puritan Revolution, millennialism "became an almost exclusively academic and theoretical concern." Neither the radical Whigs in the political opposition nor the preachers of the Methodist revival gained a reputation for millennial thought. Bloch, *Visionary Republic*, 10.

29. Stout, *The New England Soul*, 246–47, 253–55.

30. Stout concludes that the importance of millennialism in colonial New England has been "abused through overemphasis." Stout, *The New England Soul*, 8. It must be pointed out, however, that Increase and Cotton Mather anticipated Edwards's absorption with the millennium. In his last years Increase began to insist that belief in the millennium was a test of true faith. Cotton Mather, Robert Middlekauf argues, moved eschatology to the center of New England theology, displacing even the doctrines of Calvin as the key to the meaning of God's sovereignty. Middlekauf, *The Mathers*, 183, 323–24.

reality, as if written from observation."[31] Edwards cultivated a lifelong fascination with the millennial prophecies of Scripture. When he wrote his *Personal Narrative* at the age of thirty-six, he recalled being dazzled by the millennial future in his twentieth year: "Sometimes Mr. Smith and I walked there [in New York] together, to converse on the things of God; and our conversation used to turn much on the advancement of Christ's kingdom in the world, *and the glorious things that God would accomplish for his church in the latter days.*"[32] We know that Edwards's recollection of concern for eschatology in his twentieth year was not inaccurate because in a diary entry from the same year we find him lamenting the insufficiency of his prayers for the millennium.[33] This engrossment with eschatology continued throughout his life. In a letter in 1741 to a newly converted "dear young friend" in reply to a request for instructions on how to "maintain a religious life," Edwards urged her to pray that God "would carry on his glorious work which he has now begun, till the world shall be full of his glory."[34] Six years later, when David Brainerd was dying in Edwards's home, the two often discussed the coming glorious days of the church, and the young man's "vehement thirstings" for the millennial age only sharpened the pastor's own eschatological hopes (*David Brainerd*, 532). Stephen J. Stein notes that Edwards continued to make millennial entries in his private notebooks to the end of his career (*AW*, 10, 32). It is a telling sign of the fascination eschatology held for Edwards that the Revelation was the only book of the Bible on which he wrote a separate commentary.[35]

---

31. Edwards was Hopkins's chief inspiration and mentor on millennial topics. William Ellery Channing, *Works*, 6 vols. (Boston, 1841), 4:353; cited in Joseph A. Conforti, *Samuel Hopkins and the New Divinity Movement: Calvinism, the Congregational Ministry, and Reform in New England Between the Great Awakenings* (Grand Rapids, Mich., 1981), 173.

32. Jonathan Edwards, "Personal Narrative," in *Jonathan Edwards: Representative Selections*, ed. Clarence H. Faust and Thomas H. Johnson (New York, 1962), 65 [henceforth cited as "PN" in notes and text]; emphasis added.

33. *The Life of President Edwards*, vol. 1 of *Works*, ed. Dwight, 102.

34. Ibid., 151–52.

35. *AW*, 1. In contrast, it was the only book on which Calvin did *not* write a commentary. For Calvin's views of Revelation and eschatology, see Heinrich Quistorp, *Calvin's Doctrines of the Last Things* (London, 1955), and David E. Holwerda, "Eschatology and History: A Look at Calvin's Eschatological Vision," in *Readings in Calvin's Theology*, ed. Donald K. McKim (Grand Rapids, Mich., 1984), 311–42.

For Edwards the millennial age was of more than just speculative or even theological interest. Devotion to it gave him emotional satisfaction and release. In the *Personal Narrative* he relates that over the sixteen years since his twentieth year "my mind has been much *entertained and delighted* with the scripture promises and prophecies, which relate to the future glorious advancement of Christ's kingdom upon earth" ("PN," 68; emphasis added). News of the advancement of Christ's kingdom toward its earthly culmination in the millennium would, by his own admission, "much animate and refresh" the sickly and often weary pastor ("PN," 64). Ten years later, he was still finding "entertaining" the news of developments in Scotland that suggested progress in the work of redemption toward the millennium.[36] Stein infers that Edwards's millennial fixation provided comfort "throughout the years of great personal stress and turmoil," particularly in the 1740s when growing tensions between him and his Northampton congregation finally resulted in his ejection.[37]

Theologically, the millennium was crucial because of its place in Edwards's understanding of Providence. All of history was ordered by God in such a way as to lead to a foreordained result—the kingdom of his Son. As Edwards put it, the universe is like a "chariot in which God rides and makes progress towards the last end of all things."[38] So the millennium, as the last earthly stage in that process, is the culmination of all the ages of human history.

---

36. Dwight, *The Life of President Edwards*, 278.

37. *AW*, 47. It is interesting that his daughter Esther Burr used the millennial hope similarly, as a source of solace amidst daily frustrations caused by people: "What a charming place this world would be of [sic] it was not for the inhabitants—O I long for the blessed and glorious when this World shall become a Mountain of Holiness." Cited in Iain H. Murray, *Jonathan Edwards: A New Biography* (Edinburgh, 1987), 409. In their magisterial survey of Western utopias, Frank and Fritzie Manuel observe that it is characteristic of "utopian personalities," who are typically angry with the world and disgusted with society, to "withdraw from this world into a far simpler form of existence which they fantasy." We shall see below that Edwards's portrayal of the millennium was a subtle critique of eighteenth-century New England. Frank E. Manuel and Fritzie P. Manuel, *Utopian Thought in the Western World* (Cambridge, Mass., 1979), 27.

38. "Miscellaneous Observations on the Holy Scriptures" [the "Blank Bible"] (ms, Yale coll.), 169, cited in *AW*, 49.

All the changes that are brought to pass in the world, from age to age, are ordered in infinite wisdom in one respect or other to prepare the way for the glorious issue of things, that shall be when truth and righteousness shall finally prevail, and he, whose right it is, shall take the kingdom. . . . The mighty struggles and conflicts of nations, and shakings of kingdoms, and those vast successive changes that are brought to pass, in the kingdoms and empires of the world, from one age to another, are as it were travail pangs of the creation, in order to bring forth this glorious event. (HA, 346)

For Edwards, history and the millennium were inseparable. The first was preparation for the second; the second, the *telos* of the first. There-fore, neither could be understood without the other. Edwards demon-strated the inseparability of the two in his mind in two places in his "Personal Narrative." In the first instance, when describing his days in New York, he mentioned the two in the same breath: "Our [Edwards and John Smith] conversation used to turn much on the advancement of Christ's kingdom in the world, *and* the glorious things that God would accomplish for his church in the latter days" ("PN," 65). Later in the "Narrative," after saying that "the histories of the past advancement of Christ's kingdom have been sweet to me," Edwards turned immediately to the millennium and its prelude: "And my mind has been much enter-tained and delighted with the scripture promises and prophecies, which relate to the future glorious advancement of Christ's kingdom upon earth" (68). For Edwards, the process of redemption in human history was "most fundamental to Christianity."[39] And since the millennium was the last earthly stage of that history, no part of the history could be properly evaluated without consideration of its earthly *telos*. Only the future could give proper meaning to both past and present.

Edwards eagerly scanned his contemporary world for signs of progress in that process of which the millennium was the culmination. "If I heard the least hint," he wrote in the "Narrative," "of any thing that happened, in any part of the world, that appeared, in some respect or other, to have a favourable aspect, on the interests of Christ's kingdom, my soul eagerly

---

39. Wilson, introduction to HWR, 10.

catched at it. . . . I used to be eager to read public newsletters, mainly
for that end; to see if I could not find some news, favourable to the
interest of religion in the world" ("PN," 64). Stein tells us that Edwards
"retained the habit in later years" (AW, 10) and during the French and
Indian War "followed developments closely because the outcome had
implications for the view of history he had shaped in his reflections on
Revelation" (32). In 1749 Edwards begged a Scottish correspondent to
give him "information of whatever appears in your parts of the world,
favourable to the interests of the kingdom of Christ."[40] His *Notes on the
Apocalypse,* written throughout his adult life, reveal copious attention
given to world events—political, military, and ecclesiastical—that by his
lights indicated the beginning of the destruction of the Antichrist and
the worldwide outpouring of the Spirit of God.[41]

Besides seeing the millennium anticipated in contemporary history,
Edwards found it prefigured in biblical history and nature. In his private
notebooks Edwards wrote that he found typological anticipations of the
coming glorious days of the Church in the fall of Sodom and Gomorrah,
the prophecies about Israel's return to the land, Achsah's intercession with
her father, the destruction of Sisera, the reign of Solomon, the Jews'
victory in the time of Esther, and many other biblical events.[42] When he
turned to observe the beauty of the world about him, Edwards found images of the millennium there too. Both spring and the dawn, for example,
are types of the "commencement of the glorious times of the church."[43]

---

40. Dwight, *The Life of President Edwards,* 278.

41. "Notes on the Apocalypse," in *AW,* 95–305. Stein refers to Edwards's "lifelong preoccupation with the fortunes of the church militant through the ages and in the *present,* as
well as his concern with the glories of the church triumphant, anticipated on earth and fulfilled ultimately in heaven." Stephen J. Stein, "Providence and the Apocalypse in the Early
Writings of Jonathan Edwards," *Early American Literature* 13 (1978): 263. Edwards's careful
attention in his private notebooks to contemporary events belies the oft-heard claim that
Edwards was uninterested in the social and political realities of his day. For examples of this
claim, see Herbert Wallace Schneider, *The Puritan Mind* (New York, 1930), 106–7; Perry
Miller, "Jonathan Edwards's Sociology of the Great Awakening," *New England Quarterly* 21
(1948): 51; Anson P. Stokes, *Church and State in the United States* (New York, 1950), 241;
Gerhard Alexis, "Jonathan Edwards and the Theocratic Ideal," *Church History* 35 (1966):
329; and Mead, *The Old Religion in the Brave New World,* 4, 52–53.

42. *Notes on the Bible,* vol. 9 of *Works,* ed. Dwight, 224, 232, 296–99, 316, 330–31.

43. *Images,* 92, 124.

Thus Edwards was gripped by the millennium. Yet, as I have mentioned in passing, the millennium was only the penultimate goal of God's work of redemption of the elect. The ultimate goal was the final assemblage of the kingdom in heaven, far removed from earth and *after* the completion of the millennium.[44] This would be a state "manifestly different from the millennium." It would represent the return of all things to God after their beginning in God: "In the beginning of this revolution all things come from God, and are formed out of a chaos; and in the end, all things shall return into a chaos again, and shall return to God, so that he that is *Alpha,* will be the *Omega.*"[45] Thus progress in the work of redemption is ultimately circular. This is why Edwards chose the wheel as the best representation of divine providence.[46]

Although the millennium was not the ultimate goal of the history of redemption, it nevertheless excited more of Edwards's attention than any other phase in that history. This was due to the place Edwards thought he occupied within the history of providence. In his estimation the present generation was standing on the threshold of the age that would precipitate the millennium. As we shall see below, this preparatory age would last far beyond Edwards's lifetime; Edwards never expected to see the dawn of the millennium himself. But to live in the preparatory age was exciting enough. Besides, he thought that he was one of a handful of divines called by God in the latter days to teach and reprove the Church, and thus prepare it for eventual participation in the millennium.[47] So, while he knew that the millennium was only a penultimate stage before ultimate glory, anticipation of its penultimate glory was captivating enough to hold his attention for more than thirty-eight years.

Let us now attempt to imagine the spectacle that so captivated Ed-

---

44. Thus Stein notes, "Accordingly, in the sermons on Isaiah 51.8 the millennium took second place to heaven, the object of all God's dealings with the church." *AW,* 24.

45. "Notes on the Apocalypse," in *AW,* 142; "Notes on Scripture" (MS, Yale coll.) no. 389, cited in *AW,* 54.

46. *AW,* 53–54. This is the familiar Neoplatonic theme of return to the primordium. Edwards was familiar with the Neoplatonic tradition through his reading of Cambridge Platonists such as John Smith and seventeenth-century Puritan writers such as Richard Sibbes, John Flavel, and John Owen. See John E. Smith's introduction to *RA,* 53, 60–62, 65–66, 68–70; and Simonson, *Jonathan Edwards,* 33.

47. *Miscellanies,* no. 810; *AW,* 303.

wards by sketching the outlines of his millennial vision. We will begin by examining the chronology of the millennial age because (1) it demonstrates where Edwards thought he stood within the history of redemption, and (2) the time of the beginning of the millennial age has been almost universally misunderstood by students of Edwards's thought.

The Shape of the Millennium

Chronology

For Edwards the millennium would be Christ's *third* coming to set up his kingdom. His *first* coming was in the apostolic era when he set up his kingdom in a spiritual sense and destroyed his enemies by starting the church. The end of this era was marked by the destruction of Jerusalem. The *second* coming effected the "destruction of the heathen Roman empire" in Constantine's time. The *fourth* and last coming will be "his coming to the last judgment, which is the event principally signified in scripture by Christ's coming in his kingdom" (*HWR*, 351).

Contrary to prevailing scholarly opinion, this third coming of Christ in the millennium was not expected by Edwards till the distant future. And, I would argue, Edwards held this view consistently throughout his career. When he was twenty years old (in 1723), he wrote in his private notebook that he did not anticipate the final destruction of "Satan's kingdom till the year 2000" (*AW*, 77, 129). In 1747 he submitted this chronology to public scrutiny in *An Humble Attempt*. Moses Lowman was correct, he maintained, to place the Antichrist's end after 2000. One of the first series of blows against the Antichrist's reign (a worldwide series of revivals) was to come soon, but the final blow (the final destruction of the Antichrist and thus the beginning of the millennium) was not to come until the seventh millennium of human history (A.D. 2000–3000).[48]

Between his first prediction in his private notebook and his public

---

48. *HA*, 394, 410. Moses Lowman (1680–1752) was a dissenting clergyman whose *Paraphrase and Notes on the Revelation* (London, 1737) greatly interested Edwards. *AW*, 55.

forecast in *An Humble Attempt,* Edwards made another prediction that has caused commentators to stumble ever since. The problem hinges on the interpretation of a phrase in *Some Thoughts Concerning the Revival* (1742). In an oft-cited passage relating the Great Awakening to God's future work of redemption Edwards proclaimed that "this work of God's Spirit, that is so extraordinary and wonderful, is the dawning, or at least a prelude, of that glorious work of God, so often foretold in Scripture, which in the progress and issue of it, shall renew the world of mankind." The phrase in question is "that glorious work of God," which Edwards says later in the passage "must be near" (*ST,* 353). Almost every interpreter of Edwards's eschatology has construed this remark to be a reference to the millennium, and thus a prediction that the millennium was imminent.[49] If they are correct, Edwards had reversed his earlier conviction that the millennium lay in the distant future, and was taking a stand that he would contradict for the remainder of his life. Even Stein, who thinks he refers to the millennium, concedes, "This heady proclamation published in 1743 was neither in character with Edwards's earlier pronouncements on the revivals nor totally consistent with his own private reflections" (*AW,* 26).

In fact, there is good reason to believe that Edwards here referred not to the millennium but to a long period of intermittent revival that would lead up to the millennium. Four to five years earlier Edwards already had made it clear that the millennium would be a state of peace and rest—at least until the great apostasy at its end.[50] In contrast, the revivals leading

---

49. Charles Chauncy, Edwards's contemporary and adversary, was the first. *Seasonable Thoughts on the State of Religion in New-England* (Boston, 1743), 372–75. For more recent such interpretations, see, for example, Miller, *Jonathan Edwards,* 326; Goen, "Jonathan Edwards: A New Departure in Eschatology," 29–30, and introduction to GA, 71–72; Mason I. Lowance, Jr., "Typology, Millennial Eschatology, and Jonathan Edwards," in *Critical Essays on Jonathan Edwards,* ed. William J. Scheick (Boston, 1980), 191; Bloch, *Visionary Republic,* 17; and Peter Gay, *A Loss of Mastery: Puritan Historians in Colonial America* (Berkeley and Los Angeles, 1966), 16. Some may have been led astray by Goen's insertion of the heading "The Millennium Probably to Dawn in America" over the passage in question. GA, 353.

50. "Notes on the Apocalypse," in *AW,* 177–79. The dating for this is based on the work of Thomas Schafer, as described in *AW,* 78. Schafer estimates that no. 77 of "Notes on the Apocalypse" was written in the 1738–39 period.

up to it would be marked by conflict and struggle as the forces of the
Antichrist did battle with the newly emerging kingdom of the Son. So
the period *before* the millennium would be a time of change and unrest,
but the millennium itself would be a changeless epoch of peace.

> The millennium is the sabbatism of the church, or the time of her
> rest. But surely the days of her sabbatism or rest don't begin, till
> she ceases to be any longer in travail. . . . And as long as the
> church still remains struggling and laboring, to bring to pass this
> effect, her travail ceases not; . . . The church from Christ's time
> to the millennium, is in a state of warfare, or her militant state;
> but during that sabbatism, [she] shall be in a triumphant state.
> The proper time of the church's rest and triumph can't be said to
> be come, till all her enemies are subdued. (*HA*, 178–79)

The problem with the conventional interpretation is that the passage
in question, upon which the interpretation is based, describes a work of
God that is still in a process of development and change. It is "that
glorious work of God, so often foretold in Scripture, which *in the progress
and issue of it,* shall renew the world of mankind" (*ST,* 353; emphasis
added). Edwards here describes a progressive, and therefore gradual, transition in the world, during which the world will be renewed. The emphasis is on a developmental process: "which *in the progress and issue of it,*
shall renew the world." The world shall be renewed, but only "in the
progress" of that glorious work of God—that is, as the work of God
progresses through its duration. Three years earlier, in his sermons on the
history of the work of redemption, Edwards had taught quite explicitly
that the "great work of God" that would pave the way for the millennium
would be wrought "gradually" and amidst "violent and mighty opposition."[51] Yet, as we have seen, Edwards had represented the millennium

---

51. *HWR*, 392, 394. This is in a long passage describing "that glorious work," 390–
404; only on 404 does his description of the millennium begin. In this (the first) section
are many allusions to the distinction between the "glorious work of God's Spirit" and the
millennium. The prophecy of Daniel 12:11, for instance, of two periods or levels of glory,
one at the end of 1290 days, and the other at the end of 1335 days, tell us "that something
very glorious should be accomplished at the end of the former period ["that glorious

itself as a state of rest and completion that does not begin until the process of development and conflict has been completed.

It makes much more sense to understand Edwards in the *Some Thoughts* passage as he himself interpreted the passage two years later—that he was referring to the long process preceding the onset of the millennium, not the millennium itself: "It has been slanderously reported and printed concerning me, that I have often said that the millennium was already begun . . . but the report is very diverse from what I have ever said."[52] In words nearly identical to the ones we have just seen from *Some Thoughts*, he said that he had always regarded the recent awakenings "as forerunners of those glorious times so often prophesied of in the Scripture, and that this was the first dawning of that light, and beginning of that work which, *in the progress and issue of it,* would *at last* bring on the church's latter-day glory" (GA, 560; emphasis added). The "work" that would "progress," in other words, was distinct from "the church's latter-day glory." Lest anyone still think that Edwards had ever considered the millennium imminent or arrived, he added that he had also said on earlier occasions that this work would be accompanied by conflict and struggle:

> There are many that know that I have from time to time added, that there would probably be many sore conflicts and terrible convulsions, and many changes, revivings and intermissions, and returns of dark clouds, and threatening appearances, before this work shall have subdued the world, and Christ's kingdom shall be everywhere established and settled in *peace, which will be the lengthening of the millennium, or day of the church's peace,* rejoicing and triumph on earth, so often spoken of. (GA, 560; emphasis added)

In the letter quoted above Edwards denied that he had predicted an imminent millennium, and insisted that he had always assumed a long process of

---

work"], but something much more glorious at the end of the latter [the millennium]." *HA*, 393. In *HA* he said that this first period will see "a *gradual* progress of religion," and that "that great work of God's Spirit" (language almost identical to that in the *Some Thoughts* passage) "before it is finished, will issue in Antichrist's ruin." Surely that will involve process and conflict. *HA*, 410–11, 425.

52. Letter to William McCulloch, 5 March 1744, in *GA*, 560.

revival and turmoil preceding the millennium. The pattern found here is the same one found in other descriptions of the latter days: the period leading up to the millennium will be a gradual development involving both revival and opposition, whereas the millennium itself will begin only when development has ceased and peace and rest have begun.[53]

There is also the puzzling statement in part 4 of *Some Thoughts* that the New England awakenings might "prove to be the dawning of a general revival" (*ST*, 466). For Edwards, the millennium was never considered, properly speaking, a revival. Edwards understood a revival to be episodic and progressive, but the millennium as uniform and static. In a revival souls change—from unsaved to saved, darkness to light. In the millennial era, on the other hand, souls remain essentially the same: they enter the era in the light (after seeing the light during the glorious days preceding the millennium) and continue in the light until the end and beyond. The millennium will not see the emotional and religious upheavals that occur in a revival.[54] This is why Edwards never used the word "millennium" in any of the *Some Thoughts* passages that allegedly predict an American millennium—a fact which has never been satisfyingly explained.[55] He certainly was not averse to use of the word, for he had previously used it in his private notebooks and would later use it in his published treatises.[56] But he did not use it here because it was not what he meant. "General revival" was a better term for "that great work of God's Spirit," because it consisted of precisely that: a worldwide series of revivals.

The interpretation here suggested—that Edwards foresaw in the immediate future not the millennium but a long age of intermittent revival

---

53. These statements were made both before and after the writing of *Some Thoughts*, which suggests that he did not change his mind on this schema. *AW*, 177–79 (written in 1738–39); *HA*, 405, 410 (written in 1747).

54. Compare his descriptions of revivals in *Faithful Narrative* and *Some Thoughts*, particularly his portrayal of the remarkable changes wrought in both individual and corporate consciousness and behavior by conversion, with his description of the millennium, as a period of peace and stability. *FN*, 147–204; *ST*, 331–47.

55. Only Stein seems to have noted its absence, but thinks it merely evidence of Edwards's reluctance to express publicly his private millennialism. *AW*, 28.

56. For examples of usage in his private notebooks, see 177–79, 181 (1738–39); for an example from his public works, see *HA*, 410.

preceding the millennium—is supported by consideration of Edwards's predecessors in the Reformed eschatological tradition. Examination of that tradition indicates that Edwards was advancing not novel doctrine but a variation of what had become a recurring theme. Thomas Brightman (1562–1607), who was the first Englishman in the mainstream of Reformed thought to break with the Augustinian interpretation of eschatology, forecast a "Middle Advent of Christ," beginning about 1650, the first hundred years of which would see a progressive reformation in both the Church and the world. By Christ's spiritual help the Church would gradually prosper, the Jewish nation would convert, and the papist and Turkish armies would be destroyed. At the end of that century of progressive reformation, perfection would be secured. The "pleasantness" that "belong[ed] to the first beginning [before the fall]" would be enjoyed by the saints for at least another five centuries until Christ's final coming. In Brightman, then, we see a period of revival and conflict effected by divine effusions before a period of peaceful perfection.[57]

John Cotton (1584–1652) was the foremost millennialist of the New England founders.[58] Like Brightman, he predicted a period of progressively increasing blessing for the Church and gradual destruction of her enemies. (Unlike Brightman, however, Cotton looked for the personal return of Christ to inaugurate the millennium). The Church would approach "full stature and beauty" in a period of "gradual increase," and while it was gradually increasing its size and influence, the Protestant armies would be mobilized to defeat—over a period of time—the Roman and Turkish menaces, as well as the Anglican episcopacy. During this time the world would still be far from millennial perfection. Many individuals and nations would remain unconverted, and Satan would still tempt the saints. The condition of mortality would remain.[59] Cotton was

---

57. Thomas Brightman, A Revelation of the Apocalyps (Amsterdam, 1611), 626, 113–14, 634–37, 678, and A Commentary on the Canticles (London, 1644), 1077; cited in Bozeman, To Live Ancient Lives, 248. For Brightman's eschatology, see Bozeman, To Live Ancient Lives, 207–9, 248–49, and Richard Bauckham, Tudor Apocalypse (Oxford, 1978), 139–43, 205–31.

58. Stout, The New England Soul, 48.

59. John Cotton, A Brief Exposition with Practical Observations upon the Whole Book of Canticles (London, 1655), 181, and A Brief Exposition of the Whole Book of Canticles, or,

not alone among his contemporaries in projecting an age of gradually
increasing glory for the Church before the onset of the millennium. "Few
if any theorists of the 1640s and 1650s saw the millennial order as the
creation of an instant. It was the way of the Middle Coming both to build
upon previous beginnings and to propel events toward completion
through a process of gradual development."[60]

Similar projections can be found in the eschatologies of Reformed
thinkers at the beginning of the eighteenth century. Both Moses Lowman
(1680–1752) and Petrus Van Mastricht (1630–1706), whose eschatology
and influence on Edwards are discussed in more detail below, believed
that the end of history would be preceded by an era of divine effusions
gradually prospering the Church and ruining her enemies. Lowman,
whose *Paraphrase and Notes on the Revelation* was the single work most
often cited by Edwards in his apocalyptic notebook and treatises, speculated that the destruction of mystical Babylon would proceed gradually
until after the year 2000, when the millennium would commence (*AW*,
57). Van Mastricht wrote in the last volume of his greatest work that the
near future held either the Last Judgment or a "New Reformation" that
would see the internal renewal of the church and a purifying divine
judgment on the unregenerate.[61]

James Davidson's study of millennial thought in eighteenth-century
New England shows a similar pattern. Most commentators on eschatology held to an "afflictive model of progress" wherein a series of revivals,
accompanied by afflictions, would precede the millennium. Things
would get worse as the millennium drew near, for as the Church prospers,
Satan fights harder against it. The redemption of the world consists of
both merciful effusions poured out on the Church and punishing judgments poured out on the world. Even the Church will be chastised in
order to purify it. Thus the last age before the millennium will combine
mercy and judgment, deliverance and affliction. As Samuel Willard put

---

Song of Solomon (London, 1642), 221–22; cited in Bozeman, 244–45. For Cotton's
eschatology, see Bozeman, *To Live Ancient Lives*, 237–62, and Stout, *The New England
Soul*, 19–20, 48–49.

60. Bozeman, *To Live Ancient Lives*, 244.

61. Petrus Van Mastricht, *Beschouwende en Praktikale Godgeleerdheit*, trans. Henricus
Pontanus (Rotterdam, 1749), 4:481.

it, a time was coming when "the privileges of the Church both spiritual and temporal shall be great to admiration, but still it will have a mixture of darkness in it."[62]

This time of tumult stood in stark contrast to a time, of which many also spoke, when human nature would be changed, courts would not be abused, standing armies would be unnecessary, and factions would not exist. Of Edwards's contemporaries, the English dissenting theologian Thomas Ridgley (1667–1734), whose systematic theology was familiar to Edwards, perhaps came closest to distinguishing the two periods. Before the millennium, Ridgley wrote, there would be "a greater fullness of the Gentiles . . . a greater degree of the effusion of the Spirit . . . a more glorious light shining throughout the world, than has ever done." Apparently there would also be afflictions, for the millennium itself would be "perfectly free from all those *afflictive* dispensations of providence, which would tend to hinder the preaching and success of the gospel." The Antichrist will have been subdued, so the saints will be "enjoying as much peace, as they have reason to expect in any condition short of heaven."[63]

Ridgley came close to articulating the distinction, but it was Edwards who most clearly developed the two-stage chronology. Others may have assumed such a distinction without expressing it. Perhaps some, caught up by millennial enthusiasm during and after the French and Indian Wars, saw no distinction at all. Hence their audiences could be forgiven for concluding that Christ was about to come to earth to launch his thousand-year reign. Edwards, on the other hand, took care to point out that the New England revivals were signs of a long period mixed with glory and affliction, and that the millennial age, properly speaking, was still hundreds of years in the future.[64]

---

62. See Davidson, *The Logic of Millennial Thought*, 122–75; Samuel Willard, "The Checkered State of the Gospel Church" (Boston, 1701), 22.

63. Davidson, *The Logic of Millennial Thought*, 226–37. Edwards quoted from Ridgley's *Body of Divinity* in his treatise on the Trinity, cited in Thomas H. Johnson, "Jonathan Edwards's Background of Reading," *Publications of the Colonial Society of Massachusetts 28* (1930–33): 207–8; Thomas Ridgley, *A Body of Divinity*, 4 vols. (London, 1731; first American edition, 1814–15), 2:368, 373, 392.

64. Imminentism was prevalent even after the 1740s. Charles Chauncy and Jonathan Mayhew disagreed on the timing of Christ's bodily return, but both spread hopes for the speedy culmination of history. Mayhew expected a fundamental transformation of the

In sum, all of these considerations—Edwards's descriptions of the millennium as a static period of peace and rest and the preceding period as a time of change and conflict, his statement that the Great Awakening might be the prelude to a general revival, and the compatibility of this interpretation with those of Edwards's Reformed predecessors—suggest that Edwards was telling the truth when he protested that he had never predicted an imminent millennium. Instead, he had always anticipated "that glorious work of God's Spirit" which would last many generations past his own before the dawning of the millennium itself.

The significance of Edwards's denial of an imminent millennium can be seen when it is contrasted with the views of some of Edwards's predecessors and contemporaries. By postponing the millennium to the twenty-first century, Edwards was rejecting the imminentism of—among others—the Mathers. In the early part of the eighteenth century Increase Mather expected Christ to return within a matter of a few years to inaugurate the millennium. His son Cotton was even more fervent in his expectation of the end-time glory. Unlike his father, he was willing to set a date for Christ's return—1716. After that prophecy failed, he was still writing in 1724 that the millennium could begin at any time.[65]

Edwards was also rejecting the imminentism of many clerical contemporaries. Eighteenth-century revivals, both before and during the Great Awakening, were interpreted as signs that the eschaton was at hand. As early as 1706, for example, Samuel Danforth proclaimed after a revival at Taunton, "The Time of the pouring out of the SPIRIT upon all Flesh may be at the Door." Fifteen years later, Eliphalet Adams understood a rash of conversions at Windham as a sign that the times were "drawing nearer"

---

world in the near future. In the 1750s, books by Anglican Richard Clark, Scottish Presbyterian David Imrie, and seventeenth-century English Presbyterian Christopher Love used numerology, extrabiblical sources, and personal revelation to predict the beginning of the millennium in the following decade. Reprints of two seventeenth-century premillennialist Puritans, William Torry and Ezekiel Cheever, further encouraged the belief that the millennium could soon begin. Even Joseph Bellamy, Edwards's friend and disciple, was ambiguous on the timing of the millennium in his oft-reprinted sermon on the millennium. Bloch, *Visionary Republic*, 28–32, 22–28. Joseph Bellamy, "The Millennium," in *The Great Awakening: Documents Illustrating the Crisis and Its Consequences*, ed. Perry Miller and Alan Heimert (Indianapolis, 1967), 609–35.

65. Middlekauf, *The Mathers*, 181, 337, 348.

when the "whole Earth may be filled with the Knowledge of the Glory of the Lord." Great Awakening revivals produced similar expectations. In South Carolina they were hailed as the harbinger of the new age. A Pennsylvania New Side cleric pronounced them proof that "the Kingdom of God is come unto us at this Day." Weekly reports publicizing the progress of the revivals in Thomas Prince's *Christian History,* the Boston periodical published in 1744 and 1745, were punctuated periodically with millennial acclamations. The colonial victory at Cape Breton in 1745 was seen as "an Earnest of our Lords taking to himself the entire Possession of this *New World.*"[66]

The chronology of the Edwardsean millennium has two more salient features: its end and its length. The Edwardsean millennium was to be a period of absolute stability and peace for the vast majority of its duration. Only at its very end would there be a break in its bliss, when the newly freed Satan would lead a great apostasy.[67] After his rebellion is put down, the Last Judgment shall ensue. Then the Church will be lifted to the highest heavens as one glorious society, and the earth will be burned to become a furnace for the wicked.[68]

Concerning the length of the millennium, some of Edwards's contemporaries had supposed the "thousand years" of Revelation to be only a figure of speech to represent a very long time.[69] Edwards, however, insisted that the number was literal. For if it were any longer, he argued, a population explosion would render the planet unlivable. Because of the absence of wars and disease in the millennium, the human race would be "multiplying so fast"—even if it doubles but once in a century—that

---

66. Thomas Prince, Jr., *The Christian History,* 2 vols. (Boston, 1744–45), 1:111, cited in Davidson, *The Logic of Millennial Thought,* 149; Eliphalet Adams, *A Sermon Preached at Windham* (New London, Conn., 1721), vi, 40, cited in Davidson, *The Logic of Millennial Thought,* 149; Bloch, *Visionary Republic,* 16; Joseph Sewall, *The Lamb Slain* (Boston, 1745), 6, cited in Stout, *The New England Soul,* 237.

67. This is why Edwards said that during the millennium "the Christian church shall for the most part [be] in a state of peace and prosperity." *HWR,* 479. The notion of a final stand by Satan at the end of the millennium was routine in England and New England. See, for example, the description of Lowman's version in *AW,* 57.

68. *HWR,* 409, 420.

69. *Miscellanies,* no. 836. See Davidson, *The Logic of Millennial Thought,* 84–97, for the range of topics on which expositors did not interpret Revelation literally.

there would not be room enough for all to coexist comfortably after one thousand years.[70]

If the time and duration of the millennium are important for any investigation of Edwards's civil religion, the *location* of the millennium is no less important. For if the eschaton is to be precipitated by a particular nation, or centrally located in one nation, then that nation will assume preeminence in the history of redemption. Thus we turn to the geography of the millennium.

Millennial Geography

For too long scholars have attributed to Edwards, on the basis of a misreading of the *Some Thoughts* passage, the belief that the millennium would begin or be centered in America. Edwards, referring to the same "work of God" discussed above, said that "there are many things that make it probable that this work will begin in America."[71] Thus Edwards appears to have contradicted himself, since at the beginning of his career he had written in his private notebooks that the millennium would be centered in Canaan.[72] But, as we have seen, the work of God predicted in the *Some Thoughts* passage is a series of revivals and conflicts preceding the millennium, not the millennium itself. In this passage Edwards claimed only that this work of preparation, which in *An Humble Attempt* he estimated would last two hundred and fifty years (*HA*, 411), would probably begin in America.

Edwards's claim that the millennium itself would begin in Canaan was not unprecedented. In England, both Thomas Brightman (1562–1607) and Daniel Whitby (1638–1726) had claimed the same. Whitby, a liberal theologian whose eschatology Edwards read, portrayed the millennium as primarily a spiritual revival of the Jewish church. Some New England thinkers held similar views. John Cotton believed that the New

---

70. *Miscellanies*, no. 836. In contrast, Ridgley refused to take a position on whether the "thousand years" was literal or figurative. Ridgley, *A Body of Divinity*, 2:391.

71. *ST*, 353. They have also used *Images*, 147, which was written at nearly the same time as *ST* and probably refers as well to the glorious work of God to precede the millennium, not the millennium itself. Dating estimated by Thomas A. Schafer.

72. "Notes on the Apocalypse," in *AW*, 134.

Jerusalem would rise far from American shores, and Increase Mather wrote that Europe was to be the locus of the millennium.[73]

Edwards placed the center of the millennium in Canaan,[74] and described the millennium itself in international terms. "The kingdom of God . . . shall *not* be like the kingdoms of earthly kings, set up with outward pomp, *in some particular place*, which shall be especially the royal city, and seat of the kingdom" (*DM*, 235; emphasis added). Rather, it "shall universally prevail, and . . . be extended over the whole habitable earth" (*HA*, 333). No people or part of the globe shall be unaffected: "All countries and nations, even those which are now most ignorant, shall be full of light and knowledge" (*HWR*, 480). "All nations from one end of the earth to the other are subdued by the spiritual David, and firmly and quietly established in subjection to his crown."[75]

By positing an international millennium, Edwards was departing from what was more a popular—than clerical—image of the final glorious age. As noted above, John Cotton and Increase Mather rejected the notion of an American millennium. Although Cotton Mather at various points in his career looked for an American millennium, he finally realized that New England should not be confused with the New Jerusalem. Militia captain Edward Johnson, on the other hand, believed that New England was "the place where the Lord will create a new Heaven, and a new Earth in, new Churches, and a new Common-wealth together." Chief Justice Samuel Sewall was convinced that the "Divine Metropolis" would be seated on the American continent (in Mexico, to be precise). Early in the eighteenth century Joseph Morgan's *History of the Kingdom of Bara-*

---

73. Bozeman, *To Live Ancient Lives*, 218; Peter Toon, "The Latter Day Glory," in *Puritans, the Millennium, and the Future of Israel: Puritan Eschatology 1600 to 1660*, ed. Peter Toon (Cambridge, 1870), 30; Davidson, *The Logic of Millennial Thought*, 142, 145; Bozeman, 230; Increase Mather, *A Discourse Concerning the Danger of Apostacy* (Boston, 1685), 56, 61, cited in Bozeman, *To Live Ancient Lives*, 339n. On Increase Mather's eschatology, see Middlekauf, *The Mathers*, 179–87.

74. "The most glorious part of the church will hereafter be there [Canaan], at the center of the kingdom of Christ, communicating influences to all other parts." Edwards noted that Canaan was strategically located, at the center of the Old World in the midst of three continents and therefore positioned with respect to waterways that all other parts of the world could be reached easily. "Notes on the Apocalypse," in *AW*, 134.

75. "Notes on the Apocalypse," in *AW*, 181.

suah, which predicted that Christ's Kingdom would be in the New World, was popular.[76]

Edwards rejected such regionalism. That he propounded an American millennium is a notion without support in either his published works or private notebooks. He would have agreed with those critics who have dismissed the notion as parochial and tribalist—certainly ill-suited to a deity who superintends the entire cosmos. That Edwards at one point suggested that the centuries-long process precipitating the millennium might begin in America does not undermine this thesis, as will be shown below in the discussion of "that glorious work of God."

As others have noted,[77] Edwards did not construct his elaborate millennial vision in a vacuum. He fashioned his eschatology amid the turmoils of the Great Awakening and the struggles with his parishioners that culminated in ejection from his own pulpit. It will come as no surprise, then, to learn that many features of his millennium appear implicitly critical of Northampton religion, society, and economics. In this respect Edwards resembles the "great utopians" whose utopias were not otherworldly, escapist dreams but thoughtful critiques of their societies. Frank and Fritzie Manuel write, "Paradoxically, the great utopians have been great realists. They have an extraordinary comprehension of the time and place in which they are writing and deliver themselves of penetrating reflection on socioeconomic, scientific, or emotional conditions of their moment in history."[78]

Not only was Edwards's millennium a subtle reflection on eighteenth-century Northampton and New England, but it was not so bizarre that it seemed irrelevant. Like every great utopia, it "startles and yet is recog-

---

76. Cotton Mather, *Theopolis Americana* (Boston, 1710), 42, cited in Davidson, *The Logic of Millennial Thought,* 150; Johnson, *Wonder-Working Providence,* in *The Puritans,* ed. Perry Miller and Thomas H. Johnson (New York, 1938), 145; Samuel Sewall, *Phenomena Quaedam Apocalyptica* (Boston, 1697), 1–2, 45, cited in Davidson, *The Logic of Millennial Thought,* 67; Joseph Morgan's *History of the Kingdom of Barasuah,* ed. Richard Schlatter (1715; reprint, Cambridge, Mass., 1946), cited in Bloch, *Visionary Republic,* 12. Johnson and Sewall did not use the word "millennium," so it is not clear that that is precisely what they had in mind. But it is clear that they believed their land would have preeminence in God's future dispensation.

77. See, for example, Bercovitch, *The American Jeremiad,* 105.

78. Manuel and Manuel, *Utopian Thought,* 28–29.

nized as conceivable." Rather than fantasizing an unrealistic escape from the present, he sketched a future "that satisfies a hunger or stimulates the mind and the body to the recognition of a new potentiality."[79] It should be no surprise, then, that historians have attributed important social and political movements in colonial and early America to the stimulus of Edwards's millennial vision.[80]

Millennial Religion

In religion, the millennium would be everything Northampton was not. It would embody every virtue and every mark of piety that Edwards longed to see among his parishioners.[81] In the millennial time "religion shall in every respect be uppermost in the world." Political leaders would be "eminent in holiness," possessed by "vital piety." Arminianism and other deviations from Calvinism would be "exploded." Theological problems that long had perplexed the faithful would be solved: "There shall then be a wonderful unraveling the [sic] difficulties in the doctrines of religion, and clearing up of seeming inconsistencies. . . . Difficulties in Scripture shall then be cleared up, and wonderful things shall be discovered in the word of God that were never discovered before. . . . [H]eaven shall be, as it were, opened to the church of God on earth" (HWR, 480–81).

Piety would be genuine and sincere, not hypocritical: "Religion shall not be an empty profession as it now mostly is, but holiness of heart and life shall abundantly prevail." Religion would not be privatistic, confined only to the home and church, but would be "inscribed on every thing, on all men's common business and employments, and the common utensils of life."[82] In other words, businessmen, who had come under blistering

---

79. Ibid.

80. See, for example, Goen, "Jonathan Edwards: A New Departure in Eschatology"; Heimert, *Religion and the American Mind;* and Bloch, *Visionary Republic.*

81. For a lucid study of Edwards's struggles as a pastor, see Patricia J. Tracy, *Jonathan Edwards, Pastor: Religion and Society in Eighteenth-Century Northampton* (New York, 1980).

82. HWR, 481; HA, 339; HWR, 481–82. The prominence of religious piety in Edwards's millennium was not novel in New England eschatology, but illustrates the difference between the religious utopias of England and New England, on the one hand, and continental Europe, on the other. In the latter, science and knowledge, not religion, drive the shafts that turn the wheels. For the Christian Pansophists of the seventeenth

attack in Edwards's sermons for their indifference to the constraints of Christian charity,[83] would apply a zeal for holiness to their trade. Here then are examples of how Edwards's eschatological vision both was shaped by pastoral concerns and served to rebuke (implicitly) the social standards of his day.

In another implicit reproach to Northampton, whose divisiveness was legendary,[84] Edwards promised that in the millennium the church would be marked by "excellent order" (HWR, 484). It would not "be rent with a variety of jarring opinions," but the true government and discipline of the church would then be settled and put into practice (HA, 339). Northampton church members probably read between the lines, "Parishioners will respect the minister and accept his teaching and discipline."

Nor would the Church be wracked by the wild claims of "enthusiasts" to have heard voices from God. In a tacit denunciation of Great Awakening enthusiasts,[85] Edwards explained that in the "future and glorious

---

century (Bruno, Bacon, Campanella, Andreae, Comenius), the reorganization of knowledge was fundamental to the reformation of society. Though consciously religious, the Pansophists nevertheless placed their faith in the power of scientific knowledge, not piety, to modify human conduct. For Gottfried Leibniz (1646–1714), the moral and religious fate of Christian civilization depended on science, which would be the primary instrument for spreading Christianity. For Robert Turgot (1727–81), who drafted a utopian philosophy of history as a Christian apologetic, the key to progress was nonetheless not religion but intellectual and scientific innovation. Manuel and Manuel, *Utopian Thought*, 205–21, 392–410, 463–83.

83. See, for example, Edwards's condemnation of merchants who profit from the law of supply and demand: they "take advantage" of the "necessity of poor indigent people" and thereby commit the "violent" sin of "oppression." "Dishonesty, or the Sin of Theft and Injustice," in vol. 6 of *Works*, ed. Dwight, 522. Miller claimed that it was this kind of attack that led to Edwards's dismissal. Miller, *Jonathan Edwards*, 324. Calvin, in contrast, "thought well of commerce" and "praised merchants for their service to the community." William J. Bouwsma, *John Calvin: A Sixteenth-Century Portrait* (New York, 1988), 197–98.

84. As Edwards put it, "There had also long prevailed in the town a spirit of contention between two parties, into which they had for many years been divided . . . they prepared to oppose one another in all public affairs." *FN*, 144–46.

85. "Enthusiasm" may be defined as "belief in immediate inspiration by divine or superhuman power; it leads to acting on impulses thought to come directly from the Holy Spirit. In extreme cases it may lead to a sort of frenzied possession." C. C. Goen, *Revivalism and Separatism in New England, 1740–1800* (New Haven, 1962), 20n. Edwards

times of [the church's] latter-day prosperity and blessedness" there will not be "prophets, and men endowed with the gifts of tongues and of working miracles, as was the case in the times of the apostles." For the millennium will be the time for only the best, and such charismatic gifts are inferior. The Spirit of God will then be poured out in the "more excellent way" of love, not miracles or impressions of the divine voice.[86]

Millennial religion was not to be limited to the polite society of Western whites. Transcending the social mores of New England's religious liberals, Edwards proclaimed that "the Negroes and Indians will be divines" and theological treatises would be "published in Africa, in Ethiopia, in Turkey" (HWR, 480). While many in the eighteenth century acknowledged that in native intellectual and religious capacity blacks were equal to whites, most could not seem to overcome their astonishment at the blacks' "stupidity."[87] It is not clear from either his published tomes or unpublished notebooks if Edwards shared this view of blacks, but it is clear that his sights were trained on their future accomplishments. In the millennium, he claimed, blacks would attain religious virtuosity and publish learned tomes. He prophesied that "the most divine and angelic strains [will come] from among the Hottentots," an African tribe that was used in the eighteenth century as a symbol of intellectual and cultural inferiority. "The press," he went on, "shall groan in wild Tartary," the central Asian habitat known in Edwards's day for its savagery.[88]

---

argued that "immediate revelations" thought to be from God were no evidence of regeneration and could be from Satan or the natural imagination, and reproved George Whitefield on this score when Whitefield visited Northampton. RA, 142, 213–18, 286–88; Dwight, The Life of President Edwards, 147. For more on New Light "enthusiasm" during the Great Awakening, see Edwin Scott Gaustad, The Great Awakening in New England (Gloucester, Mass., 1965), 77–79, and Goen, Revivalism and Separatism, 19n, 32, 48n, 174, 182.

86. Jonathan Edwards, Charity and Its Fruits, in Ethical Writings, ed. Ramsey, 361–62.

87. Cotton Mather, The Negro Christianized (Boston, 1706), 25, cited in Winthrop D. Jordan, White Over Black: American Attitudes Toward the Negro, 1550–1812 (Chapel Hill, N.C., 1968), 187. Like Samuel Sewall and Samuel Davies, Mather believed that black "stupidity" could be eliminated by education. See Jordan, White Over Black, 101–265, for early and mid-eighteenth-century attitudes toward blacks.

88. Miscellanies, no. 26; Oxford English Dictionary, 2d ed. (1989), 7:430, 17:651.

In the seventeenth and eighteenth centuries there was some debate over the manner in which Christ would reign during the millennium—in bodily form or spiritual presence.[89] Like most of his contemporaries, Edwards came down on the side of the spiritualists. Christ's body would not be on earth but remain in heaven. His reign on earth would be "by his Spirit." This would be "more glorious and happy for his church than his human presence would be," Edwards explained, because from heaven Christ would be better able to strengthen the church's faith and "greatly to encourage & comfort them" (*Miscellanies*, no. 827).

Millennial religion, then, was to be free from hypocrisy, strife, charismatic enthusiasm, and racism. All of these qualities concern religious *relations*—no surprise for a thinker who believed, as we shall see in the next chapter, that being consists primarily in relations. Hence it was natural for him to give considerable attention to social relations in the millennial age.

Millennial Society

Jonathan Edwards spent his life pursuing the good and the beautiful, both of which he found in the union of intelligent beings devoted to being-in-general.[90] All existence, he proposed, is based on proportion, which is the relation between two things, and beauty on proportions that exhibit agreement—if you will, union—of some sort.[91] All earthly beauties are simply mirrors of the archetype of beauty, the heavenly union of beings in common consent to being-in-general (*TV*, 564–65). Union, therefore, is a signal quality of both the beautiful and the good. Edwards even maintained that all true happiness—even God's—depends upon affectionate union in a society: "The happiness of the deity, as all other true happiness, consists in love and society."[92] Little wonder, then, that when

---

89. Davidson, *The Logic of Millennial Thought*, 75.

90. Roland A. DeLattre has argued similarly in *Beauty and Sensibility in the Thought of Jonathan Edwards* (New Haven, 1968).

91. Jonathan Edwards, "The Mind," in *Scientific and Philosophical Writings*, ed. Anderson, 336; *TV*, 564.

92. Jonathan Edwards, *Treatise on Grace*, ed. Tyron Edwards (1852; reprint, Edinburgh, 1969), 64.

Edwards looked to what he considered to be God's penultimate gift to his Church—the millennium—he found it to be a society of intelligent beings in *union*.[93]

Edwards's invocations of the harmony of millennial society have a lyrical sound to them, as if midway between ordinary consciousness and poetic rapture. "A time wherein the whole earth shall be united as one holy city, one heavenly family, men of all nations shall as it were dwell together, and sweetly correspond one with another as brethren and children of the same father. . . . A time wherein this whole great society shall appear in glorious beauty, in genuine amiable Christianity, and excellent order. . . . And then shall all the world be united in peace and love in one amiable society."[94] Heimert notes that Edwards's preoccupation with oneness was a subtle critique of the divisions the Great Awakening had fostered.[95] These passages are also further evidence that the tribalism of which Edwards has been accused is inconsistent with the eschatological vision he actually held.

Edwards found the cause of this remarkable, unprecedented unity in a new sort of human heart that was then to emerge. What was just beginning to blossom in ordinary history would then be fully in bloom. The human heart would be full of "great peace and love," and therefore would overflow with all the other Christian virtues. "Then shall *flourish* in an *eminent* manner those Christian virtues of meekness, forgiveness, long-suffering, gentleness, goodness and brotherly kindness, those excellent fruits of the Spirit" (*HWR*, 483; emphasis added). Human nature would still have the same sinful nature as in all the eras before the millennium, but because of great effusions of the Spirit the religious virtue of the human heart would be exponentially multiplied. The result would be a universal diffusion of excellence of character. "Men in their temper and

---

93. *HA*, 339; emphasis added. It is no surprise, either, that God's ultimate gift to his church was also a society in union: the heavenly society in eternity after the end of the millennium. *Miscellanies*, no. 743; ibid., no. 946.

94. *HA*, 339; *HWR*, 483.

95. Heimert, *Religion and the American Mind*, 99. But he mistakenly claims for Edwards the equation of God and the Christian commonwealth. Instead, for Edwards the good Christian commonwealth is an earthly *sign* of the heavenly community of God with the church triumphant. Heimert, *Religion and the American Mind*, 124; *TV*, 564–65.

disposition shall then be like the lamb of God, the lovely Jesus. The body shall be conformed to the head" (ibid.).

The consequence would be "the most universal peace, love and sweet harmony" in society. People would donate their material resources to help their fellows in need.[96] Millennial man, energized with copious doses of Christian virtue, would revolutionize both political and ecclesiastical relations. "All nations in all parts, on every side of the globe, shall then be knit together in sweet harmony, all parts of God's church assisting and promoting the knowledge and spiritual good one of another" (HWR, 483–84).[97]

The millennial society would be the mirror image of the heavenly society of saints, angels, and the Trinity—intelligent beings united in common consent to being-in-general. And since there is "true, spiritual original beauty . . . [in] the union of minds or spiritual beings in a mutual propensity and affection of heart," the millennial society will be "a beautiful society." Beauty shall reside in each of the members as well, for "all the world [shall then be] as one church, one orderly, regular, beautiful society, one body, all the members in beautiful proportion." Compared to all ages past, this "whole great society" in its "glorious beauty" shall be the "perfection of beauty."[98]

A beautiful society is a happy society. In the millennium God's saints will become "unspeakably happy in the view of his glory" (HA, 338). For Edwards the happiness of the saints was a common theme. Although he insisted that the Christian life was a pilgrimage through a foreign land with an abundance of suffering, and observed that the Christian's life is usually more troubled than the unbeliever's,[99] he never tired of promising great joy and happiness to the faithful, both in this life and the next. The

---

96. HA, 339; HWR, 484: men will express their love in "deeds of charity." Edwards never explains, however, why charity will be needed during a time that he also claims will see universal prosperity.

97. As far as I know, Edwards never specifies what form of polity his millennial church will take—whether congregational, for instance, or presbyterian.

98. TV, 564; HWR, 484; HA, 339.

99. Edwards, "The Christian Pilgrim," in Jonathan Edwards: Representative Selections, ed. Faust and Johnson, 130–36; HWR, 283, 389; sermon on Matthew 25:46, April 1739, cited in John H. Gerstner, Jonathan Edwards: A Mini-Theology (Wheaton, Ill., 1987), 109.

happiness of the saints, he often remarked, is the intention of the Creator. God created human beings for happiness (*Miscellanies*, no. 87) and
delights in their happiness (no. 679). Early in his private notebooks he
wrote that their happiness was the highest end of the creation (*Miscellanies*, no. 3). Much later he explained that God's ultimate end in creation
"consists in two things, viz., in God's infinite perfection being exerted &
so manifested, that is, in God's glorifying Himself; and second, His
infinite happiness being communicated & so making the creature happy."
Both aspects of God's ultimate end "are sometimes in Scripture included
in one world, namely, God's being glorified" (*Miscellanies*, no. 1066). In
his notebook on Revelation Edwards wrote that even the damnation of
the wicked is for the happiness of the blessed.[100]

Millennial Economics

The last era of human history would be showered with "great temporal
prosperity." "Wealth" was to be abundant. Agriculture would be promoted "through the remarkable blessing of heaven" so that farms "shall
be abundantly fruitful." Life expectancy would increase dramatically as
human beings enjoy health and long life. With health abounding and
wars having ceased there would be "a great increase of children." The
result would be a population boom. "At the end of the thousand years,
there would be more than a million inhabitants on the face of the earth,
where there is one now." Then would be fulfilled the scriptural prophecies "that his redeemed ones should be as numerous as the drops of
dew."[101]

Edwards was keenly aware of the political manipulations that governed
the economy of his day.[102] The political and economic concerns of his

---

100. "Notes on the Apocalypse," in *AW*, 137.
101. *HA*, 339; *HWR*, 484–85; ibid.; *HA*, 340; *HWR*, 484–85; ibid.; *HA*, 342–43;
Miscellanies, no. 1131. Like most eighteenth-century utopias, Edwards's was based on an
agricultural economy. Manuel and Manuel, *Utopian Thought*, 20; Holstun, *A Rational
Millennium*, 73.
102. For a sensitive, extended analysis of Edwards's economics, see Mark Valeri,
"The Economic Thought of Jonathan Edwards," *Church History* 60, no. 1 (March
1991): 37–54.

own Hampshire County were dominated, more than most New England counties, by "a lively interplay of personal power, patronage, and paternalism." Israel Williams (Edwards's cousin) and his cronies exercised a "most imposing" influence over the social and financial affairs of the region. In Perry Miller's words, they were "grafters and land-grabbers."[103]

The Edwardsean millennial economy, in contrast, would prosper without the benefit of underhanded dealings. With his eye no doubt on the brisk river trade that plied the nearby Connecticut River, Edwards told his congregation that "the art of navigation that is now improved so much in fear, with covetousness and pride, and is used so much by wicked, debauched men, shall be consecrated to God, and improved for holy uses." Northampton merchants who profited from Valley navigation—and all who had any inkling of the economy's dependence on Valley trade and its "river gods"—must have seen the millennial ideal "as a severe indictment of a society beginning to take its cues from an amoral marketplace and the hidden hand of self-interest."[104]

In the final two sections of this portrait of the Edwardsean millennium we shall examine two topics of particular relevance to the relationship of the millennium to Edwards's public theology: knowledge and technology is one; politics, the other. Both were used by Edwards to point away from narrow nationalism to a global society, a "spiritual federalism" transcending all parochial concern for one's own land or people. Knowledge and technology in the eschaton would be used primarily to link far-flung corners of the globe in one global society, and the politics of the final earthly age would serve the harmonious relations of an international family of nations.

---

103. Gregory H. Nobles, *Divisions Throughout the Whole: Politics and Society in Hampshire County, Massachusetts, 1740–1775* (Cambridge, Mass., 1983), 35; Miller, *Jonathan Edwards*, 250.

104. *HWR*, 484; Westbrook, "Social Criticism and the Heavenly City," 409. "Edwards's exposition of the millennial expectation . . . [was] alone . . . powerful enough to check the depredations of the river gods." Miller, *Jonathan Edwards*, 321. Edwards perhaps would have been suspicious of the millennial economy of the Fifth Monarchy Men, which was based on commerce rather than agriculture. This sect was made up primarily of urban mercantilists who were conscious of developing an economic polity for an island kingdom dependent on trade. Manuel and Manuel, *Utopian Thought*, 360.

Knowledge and Technology

Millennial commerce would be aided by the explosion of knowledge to come in that age. Then the earth would see a "vast increase of knowledge and understanding" (*HA*, 338). "Great light and knowledge" would fill the world (*HWR*, 480). Inventions and new discoveries would be commonplace: "To what they know now, there will continually be something new and surprising discovered in one part of the world and another" (*Miscellanies*, no. 26). Discoveries were to be both natural and religious. Secular inventions of the eighteenth century, Edwards figured, were divinely ordained clues to the religious discoveries that were to come in the millennium. "The late invention of telescopes . . . is a type and forerunner of the great increase in the knowledge of heavenly things that shall be in the approaching glorious times of the Christian church" (*Images*, 102).

The millennium as a storehouse of knowledge was a stock in trade of both religious and secular utopias. In New England, John Cotton, Increase Mather, and Cotton Mather connected the development of knowledge with the end of the world. In England, Anglican latitudinarians and Nonconformists in the late seventeenth and early eighteenth centuries said Christians would prepare themselves for the millennium by accumulating scientific knowledge and spreading the faith. Daniel 12:4 ("Many shall run to and fro, and knowledge shall be increased") was a favorite of the millennial Puritan heirs to Francis Bacon, who were eager to advance the causes of Christ, knowledge, and empire. For seventeenth-century Pansophists on the continent such as Leibniz and Comenius, calm and orderly science was a way to God in the end-time. Secular utopians of the eighteenth century such as the Marquis de Condorcet (1743–94) fantasized unlimited progress powered by scientific knowledge.[105]

For Edwards, the purpose of this knowledge explosion was to be religious. Labor-saving devices would be developed so "that they shall have

---

105. Middlekauf, *The Mathers*, 333; Bloch, *Visionary Republic*, 10; Holstun, *A Rational Millennium*, 50; Manuel and Manuel, *Utopian Thought*, 207, 493–515. Edwards's attitude toward knowledge differed, however, from the sectarian utopists of the English Revolution. That is, unlike the Levellers, Ranters, and Diggers, Edwards was not opposed to the university system or higher degrees. See Manuel and Manuel, *Utopian Thought*, 354.

more time for more noble exercise," i.e., religious meditation and action. Communications would be improved, Edwards explained, so that there would be "more expedite, easy, and safe communication between distant regions than now." But Edwards was not satisfied with mere improvement. Thought of the millennium's glory encouraged him to expect revolutionary changes. "Who can tell but that God will yet make it more perfect so that there need not be such a tedious voyage in order to hear from the other hemisphere," for the purpose of uniting the new global community of the spirit? "And so the countries about the Poles need no longer be hid to us, but the whole earth may be as one community, one body in Christ."[106] We are therefore presented with the ironic picture of a "provincial" parson envisioning immediate intercontinental communication and the shrinking of far-flung nations to one global village. Edwards's projection of millennial technology as the infrastructure of a new global community is further evidence that in his religious imagination this supposedly insular pastor had long since exploded the bounds of his native land and nation.

Politics

Just as the geography of Edwards's millennium was nearly always conceived in international terms, the politics of his eschaton were always interpreted internationally. The millennial disposition—that is, the quantitatively improved human nature discussed above—would affect "all countries and nations." No nation would be excluded. "Now the Kingdom of Christ shall in the most strict and literal sense extend to all nations and the whole earth." "Great knowledge shall prevail *everywhere.*"[107] In one section of *An Humble Attempt* Edwards underscored the universality of the millennium's effects upon every people and nation by consecutively quoting ten biblical passages, all of which contained the word "all," some of them repeating the word over and over again: "all the

---

106. *Miscellanies,* no. 262. There was a "down side" to the communication revolution to come: it would aid the apostasy at the end of the millennium by allowing it to spread around the globe almost immediately. *Miscellanies,* no. 835.

107. *HWR,* 473, 480; Abelove, ed., "Jonathan Edwards's Letter of Invitation to George Whitefield," 488; *HWR,* 405.

nations, "all the families of the earth," "all nations" (four times), "all flesh" (three times), etc. By sheer force of repetition Edwards impressed upon his auditors his conviction that no political unit would remain unvanquished before the millennial revolution (HA, 329–30).

That revolution[108] would not, however, dissolve all political boundaries into a single world government. The many nations of the world would come into unity, but the unity would be spiritual, resulting in "sweet harmony" among nations still existing individually. In other words, this was not to be a totalitarian world government that demolishes all previous political units, but a federal system respecting the integrity of existing polities. Christ was to be head over all, and his subordinates, the political leaders of each nation, were to rule their domains in accordance with his will. "All nations" would thus remain as nations; they would even manifest "different forms of government, very many."[109] But now they would be "knit together" spiritually by the new millennial character into "one amiable society" (HWR, 483).

Edwards's spiritual federalism was analogous to his understanding of the relationship between the regenerate believer and Christ. At conversion, he taught, the believer "becomes one" with Christ, but without losing his separate identity.[110] Just as a hyperbola approaches its asymptote infinitely without ever touching it, throughout eternity the believer approaches closer and closer to perfect union with Christ, but without ever finally merging into undifferentiated unity. So too, in Edwards's spiritual federalism, each nation in the millennium would subsist in such spiritual unity with all other nations that the world of nations would become as "one heavenly family," "as one community[,] one body in

---

108. I use the word "revolution" in the same way that Edwards often used it, to denote radical changes—"overturnings," as he often put it—in every sphere of life, including political. See, for example, HWR, 430–31. Revolution in society is an analogue writ large of the revolution that takes place in a soul during conversion. This is not to suggest, however, that Edwards consciously merged history with the experiences of the private self. See William Scheick, "The Grand Design: Jonathan Edwards's History of the Work of Redemption," in Critical Essays, ed. Scheick, 177–88, and John Wilson's astute corrective in his introduction to HWR, 98–100.

109. HWR, 483–84; "Notes on the Apocalypse," in AW, 136–37.

110. As Conrad Cherry has put it, "The saint participates in, but is not absorbed in, the Holy Spirit." Cherry, The Theology of Jonathan Edwards, 88. See also RA, 341.

Christ."[111] Yet each nation would retain its separate identity and government throughout the duration of the glorious era.

The inevitable result of this international spiritual unity of nations
would be world peace. "There shall then be universal peace and good
understanding among all the nations of the world, instead of confusion,
wars, and bloodshed." International goodwill would be so demonstrable
that political leaders would dismantle their military establishments. "So
it is represented as if all instruments of war should be destroyed as having
become useless."[112] Edwards was not implicitly recommending unilateral
disarmament to George II in the interests of Christian love. For armies
were to be disbanded in the millennium because international amity
would render them "useless." But in 1739 Edwards could give no assurance to his king that all nations were dwelling "quietly and safely, without fear of enemy,"[113] and therefore in no need of armies. In fact, during
the French and Indian War Edwards demonstrated that he held to the
just war tradition and considered it sometimes obligatory for the Christian to bear arms.[114] Edwards was instead suggesting that arms and war
were necessary only in a world where Satan and sin were unchecked, and
that the coming kingdom of the Christ would be free from their horrors.

Edwards's description of the *nature* of political power in the millennium
confutes the position that the Edwardsean millennium was apolitical.[115]

---

111. HA, 339; *Miscellanies,* no. 262. The political model that I have found closest to
this among early modern utopias is Leibniz's world polity, in which individual cultures
would preserve their national characters as indestructible monads. Manuel and Manuel,
Utopian Thought, 405.

112. HWR, 482, 483; ibid.

113. Ibid.

114. "A people of G[od] may be called of G[od] to go forth to war against their
Enemies." Sermon on 1 Kings 8:44–45, 4 April 1745, Fast for Success in the Expedition
against Cape Breton, 3. In the remainder of this sermon Edwards outlined the circumstances in which a professing people may feel justified in going to war: (1) when the rights
of a public society are invaded and the preservation of the community requires it; and (2)
when a people are obliged by a "Just alliance or Covenant" contracted with another
people for their "mutual defense and Preservation." An individual is "called of God" to go
to war when he is called by "those that are in authority unless it be notoriously manifest
that the war is unjust." Ibid., 10–12.

115. Scholars such as Davidson and Hatch properly emphasize the priority, for Edwards,
of spiritual over political forces in history. Yet the political effects of those spiritual forces
were not unimportant for Edwards, as an overemphasis on the spiritual forces can imply.

"Liberty" shall reign throughout the earth, he declared. That this liberty is political and not just religious he demonstrated *implicitly* when he said that "the absolute and despotic power of the kings of the earth shall be taken away," and *explicitly* when he stated that "every nation shall be a free people, not only with a freedom from spiritual slavery, but from civil too, from the tyrannical and absolute power of men" (AW, 136–37). Edwards understood the Micah 4:4 passage ("wherein every man shall sit under his own vine tree and under his own fig tree") as referring to political liberty and "not understood only in a mystical and spiritual sense" (AW, 137).[116] Throughout his life Edwards identified the Antichrist with political powers—both the Catholic nations of Europe and the Muslim Turks. So when he called the saints to action to bring on the millennium, they could be forgiven if they understood the call to have political import.

Relying on a statement in the private notebooks (AW, 136), Davidson claims that because Edwards disavowed the overthrow of civil government in the millennium, his idea of the millennium was apolitical. Yet that statement prefaces the assertion that "the absolute and despotic power of the kings of the earth *shall be taken away,* and liberty shall reign throughout the earth" (emphasis added). At the very least, this vision of political revolution—albeit by nonmilitary means—was an implicit denunciation of all eighteenth-century political systems that exercised absolute and despotic power. Hence his millennium had political significance. But the passage most likely says more. It conflates the "glorious work of God" preceding the millennium (when "the civil . . . polities of the nations, shall be overthrown") and the millennium itself (when no "civil government shall in any measure be overthrown")[117] in order to emphasize that in the millennium "the absolute and despotic power of the kings of the earth" shall have been "taken away, and liberty shall reign throughout the earth." The denial of coups d'état *during* the millennium did not therefore rule out political revolution in the period preceding the millennium. That the millennium would be prepared by political

---

116. Bloch is therefore wrong to say that Edwards did not specify whether this liberty was a quality of civil as well as religious life. Bloch, *Visionary Republic*, 20.

117. Understanding the passage as a conflation—Edwards's combination of the two periods into one general period of transformation—is the only way to make sense of the seemingly contradictory statements contained within it.

upheaval is further confirmed by Edwards's statement in *Some Thoughts*
that Christ would "strike through kings" who opposed the Awakening
and "fill the places with dead bodies."[118] Edwards's vision of the millennium thus served to judge all polities falling short of full liberty and
warned political leaders of the perils they risked by not supporting the
revivals that would lead to the millennium.[119]

Edwards's millennium was not a critique, however, of the ruling Hanove-
rian kings. Unlike his disciples in the Revolutionary era, he considered
them to be paragons of political virtue. "Kings shall rather be as the judges
were before Saul (whose government was that which was best pleasing to
God), and as the kings of England now are in civil matters."[120]

Neither New England nor America figure in the Edwardsean millennium to any significant extent. Although the millennialism of other
Great Awakening leaders reflected "an acute sense of American religious
mission" and a strong sense of "provincial American patriotism,"[121] Edwards's references to his colony and land were almost uniformly negative.
As argued above, the discussion of America in *Some Thoughts* concerns
the long period preceding the millennium, not the millennium itself. In
The History of the Work of Redemption Edwards states, "Then shall this vast
continent of America, that now in so great part of it is covered with
barbarous ignorance and cruelty, be everywhere covered with glorious
gospel light and Christian love." The America to which Edwards here
refers is "heathenism," i.e., the native American tribes that were "wor-
shipping the devil" (*HWR*, 471–73). Their gift of glorious gospel light is

---

118. *ST*, 371. The context refers to the Awakening, which rulers were to support. This
is another indication that Edwards in *Some Thoughts* considered the Awakening to be of
the tumultuous period preceding the millennium, not the beginning of the millennium
itself. For, as we have seen, Edwards had said that the millennium would be peaceful, but
the period preceding it full of conflict.

119. Hatch's contrast between Edwards and later "civil millennialists" is too sharp.
Their millennialism was heavily charged with political meaning, but his was not without
its political implications for both future and present. Hatch, *The Sacred Cause of Liberty*,
167.

120. "Notes on the Apocalypse," in *AW*, 136. In this respect Edwards was like nearly
all of his contemporaries. Yet on some occasions, as we shall see in the next two chapters,
Edwards attacked the abuse of power by the royal court.

121. Bloch, *Visionary Republic*, 47.

not a special favor but the local application of a general, worldwide phenomenon. Throughout *The History of the Work of Redemption* the millennium is described in nothing but international terms (479–86). The last mention Edwards made of America and the millennium was in his *Humble Attempt* (1747). There America was portrayed as spiritually bankrupt, and the premillennial revivals as spiritual rescue operations for an otherwise doomed land.

> And how lamentable is the moral and religious state of these American colonies? Of New England in particular? What fierce and violent contentions. . . . How much is the gospel ministry grown into contempt, and the work of the ministry . . . in danger of sinking amongst us? How many of our congregations and churches rending in pieces? . . . What wild and extravagant notions, gross delusions of the devil, and strange practices have prevailed? . . . How apparently are the hearts of the people, everywhere, uncommonly shut up against all means and endeavors to awaken sinners and revive religion? Vice and immorality, of all kinds, withal increasing and unusually prevailing? May not an attentive view and consideration of such a state of things well influence the people that favors the dust of Zion, to earnestness in their cries to God for *a general outpouring of his Spirit, which only can be an effectual remedy for these evils?* (Emphasis added)[122]

That Glorious Work of God: The Premillennial Revivals

We have now seen the outlines of Edwards's millennium, and its implications for his public theology. This last section of the chapter explores "that glorious work of God," the long introductory period that is to prepare for and eventually bring on the millennium. An examination of

---

122. *HA*, 357–58. In the text it is clear that the "general outpouring of his Spirit" is one of the revivals to be expected in the period before the millennium. Compare this passage with *HA*, 410–11.

this period will shed further light on Edwards's public theology, particularly the critical passage in *Some Thoughts*, which, as I have argued above, refers not to the millennium but to this introductory work of God's Spirit. I will first sketch the significant features of this period, and then discuss its implications for Edwards's public theology.

As we saw above, Edwards considered the millennium to be Christ's third "coming in his kingdom." The fourth coming at the Last Judgment is the coming "principally signified in Scripture by Christ's coming in his kingdom" (*HWR*, 351), but the millennium was to be the third "great event" (ibid.) in providence by which God advances the progress of history toward its culmination. Each of these four great events are preceded by periods of revival and tumult. " 'Tis observable that it has been God's manner in every remarkable new establishment of the state of his visible church, to give a remarkable outpouring of his Spirit" (ibid., 266). The spiritual effusion that will precede Christ's third coming at the millennium is to be "the last and the greatest . . . very extraordinary, and such as never has yet been seen" (*DM*, 230).[123] In its "progress and issue" it "would at last bring on the church's latter-day glory" (*GA*, 560).

The "bringing on" would be slow and gradual. In his 1739 sermon series on the work of redemption, Edwards warned his congregation that this last great work of the Spirit would progress only gradually (*HWR*, 458). Eight years later, in *An Humble Attempt*, he dared to speculate on its actual length. It would take "one half century," he proposed, for religion "in the power and purity of it," to "gain the upper hand through the *Protestant* world." Another "one half century" would be needed to "gain the ascendant in that which is now the *popish* world." A third half-century would be necessary to "prevail and subdue the greater part of the *Mahometan* world, and bring in the *Jewish* nation, in all their dispersions." Finally, "in the next whole century, the whole *heathen* world should be enlightened and converted to the Christian faith, throughout all parts of Africa, Asia, America and Terra Australis." In other words, it

---

123. Edwards's belief that this glorious work of God's spirit would be the greatest ever seen explains how he could think that if the Great Awakening was indeed the beginning of this, then "the New Jerusalem in this respect has begun to come down from heaven." *ST*, 346.

would be two hundred fifty years before this great work of God's Spirit would accomplish all that was necessary before the millennium could begin. That great era of peace and rest for the church would not come until about the year 2000.[124]

Edwards's confidence in the progressive nature of history, particularly in this last phase, begs the question of influence on his thinking. Much scholarly attention has been given to the influence of English eschatology, particularly that of Moses Lowman, on Edwards's millennialism.[125] But credit must be given as well to Dutch Reformed scholasticism, which may have influenced Edwards indirectly through Lowman and directly through Petrus van Mastricht.

Lowman studied under disciples of Johannes Cocceius (1603–1669) at Leiden and Utrecht from 1698 to 1710. Cocceius taught a dispensational, progressive view of history that was very influential in seventeenth-century Dutch universities. Influenced by a sixteenth-century Italian Protestant who developed Joachimist speculations, Cocceius believed that Scripture foretells an impending new age in which the Antichrist will fall, the Jews will be converted, and the kingdom of Christ will come to earth by the preaching of the gospel.[126]

As a result of Cocceius' prestige, the Netherlands became a breeding ground for millennial eschatology in the late seventeenth and early eighteenth centuries. Typical of consensus thinking was Willem a Brakel's

---

124. *HA*, 411. The same process is described in more detail, but without specification of its duration, in *HWR*, 467–70.

125. See, for instance, *AW*, 22–23, 55–59; Davidson, *The Logic of Millennial Thought*, 153–57; Goen, "Jonathan Edwards: A New Departure in Eschatology." My understanding of the relationship of Edwards's millennialism to Dutch scholasticism is indebted to James Kennedy. Other treatments of Edwards and the Dutch scholastics include Bogue, *Jonathan Edwards and the Covenant of Grace*, and James P. Martin, *The Last Judgment in Protestant Theology from Orthodoxy to Ritschl* (Edinburgh, 1963).

126. *Dictionary of National Biography* (Oxford, 1917), vid. "Lowman"; Dietrich H. Kromminga, *The Millennium in the Church* (Grand Rapids, Mich., 1963), 205–6; Jürgen Moltmann, "Jacob Brocard als Vorlaeufer der Reich-Gottes-Theologie und der Profetischen Schriftauslegung der Johannes Coccejus," *Zeitschrift für Kirchengeschichte* 71 (1960): 110–29; Grete Moeller, "Föderalismus und Geschichtsbetrachtung im 17. u. 18. Jahrhundert," *Zeitschrift für Kirchengeschichte* 1931, nos. 3 and 4, 404–40; Jürgen Moltmann, "Geschichtstheologie und Pietisches Menschenbild bei Johannes Coccejus und Theodor Untereyck," *Evangelische Theologie* 19 (1959): 346–47.

Redelyk Godsdienst ([Reasonable Service], 1700), which proclaimed that history's end was near, though not imminent. The millennium would come after the Antichrist is defeated, and was to be a period of peace, godliness, and knowledge of God. The earth would be fruitful, Christ would be present spiritually, and there would be little want or suffering.[127]

Lowman probably knew of Brakel's work. Brakel may have influenced Lowman's view that the destruction of the Church's enemies was gradually being accomplished and would culminate in their total defeat, to be followed by the millennium. Since we know that Edwards "struggled mightily in his notebook with the interpretation of Lowman" (*AW*, 7), we can infer that Dutch eschatology may have influenced Edwards through Lowman.

But we have better evidence of the possibility of Dutch influence on Edwards's eschatology. In a letter that has survived, Edwards wrote to a disciple that Petrus van Mastricht's *Theoretico-Practica Theologia* was "much better than Turretine or any other book in the world, excepting the Bible, in my opinion." Mastricht (1630–1706) was a precisianist pietist who succeeded Gisbert Voetius as professor of theology at Utrecht in 1677. The 1714 edition of his *Theologia*, to which Edwards referred, contains a 240-page section entitled "Dispensation of the Covenant of Grace." This section teaches a progressive view of history in which the covenant of grace is "renewed and widened" through time, though not without waxing and waning. Like Edwards, Mastricht looked to a future Day of Wrath and the possibility of a "New Reformation," when the faith of the regenerate would quicken and judgments would be poured out on the unregenerate. Mastricht was not the first to introduce the concepts of progressive history or end-time revival to Edwards, for both were common in late seventeenth- and early eighteenth-century New England. But we can say, at least, that Edwards shared Mastricht's opinion that history was progressing toward a telos and that better times lay in store for the church.[128]

---

127. Kromminga, *The Millennium*, 206; Willem a Brakel, *Redelyk Godsdienst*, part 3 (Leiden, 1882), 287–96, 309, 325.

128. Jonathan Edwards, "Letter to Joseph Bellamy, 15 January 1747," *New England Quarterly* 1 (1928): 229; Richard A. Muller, *Post-Reformation Reformed Dogmatics*, vol. 1, *Prolegomena to Theology* (Grand Rapids, Mich., 1987), 48; Mastricht, *Beschouwende en Praktikale Godgeleerdheit*, 3:709–10; 4:481.

Edwards also agreed with Mastricht, however, that before the end the Church would have to endure much tribulation. The two hundred and fifty years before the millennium would be full of "many sore conflicts and terrible convulsions" (GA, 560). Satan was not one to surrender without a fight; he would marshal his powerful forces from all around the globe for an all-out battle against God's forces. This "afflictive model of progress"[129] was familiar to Edwards; it seemed to him a familiar pattern in history that as the Church prospered there were "dark clouds and threatening appearances." "The most glorious times of the church are always the most dismal times to the wicked and impenitent. . . . The accomplishment of the terrible destruction of God's enemies, and the glorious prosperity of his church, usually go together."[130]

The "destruction of God's enemies" related to this third coming of Christ was being effected by seven "vials of wrath," which God had been pouring out on the Antichrist since before the Reformation (AW, 11). For Edwards, as for most Protestants since the Reformation, the Roman Catholic Church was the worst enemy of the church of Christ, the very embodiment of the spirit of the Antichrist. In his private notebooks he compared the Roman papacy to "a viper or some loathsome, poisonous, crawling monster," whose nefarious influence destroyed true religion in the Middle Ages. In a 1734 sermon he referred to the pope as "the anti-[Christ]ian monster." Since the time of John Wyclif, God had been pursuing a twofold strategy to defend his kingdom against the forces of the Antichrist: while pouring out the Spirit in selective revivals to build up his Church, he simultaneously poured out vials of wrath upon the Church's enemies.[131]

God will have poured out seven vials before the Antichrist's final destruction at the end of this last "glorious work of God" (AW, 298). After reading Moses Lowman in 1739 Edwards concluded that the fifth vial had been poured out in the Reformation, when Luther and other Reformers dealt serious blows to Rome's influence and prestige. By 1747

---

129. Davidson, *The Logic of Millennial Thought,* 127–75.

130. *HWR,* 527–28; *Notes on the Bible,* 222; see also *Miscellanies,* no. 356, 810.

131. *Miscellanies,* no. hh, cited in *AW,* 11; Sermon on Matthew 18:7, 18; "Notes on the Apocalypse, in *AW,* 208; *HWR,* 420–21.

he had decided that the sixth vial, which would consist of "the taking away from the Church of Rome the supplies and help she has had from the principal powers that have hitherto supported her" (23), "may well be speedily expected" because Rome's riches were showing signs of significant depletion (*HA*, 421). The kings of Spain and Portugal had recently forbade "going to Rome for investitures, etc., thereby cutting off two great streams of the Pope's wealth [and] popish princes were now taxing the clergy" (*AW*, 300). Another sign was "the late peeling and impoverishing the Pope's temporal dominions in Italy, by the armies of the Austrians, Neapolitans, and Spainards" (*HA*, 421).[132]

The sixth vial would be poured out for most of the duration of the two hundred fifty years of the glorious work of God. By these executions of God's wrath, and the revivals his Spirit would produce, Deism, Roman Catholicism, Islam, and Judaism would gradually diminish in power and influence. Then, just before the end of this period, would occur a final great battle. "All the forces of Antichrist, and also Mohammedanism and heathenism, should be united, all the forces of Satan's visible kingdom through the whole world of mankind. . . . This will be, as it were, the dying struggles of the old serpent, a battle wherein he will fight as one that is almost desperate." The fighting will be desperate and "violent," but "Christ and his church shall in this battle obtain a complete and entire victory over their enemies." The hidden weapon that gives Christ the winning edge is the last and seventh vial, whose pouring out was finally to ensure the victory.[133]

America's Role

Edwards's description of this last great work of God before the millennium, which I have just summarized, makes little mention of New England or America. In fact, with the exception of the oft-quoted *Some Thoughts* passage, America plays no role at all in his public descriptions of this era—the era, by the way, of most immediate relevance for him and his readers. In the passage from *Some Thoughts*, as we have seen, Edwards

---

132. See also *AW*, 305 (written at about the same time as *HA*, 421).
133. *HWR*, 463–64; see also *HA*, 196–97, 394.

wrote that the "glorious work of God" might begin in America, and soon. If there was any inconsistency in Edwards's thought, it was here. Only in this work, in 1742, did he highlight America's role in the final ages;[134] neither before nor after this time did Edwards give America or New England a positive role to play in God's shepherding of history.

Yet even here, where America was to be the probable scene of the beginning of that glorious work of God, American leadership was ironic. God would start with America only because she was the "utmost, meanest, youngest, and weakest part" of the world, in order "to make it plain the work was of him."[135] This is a restatement of what he had recorded in his private notebooks at about the same time, where he stated that in the latter days the Church would enter prosperity and spiritual joy by "successive seasons of the pouring out of the Spirit of God . . . and the first outpouring of the Spirit will be the *least glorious*" (emphasis added). As if to underline the ambiguous meaning of America's "leadership" role, Edwards described the return of the church of God in the latter days "by several companies that will come in one after another in successive seasons of the pouring out of the Spirit of God, with a space between [each]: . . . They that are brought in [first] are not only inferior among men, but the least pure, beautiful, and amiable as Christians in their experience and practice."[136]

---

134. It must be noted, however, that at about the same time as ST (dating estimated by Thomas A. Schafer), Edwards penned in his private notebooks an allusive reference to America and the latter-day glory. America, he wrote, was "a type and forerunner of what is approaching in spiritual things." *Images*, 102. In this period he also changed his interpretation of the "distant isles" of Isaiah 60:9. Earlier, he had thought them to "principally" refer to Europe; *Miscellanies*, no. g; "Notes on the Apocalypse," in *AW*, 142. But in ST he identified them as a reference to America. *ST*, 353.

135. This accusation may seem inconsistent with Edwards's praise for America's spiritual privileges, which we saw in the last chapter. But for Edwards there was no inconsistency. Americans had been given greater spiritual privileges than any other people, but because they had abused those privileges, their guilt was correspondingly greater.

136. *ST*, 356; *Notes on the Bible*, 232; ibid. This latter entry, which is no. 417, has been dated by Schafer at approximately late 1742 or early 1743. It suggests that Edwards has America in mind because Edwards had in the same period written, in *Some Thoughts*, that the Great Awakening was the "first fruits of that glorious day." *ST*, 354. Furthermore, in his private notebook he wrote that the recipients of the "first outpouring of the Spirit" were full of "spiritual pride and self-confidence," the same charge he leveled at New

In the passage from *Some Thoughts*, Edwards further underscored the ambiguity of America's role by arguing that she was chosen out of regard for aesthetic "balance." Since "the old continent has crucified Christ . . . 'tis probable that, in some measure to balance these things, the most glorious renovation of the world shall originate from the new continent." Edwards's God is concerned about continental "equality." His "providence observes a kind of equal distribution of things." Hence, since the Gentiles "first received the true religion from the Jews," God has so ordered it that the Jews should now receive the Gospel from the Gentiles—in order "that there might be a kind of equality in the dispensations of providence."[137]

The tone throughout the discussions of America and the millennium in *Some Thoughts* is consistently tentative. Most projections were conjectural, introduced by the particle "if."[138] This hesitancy increased toward the end of the work, as if Edwards became less optimistic during the course of his writing—a period that coincided with the further development of contention and division in New England.[139] On the last page of the work Edwards's uncertainty was most marked. Suddenly new conditions were added that had to be fulfilled before this glorious work of God could be said to have begun in America. The country must "*fully* and *freely* . . . acknowledge his glorious power and grace" in the awakening, "and engage with one heart and soul, and by due methods, the endeavor to promote it" (*ST*, 530). In short, the gainsayers and fence sitters of New England had to stop opposing the revival, and jump on the bandwagon to support it enthusiastically—hardly a realistic hope at the end of 1742. From Edwards's pessimistic evaluations of his fellow countrymen we can infer that as the writing of *Some Thoughts* progressed, the author may have begun to lose confidence in his earlier prediction of a probable American beginning for that glorious work of God's Spirit.

Englanders just a year later in a letter to a Scottish correspondent: "[God] saw our spiritual pride and self-confidence." *Notes on the Bible*, 232; letter to William McCullough, 5 March 1744, in *GA*, 559.

137. *ST*, 354–55.

138. Stein first noticed this. *AW*, 28.

139. In the summer of 1742, for instance, "James Davenport was wrecking the Awakening." Miller, *Jonathan Edwards*, 203. See Gaustad, *The Great Awakening*, 61–79, and Goen, *Revivalism and Separatism*, 48–67.

When we turn from *Some Thoughts* to his other works in which he discussed the millennium or the great work preceding it, we find that America is never mentioned. In *Faithful Narrative* (1737) Edwards ascribed no eschatological significance to the 1735–36 awakening in the Connecticut Valley—even while two British and four American ministers did, and in the prefaces to the same work.[140] In his 1739 sermons on the history of the work of redemption, Edwards refused to speculate on the timing or the location of the glorious work of God to come: "We know not where this pouring out of the Spirit shall begin, or whether in *many* places at once, or whether what has already taken place ben't some forerunner and beginning of it" (*HWR*, 460). In his letter to Whitefield in 1740 the Northampton divine could only "*hope* this is the dawning of a day of God's mighty power."[141] When writing a Scottish friend about the awakenings, he made no connection between America and either the millennium or revivals introducing it (*GA*, 558–60). In *An Humble Attempt* (1747) particular nations faded into insignificance before the dominating universality of "those great effusions of the Holy Spirit" (333) that would "bring on that advancement of Christ's church and kingdom" (320). When New England and America were mentioned, they were held up as the most egregious examples of nations that were spiritually bankrupt, of nations most in need of awakenings to save them from perdition (357–58).

In all of Edwards's descriptions of the long period of revivals and international tumults that were to precede the millennium, then, America was either absent, vilified, or given leadership by default.[142] When

---

140. *GA*, 208, 210, 131–32, 137, 141; there are also Edwards's letters to Benjamin Colman, cited by Stein in *AW*, 20.

141. Abelove, "Jonathan Edwards's Letter," 488.

142. The fact that Edwards's closest disciples (Joseph Bellamy, Samuel Hopkins, and Jonathan Edwards, Jr.), who carefully read their mentor's published works and private notebooks, developed eschatologies that were decidedly untribalist supports my contention that Edwards's eschatology transcended provincial, nationalistic concerns. Mark Valeri reports that "like most New Divinity preachers and unlike many Old Light, Arminian and Separatist pastors, Bellamy resisted the kind of civil millennialism or civil religion that flowered during the American Revolution." Bellamy, Hopkins, and Edwards, Jr., interpreted the millennium as the ultimate establishment of benevolence, not primarily as the triumph of an American, nationalistic order. This explains, writes Valeri,

the political dimensions of that glorious work are examined, what stands out is its international scope. "And doubtless one nation shall be enlightened and converted after another. . . . [T]he gospel shall be preached to every tongue and kindred and [nation and people] before [the] fall of Antichrist; so we may suppose that it will soon be gloriously successful to bring in multitudes, and from many nations" (*HWR*, 459, 461). Even the means used to bring on the glorious work would involve international cooperation, with no mention of any one nation as leader: "In the text we have an account *how* this future glorious advancement of the church of God should be brought on, or introduced; viz., by great multitudes in different towns and countries taking up a *joint resolution,* and coming into an express and visible *agreement,* that they will, by united and extraordinary *prayer,* seek to God that he would come and manifest himself, and grant the tokens and fruits of his gracious presence" (*HA,* 314; Edwards's emphases).

Not only is the glorious work international in scope throughout its duration, and effected by prayer societies from many lands, but the forerunners of this work are international as well. Edwards found revivals in England, Scotland, Russia, and India to be portents of the glorious work to come.[143] In a 1748 letter to a Scottish correspondent he opined that recent religious stirrings among British politicians and clerics "appear to be happy presages and forerunners of yet better and greater things that are coming."[144] Thus six years after *Some Thoughts* he found "forerunners" (the same word used of the New England revivals in *Some Thoughts*) of the glorious work thousands of miles away from New England. At roughly the same time he began to see other forerunners close to home, but among a people other than his fellow Yankees. The awakening among native Americans taught by David Brainerd was also "a *forerunner* of

---

why during the 1780s and 1790s New Divinity preachers were critics of populist and democratic nationalism. Mark Valeri, "Joseph Bellamy: Conversion, Social Ethics, and Politics in the Thought of an Eighteenth-Century Calvinist" (Ph.D. diss., Princeton University, 1985), 175, 176–77.

143. See Johan Anthony Dejong, *As the Waters Cover the Sea: Millennial Expectations in the Rise of Anglo-American Missions, 1640–1810* (Kampen, 1970), 127; Miller, *Jonathan Edwards,* 317.

144. Dwight, *The Life of President Edwards,* 262.

something yet much more glorious and extensive of that kind" (*David Brainerd*, 533). And Brainerd's "vehement thirstings of soul" for a glorious work was another sign to Edwards that "God has a design of accomplishing something very glorious for the interest of his Church before long" (534). After *Some Thoughts*, then, Edwards de-Americanized his premillennial schema, and saw God planting seeds of the future revivals all around the earth.

Some scholars have seen in Edwards's repeated calls to the Church to pray for the glorious work to begin, and his faith in the efficacy of such prayer, an identification of eschatological revivals as the fruit of human achievement. James Holstun calls this "catalytic millennialism." The catalytic millennialist shows the way to the reign of Christ on earth, or even how to constitute that reign. He aims to create the virtuous citizen by creating the ideal social order. As James Harrington put it, " 'Give us good orders, and they will make us good men' is the maxim of a legislator and the most infallible in the politics." Holstun cites Czech pedagogue John Amos Comenius (1592–1670) as a catalytic millennialist because Comenius thought he would create a regenerated millennial nation by an educational reformation.[145]

Alan Heimert attempts to cast Edwards as a catalytic millennialist by using texts like the following: "All will not be accomplished at once, as by some great miracle, as the resurrection of the dead at the end of the world will be at once. But this work is a work that will be accomplished by means, by the preaching of the gospel, and the use of the ordinary means of grace."[146] This analysis, however, presupposes that Edwards's referent was the millennium instead of the long series of revivals preced-

---

145. Holstun, *A Rational Millennium*, 43, 46–47. Other examples of this sort of millennialism cited by Holstun were John Eliot, the early Winstanley, and Harrington; cited in Holstun, 46. The seventeenth-century Pansophists (Giordano Bruno of Nola, Francis Bacon, Tommaso Campanella, and Johann Andreae) demonstrate the same pattern; Manuel and Manuel, *Utopian Thought*, 205–21.

146. *HWR*, 458–59; Heimert, *Religion and the American Mind*, chap. 2. Davidson makes a similar claim: Edwards "was one of the first Americans to argue explicitly that a noncatastrophic interpretation of Christ's coming would provide believers with the confidence necessary to establish the kingdom." Davidson, *The Logic of Millennial Thought*, 270. Edwards argued that believers should have the confidence to pray for the coming of the kingdom, not establish it by their own efforts. *HA*, 395.

ing the millennium. It also ignores the next paragraph, in which Edwards suggested the dependence of ordinary or "natural" means on the Holy Spirit for efficacy: "But I proceed now to show how this glorious work shall be accomplished. 1. [God's] Spirit shall be gloriously poured out for the wonderful revival and propagation of religion" (HWR, 460).

Two paragraphs later Edwards suggested what he knew from personal experience, that preaching without the power of the Spirit cannot bring revival: "And there shall be a glorious pouring out of the Spirit with this clear and powerful preaching of the gospel, to make it successful for reviving those holy doctrines of religion which are now chiefly ridiculed in the world" (461). Elsewhere Edwards made this more explicit. After saying that God "is pleased to represent himself as it were at the com-mand of his people" (HA, 353), several pages later he qualified that in a discussion of the grace that brings revival: "There is very much to con-vince us, that God alone can bestow it, and show our entire and absolute dependence on him for it. The insufficiency of human abilities to bring to pass any such happy change in the world . . . does now remarkably appear" (359).

These passages demonstrate that Edwards was what Holstun calls a "hermeneutical millennialist," one who recognizes the "irreducible dis-tance" between future final events and one's attempts to clarify and prophesy them.[147] For Edwards the glorious work of God to precede the millennium could never be at the beck and call of human beings, much less degenerate Americans. God would send it in answer to prayer, but both the prayer and its answers were nevertheless still the fruit of God's sovereign grace. He thus preserved a fundamental discontinuity between human achievement—American or Hottentot—and the eschaton.

Edwards reinforced this discontinuity by noting the disjunction in all revivals between religious states before and after an awakening. "It has usually been so from the beginning of the world, that the state of the church has appeared most dark, just before some remarkable deliverance and advancement" (HA, 360). This disjunction underlined for Edwards

---

147. Holstun, A Rational Millennium, 45–46. Holstun cites Richard Baxter, the radical medieval sects described in Norman Cohn's Pursuit of the Millennium, and the Anabaptists at Muenster, as hermeneutical millennialists.

the absence of any necessary connection between human effort or good-ness and the divine effusions, either in the eschaton or at any other time: "[This] has often been God's opportunity for the magnifying his power, mercy and faithfulness towards her . . . [so] as to magnify God's free grace and sovereign mercy" (361).

Perhaps the most intriguing passage in the Edwards corpus that bears on this subject is an entry in his private notebook written at the end of the 1730s, just before the beginning of the Great Awakening. The entry suggests that Edwards thought of himself as a latter-day prophet whose mission was to correct the Church of her errors, the worst of which was her presumption of virtue and exalted status. "Before the end of the church's suffering state," he wrote, God will raise up "a number of emi-nent ministers . . . [to] reprove his own [church] & show her her errours." Their ministry will be similar to that of Elihu, who showed Job's three friends their errors, and their "spirit and power" will be that of "Elias." They will "convince his professing people of their meanness emptiness blindness & sinfullness & his sovereignty & greatness."[148]

That Edwards saw himself as one of these eminent ministers is hinted when he explains that "the church *now* exceedingly needs" the re-proaches of these men.[149] When Edwards wrote a Scottish correspondent several years later (1743), it was more apparent that he had self-consciously taken upon himself the prophetic mantle: "God is now going and returning to his place, till we acknowledge our offense, and *I* hope to humble his Church in New England, and purify it, and so fit it for yet greater comfort, that he designs in due time to bestow upon it" (GA, 540;

---

148. *Miscellanies*, no. 810; see a parallel passage in *AW*, 303. This notion of the necessity of a great man to effect world-historical movement in a final age is common to seventeenth- and eighteenth-century utopias, both religious and secular. Leibniz, for example, thought of himself as chosen by God to be the great intermediary between China and Europe as adviser to Peter the Great. Turgot considered the "genius" to be the dynamic agent of progress as history moves toward perfection. Condorcet believed that at crucial moments in history the intervention of genius was necessary to point out the value of a new and better way of doing things. Manuel and Manuel, *Utopian Thought*, 393, 408, 469–70, 495.

149. John Calvin felt he had a similar calling, as a prophet and teacher "to bring the world to order." His calling, however, did not have the eschatological urgency of Ed-wards's. Bouwsma, *John Calvin*, 191.

emphasis added). Perhaps this self-appointed role can help explain why such a substantial part of his spoken ministry consisted of stern reproofs to his parishioners for their failure to integrate their beliefs.

The most interesting part of the *Miscellanies* entry is its identification of pride and self-righteousness as the greatest sin of an eschatological people: "her greatest errour being her being so insensible of these things & her entertaining so many conceits to the contrary of these things" (*Miscellanies*, no. 810). The 1743 letter indicates the same. Edwards told his correspondent that he hoped to "humble" the church in New England (GA, 540). As he saw it, pride was the most besetting sin of New England after the awakenings. It was also a sign of greater danger. For a professing people to be ignorant of its corruption was itself symptomatic of moral and religious ruin.

The entry in the *Miscellanies* thus states, approximately three years before *Some Thoughts*, that the most heinous sin for an eschatological people to commit is to think more highly of itself than it ought to think. Presumption of exalted status in the history of redemption is therefore ungodly hubris, and the sort that could prove mortal. If America gloated over her religious favors, forgetting her profligacy, then judgment and destruction threatened. Edwards's most important duty, as an eschatological prophet, was to expose and condemn all self-righteousness and pride. The Northampton theologian may himself have succumbed to pride and self-righteousness by writing such an entry, but he knew that he could not identify his people with God's end-time purposes without risking the betrayal of his prophetic calling.

The Significance of Edwards's Millennialism

Jonathan Edwards's millennialism represents a "new departure"[150] in two respects. First, as this chapter has shown, for Edwards the millennium

---

150. As this chapter has indicated, Goen misconstrues the nature of Edwards's "new departure." Edwards was by no means the first postmillennialist in New England, and he did not prophesy an imminent American millennium. Goen, "Jonathan Edwards: A New Departure in Eschatology."

was central to his theology. For many thinkers in the Reformed tradition the millennium was often a theological appendage. Although it cannot be claimed that the millennium was the *center* of Edwards's theology, this chapter has argued that eschatology was consistently prominent in, and even essential to, much of his thought. His philosophy of history and his use of biblical typology, for instance, cannot be understood apart from the millennium. Eschatology was such a prominent constituent of Edwards's thought that it spilled over into his private life, providing both "delight" and emotional solace during his many years of professional conflict at Northampton and Stockbridge. That Edwards's theology was future-oriented and even partially determined by consideration of the future, is perhaps better understood in this century when both biblical and systematic theologies have been shaped by eschatological concern.

Second, Edwards's eschatology functioned as social critique. The prominence of eschatology in his thought and the great prestige of the man in his own time[151] combined to give Edwards's millennialism a prophetic voice of considerable power. So when this scrupulous visionary trained his potent imaginative sights on the future global society, his American auditors knew that he would never countenance any nationalism devoid of benevolence to "the universal system of being" (*TV,* 554). And if their consciences were not pricked by his vivid depiction of a millennial society that implicitly judged their own, their indignation was stirred against this preacher whose eschatological vision boldly challenged their motives and mores. Perhaps Northampton never would have expelled its pastor if he had been less severe in his denunciations of their sins. But that was hardly possible, given his own estimate of the eschatological calling he had been given. His conviction that God had called him as an end-time prophet to deflate America's exalted claims for herself only sharpened his criticisms and foreclosed any chance of reconciliation.

Edwards's social critique was stirred by his eschatological vision. But when he turned from derogation to prescription, he looked first through the prisms of philosophical ethics and theology. That is, it was one thing to use the millennium as a template against which to judge New England

---

151. See the end of Chapter 5 for a discussion of Edwards's influence in the eighteenth century.

society. But it was quite another to prescribe how mid-eighteenth-century New England society actually ought to be structured and operated. For this task Edwards drew from his deliberations on being, love, and God. To an examination of these deliberations we now turn.

3 Private Affection and Publick Spirit: The Edwardsean Social Ethic

"X [Christ] has had little honour from *most* of the rulers," complained Jonathan Edwards in 1743. "*Many* of those that are in power are governed by their Private Interests."[1] Twelve years later the sage of Stockbridge[2] lamented the implications of Braddock's defeat for popular liberties: "The civil & religious Liberties & priviledges of the British Plantations in America & all that is dear to us . . . is so threatened[,] never as at this time."[3]

If these remarks suggest that Edwards was suspicious of existing political authorities and at the same time a champion of popular liberties, they fit few current interpretations of the Northampton pastor's political theory. Generally, scholars have taken one of three positions on Edwards's politics, none of which adequately illuminates the above quota-

---

1. Sermon on Isaiah 47:4, 29 September 1743, 28, 29.
2. This is John Wilson's phrase in Wilson, "Religion at the Core of American Culture," in *Altered Landscapes*, ed. Lotz, 373.
3. Sermon on Psalms 60:9–12, 28 August 1755, 21.

tions.[4] The first is that Edwards either "cared little about political matters" or, if he did, never bothered to apply his prodigious intellectual resources to their analysis.[5] The result is that, as Perry Miller put it, "in Edwards, social theory seems conspicuous by its absence."[6] Thus, according to Gerhard Alexis, "neither the casual reader nor the assiduous student of Edwards will find much in his life or writings that concerns the political order or the tenure of kings and magistrates."[7] The Edwards portrayed by these interpreters is an ivory-tower theologian who refuses to concern himself with matters beyond the walls of his church.[8]

Other Edwards scholars claim to have found traces of political theory in Edwards's writings, but conclude that it is "feudal" in character.[9] According to Clyde Holbrook, Edwards believed that magistrates are "wiser and stronger" than their subjects. Since subjects receive "being

---

4. A principal reason why scholars have missed or misunderstood Edwards's social and political theory is that they have not used his unpublished sermon manuscripts, where a large portion of his social thought is buried.

5. Stokes, *Church and State*, 241.

6. Miller, "Jonathan Edwards's Sociology," 51.

7. Alexis, "Jonathan Edwards and the Theocratic Ideal," 329.

8. For other representatives of this view, see Schneider, *The Puritan Mind*, 106; Joseph Haroutunian, *Piety Versus Moralism: The Passing of the New England Theology* (New York, 1932), xxi; Roland A. DeLattre, "Beauty and Politics: A Problematic Legacy of Jonathan Edwards," in *American Philosophy from Edwards to Quine*, ed. Robert W. Shahan and Kenneth R. Merrill (Norman, Okla., 1977), 20; Westbrook, "Social Criticism and the Heavenly City," 396; David L. Weddle, "The Democracy of Grace: Political Reflections on the Evangelical Theology of Jonathan Edwards," *Dialog: A Journal of Theology* 15 (1976): 251; H. Richard Niebuhr, *The Kingdom of God in America* (New York, 1937), 123, 144–45; Heimert, *Religion and the American Mind*, 398; Dennis M. Campbell, *Authority and the Renewal of American Theology* (Philadelphia, 1976), 15; Joseph A. Conforti, "Samuel Hopkins and the New Divinity: Theology, Ethics, and Social Reform in Eighteenth-Century New England," *William and Mary Quarterly*, 3d ser., 34 (1977): 572–89; Norman Fiering, *Jonathan Edwards's Moral Thought and Its British Context* (Chapel Hill, 1981), 348–49; John Corrigan, *The Hidden Balance: Religion and the Social Theories of Charles Chauncy and Jonathan Mayhew* (Cambridge, Mass., 1987), 2; and William G. McLaughlin, *Revivals, Awakenings, and Reform: An Essay on Religion and Social Change in America, 1607–1977* (Chicago, 1978), 71.

9. Clyde A. Holbrook, *The Ethics of Jonathan Edwards: Morality and Aesthetics* (Ann Arbor, 1973), 203 n. 5; Haroutunian alludes to a feudal political theory for Edwards in his discussion of the Edwardsean doctrine of the atonement; Haroutunian, *Piety Versus Moralism*, 159–60.

from their rulers," they do not have rights of their own, independent of their relationship to their rulers.[10] If this interpretation is correct, Edwards was a political traditionalist, unaware of—or opposed to—the new political theories of the mid-eighteenth century.

The final and most extreme view yet offered was articulated most clearly by Sidney E. Mead. Mead claimed that rather than being indifferent to politics or possessed by regressive political views, Edwards was self-consciously and militantly opposed to Christian political participation at all. In what Mead called "one of the most momentous changes that has ever taken place in Christendom," Edwards allegedly privatized religion by separating "salvation from one's life in the 'natural world.' " But the separation was hostile, not friendly. Edwards's "exclusive sectarian company of the converted" in principle was "at war with the 'worldly' social and political affairs of the commonwealth in which it existed."[11] By Mead's lights, Edwards was a narrow-minded zealot who saw no possibility of peaceful coexistence between the Church and the larger society.[12]

All of these interpretations fundamentally misrepresent Edwards's conceptions of the civil polity and the Christian's relation to it.[13] I contend

---

10. Holbrook, *The Ethics of Jonathan Edwards,* 80.

11. Mead, *The Old Religion in the Brave New World,* 4, 52–53. For Mead, Edwards was a stellar example of "sectarians" who, by defending their privatized religion, implicitly attacked "a fundamental principle of the Republic" [common concern of all citizens for the welfare of the commonwealth]. By so doing, they "undermined respect for all authority and institutions." Ibid., 40–41, 53.

12. Alexis argues, similarly, that Edwards differed from Anabaptist withdrawal from the world only in that he upheld the magistrate's use of the sword and opposed the use of the sword by the saints to bring in the Kingdom. He contends that there is no theocratic ideal in Edwards because Edwards did not expect the saints to express God's will for the whole of culture. As the next three chapters demonstrate, however, Edwards expected the Christian magistrate and citizen to participate in, and ameliorate, the community beyond the confines of the Church. Alexis, "Jonathan Edwards and the Theocratic Ideal," 341–43. See also Campbell, *Authority,* 19.

13. Some scholars have found elements in Edwards's thought relevant to social theory, but interpret them so as to construe Edwards as still uninterested in his own society. Westbrook, for instance, claims Edwards's only real interest was in the next world, and Holbrook finds the impact of Edwards's "social outthrust" restricted to his influence on Samuel Hopkins and nineteenth-century social reform. Westbrook, "Social Criticism and the Heavenly City," 397; Holbrook, *The Ethics of Jonathan Edwards,* 95. Other scholars detect social theory in Edwards, but do not elaborate to any significant degree. Conrad

that Edwards's public theology does indeed encompass social and political theory, and that in fact it is at least as fully developed as the most prominent liberal[14] social theories of his day. In this chapter I will examine the ethical foundation for Edwards's political theory. I will investigate Edwards's understanding of God and being (ontology), the relation of virtue to the system of being, and the implications of Christian love for virtue. I propose that the structure and principles of his ethics demand the same responsible political participation that is urged in his discussions of magistracy and citizenship. In Chapter 4 I will delineate Edwards's understanding of the magistracy. I argue that Edwards resembled Country ideologues in his suspicion of political power, but that his theological understanding of the magistracy added a religious dimension to the skepticism. In Chapter 5 I contend that, rather than advocating Christian withdrawal from the public square, Edwards promoted wholehearted participation in the civil community—regenerate working together with unregenerate to achieve common moral goals. I further suggest that because of the enormous stature which Edwards possessed in colonial America, his theological understanding of citizenship and magistracy must be considered as a factor in the preparation of the American mind for resistance against Great Britain.

Edwards's political and social views are rooted in, and can be consistently developed from, his general ethical principles. Before we examine Edwardsean ethics, however, we need to examine the dynamics of his ontology (the system of being), upon which part of his ethical theory is

---

Cherry points out that Edwards's religion was not privatistic, but does not relate this to social theory. Cherry, *The Theology of Jonathan Edwards*, 216. Stein and Murray have demonstrated that Edwards was quite interested in the social and military realities of his day, but, again, do not go on to place that interest within a larger social theory. *AW*, 32, 46, 74; Murray, *Jonathan Edwards: A New Biography*, 390. Fiering states that participation in a community of love was the first principle of salvation for Edwards, and that Edwards saw the necessity for a civic morality, but he, too, does not develop Edwards's political theory. Fiering, *Jonathan Edwards's Moral Thought*, 336, 260.

14. I follow Stout and Heimert in their depiction of liberals as those religious leaders who were Arminian in theological tendency and elitist in social orientation, and who preached from extensive notes. Evangelicals, on the other hand, were Calvinists, more dependent on popular response, and more extemporaneous in preaching. Stout, *The New England Soul*, 212–32; Heimert, *Religion and the American Mind*, 159–236.

based. For even his ontology has important implications for social and political theory.

God and Being

Edwards's ontology, or philosophy of being, has implications for his political theory because of his conception of the nature of all being, and therefore human being, as active, propensive, and directed toward other beings.[15] But in order to understand his conception of the being of human beings and other beings, we must first examine his notion of God's being, of which all other being is an image.

Edwards spoke of God's being as "disposition" or "habit."[16] That is, God's essence is a constantly exercised inclination to repeat his already perfect actuality through further exercises. God's actuality is already perfect because it is completely exercised in and through the inner-trinitarian relationships. God's action in the world is therefore the spatiotemporal repetition of God's already-realized actuality.

The notion here, which is significant for Edwards's social theory, is that the divine disposition is ontologically productive and relational. Although he does not add to his actuality, God is continually involved in a process of self-extension by creating, and then relating to, other beings.[17] (We shall see below that human being, since it is patterned after divine being, is also relational and able to add to its own being by relating to other beings.)

The rationale Edwards proposed for this self-extension is intriguing. God's most basic disposition, Edwards asserted, is to delight in himself. He created the world in order to find himself in temporality, so that he

---

15. This section is heavily indebted to Sang Hyun Lee's masterly analysis, *The Philosophical Theology of Jonathan Edwards* (Princeton, 1988).

16. The two words were used interchangeably by Edwards. Lee, *Philosophical Theology*, 34–46.

17. *Miscellanies*, no. 117, in Harvey G. Townsend, ed., *The Philosophy of Jonathan Edwards from His Private Notebooks* (Eugene, Oreg., 1955), 258; *Miscellanies*, no. 448, in Townsend, ed., *Philosophy*, 133.

might delight in himself *ad extra*. Another motive for creation was God's own goodness, or the disposition to communicate good, which "will move a being to make occasion for the communication." So God created beings to whom he could communicate good, the essential nature of which is God's own being. God is in a never-ending process of enlarging his own being by creating new relationships. Hence created existence is the spatiotemporal repetition of God's inner-trinitarian fullness, a process that will be everlasting in duration.[18]

Just as God is dispositional, the essence of all being is disposition or habit. Like God, that is, created being is inherently dynamic. Disposition, or the dynamism of a thing, is not a quality possessed by a thing, but is the *essence* of the thing. Therefore, the laws that describe the motion of a thing constitute the essential definition of the thing.[19] Thus Edwards's ontology, which pictures a world of constant movement and action,[20] presents a startling contrast to Aristotle's world of essentially static substances. Aristotle, who was probably the first to give "habit" (or *hexis*, as he called it) a philosophical usage, conceived of habit as a principle of operation, accidental to the being of a substance.[21] Edwards's habit, on the other hand, is a principle of being, constitutive of an entity's essence. The Greek philosopher might have said that substance owns a property, but the New England philosopher said substance is a doer of deeds.[22]

---

18. *Miscellanies*, no. 448, in Townsend, ed., *Philosophy*, 133; *Miscellanies*, no. 1218, in Townsend, ed., *Philosophy*, 149–52. Since this world is in part a communication of God's being *ad extra*, M.D. Bryant and Robert Westbrook are mistaken when they imply that Edwards's fascination with the millennium led him to slight the importance of history. For Edwards the history of the work of redemption, which encompasses both "sacred" and "secular" history, is a genuine though proleptic realization of the final end, which transcends even the millennium. See Chapter 2, "Social Criticism and the Heavenly City." Westbrook, 396; Bryant, "America as God's Kingdom," 54–94.

19. Jonathan Edwards, "Subjects To Be Handled in the Treatise on the Mind," nos. 36, 50, in *Scientific and Philosophical Writings*, ed. Anderson, 391–92.

20. According to Edwards, solidity is nothing other than the act of resisting. Bodies are God's actions. "Of Being," in *Scientific and Philosophical Writings*, ed. Anderson, 205; "Of Atoms," in *Scientific and Philosophical Writings*, ed. Anderson, 215.

21. Lee, *Philosophical Theology*, 17–22.

22. This is a paraphrase of a statement by Anderson in *Scientific and Philosophical Writings*, ed. Anderson, 67.

Second, created being is relational. Edwards construed the world as a dynamic network of relationships, so that every entity is necessarily in relation to other—in fact, all—entities. As one scholar has put it, "A thing *is* only as it is related to other things."[23]

This relational character of being is directional. That is, being drives toward a goal, which is union with other beings. Being is continually in the process of moving from "virtuality" to full actuality, which is achieved for intelligent beings by a union of mutual consent. But this directional activity of being toward union is not limited to intelligent beings. Edwards considered Newton's discovery of the law of universal gravitation (the "mutual tendency of all bodies to each other") to be "a type of love in the spiritual world." So even inanimate being is directional in its disposition, and thereby functions as a symbol of the coming union of intelligent beings.[24]

Because human being, like divine and all other being, is habit or disposition, human nature is active and dynamic. This is all the more true for the regenerate human being. The Christian life is defined more by "transitive practical acts" than by the "unition and adherence itself." That it should be so is a law of necessity, for "all habits [are] a law that God has fixed, that such actions upon such occasions should be exerted."[25] Thus Christian practice is not a subsequent response to Christian experience, but the constitutive essence of Christian experience. "Godliness in the heart has as direct a relation to practice . . . as a habit or principle of action has to action" (RA, 398). Without Christian practice there is no Christian life.

It is not only the nature of habit, however, that makes Christian practice a necessary result of Christian experience. God's nature, as well, requires it. For God's own propensive, dispositional nature requires that the divine fullness be repeated in time, for the sake of God's own goodness and joy. Sang Hyun Lee writes, "Edwards's insistence upon the inevitability and necessity of the practical consequences of the regenerate

---

23. Lee, *Philosophical Theology*, 50.

24. Ibid., 95; *Images*, 79.

25. *Miscellanies*, no. 819, cited in Lee, *Philosophical Theology*, 109; *Miscellanies*, no. 241, cited in Lee, 35.

is rooted in the inevitability with which the sovereign God will accomplish his own aim."[26]

Besides being active and dynamic, human being is, like God and all being, relational. It is God's nature to communicate himself to finite beings, and human beings are made in God's image. Therefore, human beings delight in relations, not "because of our imperfection but because we are made in the image of God."[27] Regenerate human being is even more disposed to relations because its disposition is actually God's disposition infused into it. And God's disposition is "the tendency to an infinitely complex and extensive system of relationships."[28] So the regenerate person has the same tendency to reach out to other human beings to know and love them. By this tendency the being of the regenerated person, according to Edwards, is enlarged, just as God enlarges himself as he extends himself in more and more relationships.

The implications of Edwardsean ontology for social ethics should be clear. Without need for any "ought" the very nature of being (the "is") already pushes toward a consensual union of beings.[29] Because being is habit, it is active and relational, and drives toward union. Regenerate human being is joined with the divine disposition, and therefore by a sort of necessity reaches out to other intelligent beings to know and love them. Hence the Christian is "impelled" to work today to build the Kingdom of God; he or she will not wait passively for a millennial future. Those students of Edwards's social theory who claim that Edwards's millennialism discouraged serious engagement with history miss the implications of his ontology for the importance of temporality.[30] Edwards would not brook a Christian flight from history, or any retreat from a responsible and wholehearted commitment to action within history. For the Chris-

---

26. Lee, *Philosophical Theology*, 233.

27. *Miscellanies*, no. 96; in Townsend, ed., *Philosophy*, 195.

28. Ibid., 113.

29. Of course Edwards denied that full union with being could be achieved by unregenerate intelligent beings. Nevertheless, inanimate being and even the unregenerate, by their imperfect movement toward union, provide for us an analogy (a "type") of spiritual union of the regenerate with being-in-general. *Images*, 79.

30. See, for example, Westbrook, "Social Criticism and the Heavenly City," 397, and Alexis, "Jonathan Edwards and the Theocratic Ideal," 343.

tian is driven by the propensive, relational, and enlarging nature of the divine being that has now infused his or her own disposition. We shall see below, both at the end of this chapter and in the following chapters, that Edwards's own life illustrated the Christian's active engagement in history. Edwards was a model of compassion for the poor and used his pulpit to defend the rights and dignity of society's marginalized.

Virtue and the System of Being

Edwards's social ethic is derived from two sources: the ontology just described and his notion of Christian love. That part of his social ethic drawn from his ontology is described in this section; that based on his theology of love, in the next (and last) section of this chapter. The relationship between Edwards's ontology and social ethic may be better understood by distinguishing them in two ways. First, they have different functions. Edwards's ontology, like all ontologies, explicates the "is" of reality, whereas his ethic moves from what is to what ought to be. His ethic, naturally, is explicitly moral, but his ontology is not. Second, each describes a different aspect of the system of being. The ontology, as we have seen, is an analysis of the *nature* of being. The Edwardsean social ethic, on the other hand, appeals to the *structure* of being.

In *The Nature of True Virtue* (1755) Edwards described the structure of being as a vast network of interrelations wherein every entity is related to every other. This is particularly true of intelligent being: "Every intelligent being is some way related to being in general, and is a part of the universal system of existence; and so stands in connection with the whole" (*TV*, 541). From this "is" Edwards derives an "ought": it is the moral obligation of every intelligent being to acknowledge its place within this structure and, in addition, to give "cordial agreement" to it (565).

Cordial agreement is more than intellectual assent. It involves active "benevolence to Being in general" (*TV*, 540),[31] which means that the truly virtuous person will have "that affection or propensity of the heart

---

31. By "being in general," Edwards meant *intelligent* being in general. *TV*, 542.

to any being, which causes it to incline to its well-being, or disposes it to desire and take pleasure in its happiness," even if it is not beautiful. Benevolence based on the beauty of the object is an inferior kind of benevolence, which Edwards called "love of complacence." But the highest kind of benevolence will seek the good of *every* being unless that being opposes the highest good of being in general.[32]

It is not enough, however, to incline to the well-being of human beings alone. For the "Being of beings, infinitely the greatest and best" of all beings, is God. True benevolence must "chiefly consist in love to God," as the "sum and comprehension of all existence," the "fountain" which moment by moment gives existence to all beings.[33] To fail to love God would be to violate the structural principle of Edwards's philosophical ethics: one *ought* to acknowledge gratefully that one *is* related to all of being, and therefore preeminently related to and dependent on the sum and comprehension of all being (God). The result of love to being in general is "union" with it[34] and love for particular intelligent beings in one's life: "He that loves Being, simply considered, will naturally . . . other things being equal, love particular beings" (*TV*, 571).

The relevance of all this to political ethics appears when Edwards contrasts "publick spirit"—which he uses as a synonym for, or manifestation of, love to being in general—with "private affection." Private affection is love for any group of beings short of intelligent being in general. It is affection for any "private system of being," that is, "any system or society of beings that contains but a small part of the great system comprehending the universality of existence" (*TV*, 554n.). It is noteworthy that in this context Edwards relegates a certain form of patriotism to the status of inferior virtue.

> [Patriotism] limited to a party that is very large, or to the country or nation in general of which they are a part, or the public community they belong to, though it be as large as the Roman

---

32. *TV*, 542–43, 545.

33. Ibid., 550–51. On Edwards's doctrine of God's continuous creation, see *Miscellanies*, no. 346, in Townsend, ed., *Philosophy*, 130.

34. *TV*, 541. Edwards describes "cordial agreement" as "union and consent with the great whole."

Empire was of old . . . exclusive of union of heart to general existence and of love to God, nor derived from that temper of mind which disposes to a supreme regard to him, nor subordinate to such divine love, it cannot be of the nature of true virtue. (*TV*, 602–3)

In nearly every other case in which Edwards used the private-publick distinction, he seems to have had political relations in mind. When he sought to explain *why* "private affections . . . cannot be of the nature of true virtue," he used a political model. Private affection not subordinated to love for being in general is like affection to "another [rival] prince," and thus makes the person treat "his prince wholly as a subject" (*TV*, 555–56). In *Charity and Its Fruits* the "public-spirited" person is "concerned for the good of the public community to which he belongs, and particularly of the town where he dwells," but the person of "narrow, private" views has no such concern.[35] The political use of the publick-private dichotomy is especially frequent in Edwards's fast and thanksgiving day sermons.[36]

Besides being political in reference, the publick-private distinction always puts a negative connotation on "private." Private affection makes a person an "enemy" to general existence. Private affection is rooted in the self because it comes ultimately from self-love, whereas true virtue is "publick," united with others and "the great system."[37] The one is embracing and expansive, the other grasping and self-reducing.

All of this may seem rather obvious from the nature of the terms, but their placement in the twin contexts of political relations and the meta-

---

35. *Charity and Its Fruits*, by Jonathan Edwards [henceforth cited as *CF* in notes and text], in Paul Ramsey, ed., *Ethical Writings*, vol. 8 of *The Works of Jonathan Edwards* (New Haven, 1989), 260.

36. See, for instance, sermon on Isaiah 47:4, 13 October 1743, 29; sermon on Proverbs 14:24, 1729, 6; and sermon on Joshua 7:12, 28 June 1744, 6.

37. *TV*, 554, 555, 602, 611–12. This dichotomy of "private" versus "public," with "private" seen as detrimental, was not new, but in accord with the seventeenth-century New England tradition, in which "public service," along with "mutuality" and "subordination" constituted "a kind of sacred trinity of all respectable societies, Puritan or otherwise." Stephen Foster, *Their Solitary Way: The Puritan Social Ethic in the First Century of Settlement in New England* (New Haven, 1971), 18.

physical system of being has implications for political ethics. The first implication is that Edwards considered opposition to true virtue to be manifested prominently in political relations. Thus Edwards was no ivory-tower scholastic reveling in metaphysical speculation abstracted from sociopolitical reality. He was concerned about the relationship between ethics and society. Second, for Edwards true virtue must manifest concern for the public good, the commonwealth that Edwards is supposed to have ignored. Privatistic religion that ignores "the political problem"[38] is secondary virtue and therefore false religion.

Edwards's philosophical ethics then turned from an analysis of the structure of universal being to its microcosm in human being. In what might be called a phenomenological analysis of the human person, Edwards identified faculties and dispositions that are common to all humans and, consequently, grounds for each human's benevolence toward other humans. We are "related to all mankind," he averred, by the "same nature, like faculties, like disposition: like desires of good, like needs, like aversion to misery, and are made of one blood." Therefore, "men should love their neighbours" by giving to those who are poor.[39] Again, Edwards derived the "ought" from the "is."

Edwards identified four forms of consciousness that are common to all human beings. The first is aesthetic perception. God has put in all persons a "law of nature" that gives them pleasure when they see beauty (*TV*, 565–66).[40] The second is conscience. Edwards sometimes calls this "public conscience," and at other times "natural conscience." It is a sense of moral good and evil natural to all humans, a "law of nature" that God has planted as an "instinct" in the human person. It is the basis for human concern for justice, duties to family and neighbor, and patriotism.[41]

---

38. H. Richard Niebuhr, *The Kingdom of God in America*, 123.

39. "Christian Charity: or the Duty of Charity to the Poor, Explained and Enforced," in vol. 6 of *Works*, ed. Dwight, 538, 541.

40. Here Edwards means "natural" beauty of proportion and agreement, not the divine beauty of holiness, which is perceived only by the regenerate who have been given a new "sense of the heart."

41. *TV*, 592–94, 564, 365–66, 596–97, 569–70, 578, 602–3. This is common in the Reformed tradition. There is very little difference, for instance, between Edwards's con-

Unlike the eighteenth-century benevolists, who argued that human beings are inherently benevolent and that this benevolence is rooted in natural feeling,[42] Edwards did not consider this moral sense to be the origin of true, disinterested virtue. He agreed with the benevolists that the moral sense was a register of the will and command of God, and therefore not properly derived from self-love. But he insisted that it is nevertheless related to a sense of personal inconsistency and desert rather than pure, disinterested love. It is the natural man's "relish of uniformity and proportion." It approves of the same general benevolence that is the goal of pure, disinterested virtue, but only because of the *natural* uniformity, equality, and justice of it. Natural moral sense arising from conscience does not see "the true beauty of it [general benevolence]." Thus it agrees with God "as to the object approved, though not as to the ground and reason approving," which for Edwards is the beauty of divine holiness.[43]

A third form of consciousness shared by all humans is "natural pity," which God has given to humankind for its preservation (*TV,* 607).

The fourth form is religious knowledge. Because every person knows God's eternal law in the conscience, he or she can have true religious knowledge. Socrates and Plato, for example, correctly acknowledged the blindness of human nature and the necessity of a divine instructor. The Greeks, Romans, and Chinese knew something of "true religion," and this they were "taught traditionally." Plato "ran higher towards truth in his sentiments of religion, than others . . . [but] durst not speak out all he knew."[44]

---

ception of justice based on conscience as the law of nature planted in the human heart, and Calvin's notion of natural law as God's eternal law engraved on the conscience. John Calvin, *Institutes of the Christian Religion,* trans. Ford Lewis Battles, ed. John T. McNeill (Philadelphia, 1960), 2.2.13, 2.2.24, 2.8.1, 3.7.8, and 4.20.15.

42. The most prominent were the third earl of Shaftesbury and Francis Hutcheson. See Fiering, *Jonathan Edwards's Moral Thought,* 10, 175, 252.

43. *TV,* 596–97, 592–94, 573, 594, 595, 612–13.

44. "The Insufficiency of Reason," from "Miscellaneous Observations on Important Theological Subjects," in *The Works of President Edwards in Eight Volumes,* ed. Edward Williams and Edward Parsons (Leeds, 1806–11), 8:215–16. In his attribution of true religious knowledge to the unregenerate, Edwards was simply following the Reformed tradition in its understanding of common grace and natural law. Calvin had the same understanding of limited but truthful religious knowledge given to all human beings. See

Edwards's belief that God gave an abundance of good gifts to regenerate and unregenerate alike belies Mead's claim that for Edwards the regenerate have nothing in common with the unregenerate.[45] Edwards believed that both approve the same moral goals because of a common conscience that points uniformly to the same moral ends. Therefore there are moral and epistemological grounds for the Christian working together with non-Christians in the public square in pursuit of the same moral ends.[46]

Finally, Edwards noted the structural interdependence of human existence, and from this drew a lesson. "God has made us with such a nature, that we cannot subsist without the help of one another. Mankind in this respect are as the members of the natural body; one cannot subsist alone, without an union with, and the help of the rest." Therefore, he concluded sharply, "He who is all for himself and none for his neighbors, deserves to be cut off from the benefit of human society, and to be turned out among wild beasts, to subsist by himself as well as he can. A private niggardly spirit [note that "private" is once more an opprobrium] is more suitable for wolves and other beasts of prey, than for human beings."[47]

We see, then, that Edwards described the fully actualized human person as one who continually reaches out in new relationships to know and to love, regardless of the beauty of the object loved. We have seen also that Edwards described true virtue as benevolence to all intelligent beings, and explicitly condemned nationalisms that restrict benevolence to the beings within one polity. For the structure of being and the shared gifts of consciousness among all human beings make it only "reasonable"[48] that humans should exercise benevolence beyond the limits of their own church and nation.

Institutes, 1.3.2–3, 1.5.2–3, 2.2.24, 3.8.4, 3.10.4, 3.20.34, 4.14.8, 4.18.15, note 41 above, and John E. Smith's introduction to RA, 6.

45. Mead, The Old Religion in the Brave New World, 66.

46. In the passage from Religious Affections that Mead cites, Edwards distinguished natural and supernatural sources of religious affections, not their moral goals or the behaviors which they motivate. RA, 205.

47. "Christian Charity," in Works, ed. Dwight, 6:541.

48. Ibid.

Christian Love and Virtue

Edwards did not derive ethical principles only from his philosophy of being. He also made abundant use of his theological principles to ground a specifically Christian ethic of public responsibility.[49] Two fundamental conceptions anchor this ethic: the spirit of Christian love, and God's relation to his creation. In brief, the spirit of Christian love moves the Christian to concern for the interests of others. The Christian will be concerned not just for the spiritual needs of others, but for their material needs as well. And the Christian will be concerned for the interests of all human beings, regenerate as well as unregenerate. God's relation to his creation, on the other hand, is incarnational. That is, he is present in one's neighbor, and especially in the poor. Therefore the most direct and pleasing way for the Christian to love God is to serve people in society and give to the poor.

Now let us examine the strategies by which Edwards came to these conclusions. First, we will explore his understanding of Christian love. For Edwards, Christian love is fundamentally a reaching beyond self to the other. It is a reorientation of concern from self to neighbor. In *Charity and Its Fruits*, the work in which he most fully developed his conception of love, Edwards explained, "They who have a Christian spirit seek not only their own things but also the things of others" (CF, 259). In this work Edwards gave specifically political expression to this concern for others. He explained that love would dispose the Christian to active participation in his civil community, for the sake of improving its quality of life: "It disposes persons to be publick-spirited. A man of a right spirit is not a man of a narrow, private spirit; but he is greatly concerned for the good of the public community to which he belongs, and particularly of the town where he dwells. . . . A Christian spirited man will be also concerned for the good of his country, and it disposes him to lay out himself for it" (CF, 260–61).

---

49. Edwards nowhere systematically presented such an ethic, but in several works (CF, "Christian Charity," and the "Strong Rod" funeral sermon for Col. John Stoddard) he gave detailed attention to the public ethical implications of a Christian's commitment to God. What follows is a distillation of what I found in these and other works in his corpus.

Christian love, for Edwards, was directed to one's neighbor not only by its own inner nature, but teleologically as well. God has purposed from eternity that the individual is to live for others: "And he who has made you has made you for himself, and for the good of your fellow creatures, and not only for yourself" (CF, 268).

In his notion of love attempting to improve the world, Edwards implied what he later stated explicitly, that love is by nature *active*, "a principle that we always find is active in things of this world." Thus grace, which is a theological term for God's love, "is a principle of holy action." Since love is always active, and the Christian's heart is possessed by love, true Christian faith will always issue in practice. As he titled his eleventh sermon in *Charity*, "Grace tends to holy practice." Therefore there is no place for speculative contemplation divorced from holy practice; all vision of God necessarily issues in the practices of God's love in the world: "As to a speculative knowledge of things of religion, there are some wicked men who have attained to great measures of it. . . . [But] a true knowledge of God and divine things is a practical knowledge." Accordingly, every one of the great Christian virtues (trust, repentance, humility, fear of God, thanksgiving, praise, heavenly mindedness, hope) "tends to holy practice."[50]

Edwards made it clear that when he spoke of Christian love, and the public service that it engenders, he intended benevolence not just to those in the church but to all human beings. This is particularly clear in his sermon "Christian Charity," which commends charity to the poor as a duty second to none in the Christian life. It may be recalled from above that the rationale given for charity was "the general state and nature of mankind . . . [all] men are made in the image of our God, and on this account are worthy of our love." Thus charity given only to church members violates the unity of all humankind. Edwards was insistent that charity should be rendered to all the poor, regardless of their moral states:

---

50. CF, 301, 298, 293, 296, 301–8. This emphasis on practice was common to the Reformed tradition. Yet Edwards's emphasis on practice was even greater than his predecessors', and is seen most clearly in his great definition of true religion, *Religious Affections*, particularly the twelfth and "chief" sign of grace. RA, 40–42, 383–461. This has led Smith to suggest that Edwards was partly responsible for the "robust sense of activity in the world" of later American Protestantism. RA, 43.

"[We are to help them even if they be] an ill sort of person . . . of a very ill temper, of an ungrateful spirit . . . our enemies . . . we are particularly required to be kind to the unthankful and to the evil; and therein to follow the example of our heavenly Father, who causes his sun to rise on the evil and on the good, and sendeth rain on the just and on the unjust."[51]

Edwards reiterated the indiscriminate scope of Christian love in his sermon "End of the Wicked Contemplated by the Righteous," in which he proclaimed that the Christian is to love every man regardless of his spiritual or moral estate because one never knows what his eternal destiny might be. Who knows but that he might not be a "companion in eternity?"[52] In his Farewell Sermon to the Northampton congregation, he admonished his parishioners not to think of themselves as Christians unless they "fervently love all men, of whatever party or opinion, and whether friendly or unkind, just or injurious, to you or your friends, or to the cause and kingdom of Christ."[53]

Lest love be interpreted as simply concern for the "souls" of the unregenerate, Edwards insisted that true love cares for their "bodies" as well. In *Religious Affections* he wrote that true religion cares for the material, as well as spiritual, needs of others. He criticized those who "pretend a great love to men's souls, that are not compassionate and charitable towards their bodies . . . [because] they must part with money out of their pockets. But a true Christian love to our brethren, extends both to their souls and bodies. . . . *And if the compassion of professing Christians towards others don't work in the same ways* [i.e., "to their bodies"], *it is a sign that it is no true Christian compassion*" (RA, 369; emphasis added).

Edwards's call to the church to help society's poor was, of course, not revolutionary. He did not advocate structural change, but merely charity that would in the long run and in most instances probably leave the poor still poor. Neither was this new to the Christian tradition. From the

---

51. "Christian Charity," in *Works*, ed. Dwight, 6:559–62.
52. "End of the Wicked Contemplated by the Righteous," in *The Works of President Edwards*, ed. S. Austin, vol. 4 (New York, 1843), 293–94, cited in Holbrook, *The Ethics of Jonathan Edwards*, 32.
53. "Farewell Sermon," in *Works*, ed. Williams and Parsons, 4:379.

earliest documents of the church,[54] Christians had been exhorted to
share their wealth with the less fortunate. Charity was commonly exhorted in the Middle Ages,[55] and Puritan rhetoric contained many such
exhortations.[56] Yet, as we shall see in Chapter 5, Edwards preached this
duty more than some of his better-known contemporaries. It is not clear
why Edwards should have been so concerned, but we can guess that the
social structure of Northampton may have been a factor. Northampton's
economic classes had become increasingly distinct since the turn of the
eighteenth century. The more affluent parts of the citizenry had stopped
supporting the poor in ways that had been practiced by earlier generations. In addition, Northampton, like most of New England, was running
out of land for its sons. High prices for land, its decreasing productivity,
and a rapidly swelling population meant reduced income for many. No
doubt Edwards was aware of the economically unfortunate both in his
own town and elsewhere throughout New England.

In sum, Edwards's doctrine of Christian love required active participation of the Christian in the civil affairs of the community for the purpose
of improving its quality of life. The Christian's concern for his unregenerate compatriots was to extend beyond their need for conversion, encompassing their "temporal prosperity" as well.[57]

---

54. James 2:14–17, 5:1–6; Matthew 19:21; Galatians 2:10.

55. M. M. Postan, ed., *The Cambridge Economic History of Europe*, vol. 3, *Economic
Organization and Policies in the Middle Ages* (Cambridge, 1963), 559; *The Little Flowers of
St. Francis: The Acts of Saint Francis and His Companions*, trans. E. N. Blaiklock and A. C.
Keys (Ann Arbor, 1985), 4–5, and passim.

56. See, for example, Winthrop, "A Model of Christian Charity," in *The Puritans in
America*, ed. Heimert and Delbanco, 84–85; Cotton Mather, *Psalterium Americanum*
(Boston, 1718), 33. On Mather's concern for the poor, see Richard F. Lovelace, *The
American Pietism of Cotton Mather: Origins of American Evangelicalism* (Grand Rapids,
Mich., 1979), 198–250, esp. 228–34. On Puritan benevolence, see also Charles H.
George and Katherine George, *The Protestant Mind of the English Reformation* (Princeton,
1961), 83–85, 89–90, 104, 131–39, 156–58, 162–69.

57. Alexis overemphasizes Edwards's disillusionment with theocracy when he says that
Edwards differed from Anabaptist withdrawal from the world only in that he upheld the
magistrate's use of the sword, and opposed the use of the sword by the saints to bring in
the Kingdom. Actually, even the latter statement is misleading, for, as we have seen in
Chapter 2, Edwards believed that God supported England in her eighteenth-century wars
against France and Spain, the military-political arms of the Antichrist.

God's Presence in One's Neighbor and the Poor

The second fundamental theological concept that anchors Edwards's political ethic is his construal of God's relation to his creation. We must first remember that Edwards conceived of the world as re-created at every moment by God, and in such a way that even what is created is not a substance but an instance of God's acting. This is why Edwards can say that, strictly speaking, there is no substance but God. Yet in Edwards's conceptualization of the Christian's love for God, Edwards so particularized God's being in the world as to restrict it, for the purpose of this doctrine, to the person of one's neighbor. In the Christian's neighbor God is found. So if the Christian wants to express love for God, he (she) must serve and love his (her) neighbor. For one's neighbor is God's "receiver": "We can't express our love to God by doing anything that is profitable to God; God would therefore have us do it in those things that are profitable to our neighbours, whom he has constituted his receivers" (*ST,* 523–24).

The Christian particularly finds God, Edwards believed, in the poor neighbor. If she wants to give to God, let her give to the poor: "For though Christ is not here [on earth], yet he has left others in his room, to be his receivers; and they are the poor. . . . God hath been pleased to make our needy neighbours his receivers."[58]

Not only is love of neighbor the chief expression of love of God, but it is in fact the "soul" of faith, faith's "working, operative nature." According to Edwards, love belongs to the "essence" of faith (*CF,* 330). Edwards's placement of love at the center of faith has caused one student to accuse him of adopting "the doctrine of Rome openly that love is the form and soul of faith."[59] By Rome's doctrine is meant that of the medieval church, with Thomas Aquinas its chief representative. Edwards's relation of faith and love, however, is different from Thomas's in an important respect. Thomas regarded faith and love as essentially separate. Love, or charity, he wrote, is the form of faith and makes the act of

---

58. *ST,* 526; "Christian Charity," in *Works,* ed. Dwight, 6:544.

59. Jan Ridderbos, *De Theologie Van Jonathan Edwards* ('s-Gravenhage [The Hague], 1907), 254, cited in Cherry, *The Theology of Jonathan Edwards,* 134.

faith perfect. Charity is not inherently related to faith because "what brings faith to its form, or makes it alive, does not belong to the essence of faith."[60] For Edwards, on the other hand, faith and love are two names for the same act when considered from two points of view (CF, 330–31). Love therefore belongs to the very nature and essence of true faith (330). Love is the soul and life of faith, but it does not come as a separate entity to form an unformed faith. Instead, love and faith are two aspects of the same act from the beginning.[61]

Since love is of the essence of faith, it is a *sine qua non* of true religion. This position of Edwards, so clearly seen in his post-Awakening writings (particularly *Some Thoughts Concerning the Revival* and *Religious Affections*), seemed to have evolved from his experiences during the revivals. For in the 1738 sermon series later published as *Charity and Its Fruits*, Edwards's list of tests of true conversion was far more heavily weighted toward forms of consciousness than forms of practice: grief over moral failure, dread of sin, sensibility of the beauty of holy practice, delight in holiness, hunger and thirst for holy practice, constant efforts to live a holy life, desire to know more of one's duty (CF, 310–12). Edwards wrote in *Charity* that love is an active principle, but he seemed reluctant to settle on certain kinds of behavior as tests of grace.

Some Thoughts (1742) and *Religious Affections* (1746), both written after Edwards had been soured by the ambition and selfishness in many of his "converts," displayed no such reluctance. Edwards called practice the "chief" test of grace and rejected a number of "private" affections. It did not matter if religious experiences were exalted, involved physical sensation, resulted in much talking, were spontaneous, involved "miraculous" use of scriptural texts, followed a customary order, resulted in long private devotions or much verbal praise of God, or provided great psychological assurance of their validity. None of these phenomena was a neces-

---

60. Thomas Aquinas, *Nature and Grace: Selections from the Summa Theologica*, trans. A. M. Fairweather, The Library of Christian Classics, vol. 11 (Philadelphia, 1954), 268, 270.

61. Edwards's emphasis on love as belonging to the essence of faith can probably be attributed to his disillusionment with many who professed conversion during the awakenings, but subsequently showed little or no evidence of genuine love. See the Edwards correspondence collected in GA, 536–38, 554–57, 558–59, esp. 565–66.

sary sign of grace.[62] Edwards had lost confidence in subjective forms of consciousness, which could be sources of self-deception. Now only publicly manifested Christian practice could be relied upon as a test of true religious experience.

When the post-Awakening Edwards listed the standards by which true religious experience was to be judged, each one was centered in a loving demonstration of concern for the needs, both eternal and temporal, of others: "They [the truly regenerate] may appear to be . . . universal in fulfilling rules of love to men, love to saints and love to enemies; . . . rules of mercy and charity, and looking not only at our own things, but also at the things of others; rules of doing good to men's souls and bodies, to particular persons and to the public; . . . to be earnestly engaged in the service of God and mankind" (RA, 419).

The chastened Edwards told ministers that they had no warrant from Christ to affirm the religious experience of anyone who did not seek to relieve the poor, though "they tell a fair story of illuminations and discoveries" (RA, 335). One could be said to have been truly converted only if she confessed to a "general benevolence to mankind" (411). When he held up model saints as living demonstrations of true religion, he was careful to point out that moral practice was primary for each. His wife Sarah, the anonymous "person" whose piety was described in Some Thoughts, was said to have realized the importance of moral and social duties, particularly during her times of religious ecstasy (ST, 335–36). The David Brainerd whom Edwards held up before the world was a model of the same devotion to moral practice. Norman Pettit writes, "Edwards in this work identified true sainthood with total commitment to making the condition of mankind as 'excellent' or 'beautiful' as God had intended" (David Brainerd, 13).

As has been hinted by some of the passages already quoted, Edwards put a premium on charity to the poor as a signal expression of love to neighbor and therefore a preeminent test of true religion. This is a duty, Edwards preached to his church, as important as prayer or church attendance. No commandment in the Bible is "laid down in stronger terms"

---

62. RA, 443, 121–91.

than the commandment of giving to the poor.[63] It is therefore an all-important test of grace. "And the Scripture is as plain as it is possible it should be, that none are true saints, but those whose true character it is, that they are of a disposition to pity and relieve their fellow creatures, that are poor, indigent and afflicted" (RA, 355).

This is an objective standard by which every Christian would be judged. And effort alone was not enough; Edwards judged the sufficiency of Christian charity by the number of poor remaining in a community.[64] Unless there were "none" in the community "that are proper objects of Charity . . . [suffering] in pinching [want]," Christians in the community had not done enough. "Rich men" were urged by Edwards to establish and support schools "in poor towns and villages" and to support ministerial students from poor families. Edwards called upon these men to give at least "one-quarter of their estates" to support the revival, but warned those who complied against complacency. Giving even that size a gift would be but to "act *a little* as if they were designed for the kingdom of heaven" (emphasis added).[65]

A time of revival, pronounced the post-Awakening Edwards, was particularly the time when charity ought to be practiced. For little else would bring the Kingdom of God to earth so effectively: "So amiable would be the sight, in the eyes of our loving and exalted Redeemer, that it would soon as it were fetch him down from his throne in heaven, to set up his tabernacle with men on earth, and dwell with them."[66]

When Edwards sought to promote his revivals by relating the case histories of exemplary converts, he was careful to point out their compassion for the poor. Edwards commended four-year-old Phebe Bartlet, for example, for her "uncommon degree of a spirit of charity." He told of the

---

63. "Christian Charity," in *Works*, ed. Dwight, 6:540.

64. Apart from their context these statements might imply that Edwards believed that the poor were not true Christians. Yet in his "Christian Charity" sermon Edwards stated that "poor" at some point becomes a relative term, standing for anyone who is less fortunate than oneself: "Though we may not have a superfluity, yet we may be obliged to afford relief to others who are in much greater necessity." "Christian Charity," in *Works*, ed. Dwight, 6:562.

65. Sermon on Malachi 3:10–11, July 1743, 29; ST, 515.

66. ST, 523–24, 527.

time she heard of "a poor man that lives in the woods" whose family had lost their cow. The young convert begged her father to give the man one of their own cows. When her father replied that he could not afford to give up the animal, Phebe then pleaded with him to take the poor man and his family into the Bartlet home. (*FN*, 204–5). Sarah Edwards was portrayed by her husband in *Some Thoughts* as having "a great sense often expressed, of the importance of the duty of charity to the poor, and how much the generality of Christians come short in the practice of it" (*ST*, 339).[67]

If we can trust Samuel Hopkins, Edwards's closest disciple and first biographer, Edwards practiced what he preached. Hopkins marveled at the "uncommon regard he showed to liberality, and charity to the poor and distressed. He was much in recommending this, both in his public discourses and private conversation." According to Hopkins, his mentor remarked how Christians in his day were very deficient in this duty, in fact much more than in "other parts of external Christianity [nominally Christian countries]." The disciple wrote that Edwards often talked about how much charity was urged, particularly in the New Testament, and that he recommended that every church keep a large fund for this purpose, for this was the principal duty of the deacons. Hopkins, who lived in the Edwards home for close to six months, testified that Edwards was a stellar example of giving to the poor, but usually gave secretly. If all of his giving were ever revealed, it "would prove him to be as great an instance of charity as almost any man that can be produced." To illustrate Edwards's practice, Hopkins told of a time that Edwards heard of a family in another town that had fallen into poverty because the father had become sick. Edwards made arrangements to have the man receive a bundle of money without knowing from whom it came.[68]

Edwards's deathbed remarks confirm Hopkins's testimony. Among his

---

67. Apparently this was a conviction that ran through the family. Sereno Dwight remarked that Edwards's daughter Jerusha was known for her charity to the poor. Dwight, *The Life of President Edwards*, 117.

68. Samuel Hopkins, *Memoirs of the Life, Experience and Character of the Late Rev. Jonathan Edwards . . .* , in *Works*, ed. Williams and Parsons, 4:48. Edwards's charity was all the more remarkable when it is remembered that, because of his large family and need for expensive books, he suffered financial strain through most of his career.

last words were the following: "May my funeral be like Mr. Burr's, with-out pomp and cost. Any additional sum of money, that might be ex-pected to be laid out that way, I would have it disposed of to charitable uses."[69]

This analysis of Edwards's theological ethics demonstrates that Ed-wards's theory of citizenship, which will be treated in Chapter 5, was not a response to the political crises of his day, but a consistent development of his theological principles. Both his theological ethics and his theory of citizenship portrayed the Christian citizen as one who fully and responsi-bly engages in civil affairs for the purpose of improving the quality of life in the community. Edwards did not tolerate privatistic religion that ig-nores social and political problems.

---

69. Dwight, *The Life of President Edwards,* 578. Edwards's practice of charity belies Holbrook's conclusion that the mingling of religious and aesthetic sensibilites in the Northampton divine led to passive contemplation, not action. This chapter demonstrates that Edwards's contemplation issued in action. Holbrook, *The Ethics of Jonathan Edwards,* 177.

4 The Importance and Functions of Strong Rods: Edwards on the Magistracy

Edwards's view of the magistracy has been said to "reflect the medieval feudal culture," in its "description of government and society in terms of a sovereign ruler and serflike creature or subject."[1] This interpretation stands on a passage from Edwards's private notebooks where rulers are said to be "the wiser and stronger, and [God] has appointed those to be in subjection, who are less knowing, and weaker, and have received being from their rulers, and are dependent, preserved and maintained." On the face of it, this quotation seems to support the claim of medieval feudalism, where there was at times a tendency "to think of the king as the only conceivable representative of the kingdom."[2] But when the

---

1. Holbrook, *The Ethics of Jonathan Edwards*, 203 n. 5.

2. Ewart Lewis, *Medieval Political Ideas*, 2 vols. (New York, 1954), 1:195. At other times vassals had rights and participated in the making of law. In addition, certain thinkers in the fourteenth century (John of Paris, Marsiglio of Padua, and Bartolus of Sassoferrato) and the fifteenth-century conciliarist movement placed ultimate political

passage is read in context it takes on a different meaning. For the "rulers" are parents, not magistrates; "those to be in subjection" are children, not citizens in a polity. This is apparent from what immediately precedes the passage. Edwards had been describing "human moral governments among men" in general. Then he turned to a specific application—the nuclear family of parents over children. Parents "govern" their children as "rulers," he writes, because they are wiser and stronger than their offspring. Then follows the passage at the beginning of this paragraph.[3]

If anyone in Edwards's era held anything close to "medieval feudal" political views, it was New England's "Court" party. After the turn of the eighteenth century, New England society, following the Country-Court division of political parties in England, split into similar factions. In England after 1675 "Court" described the attitude and lifestyle of people who owed their positions to patronage and supported the position that there existed royal prerogatives not subject to the will of Parliament. The New England Court was an elite group who rejected the voluntaristic elements of Puritan political theory and adopted English manners, morals, and dress.[4] Most urban ministers in early eighteenth-century New England were of the Court persuasion. Insecure because of the waning status of their profession, threatened by growing disorder within their churches, and fearful that popular demands for inflated currency would devalue their fixed incomes, these clergymen looked to the magistrate as a guarantor of social order. They denounced resistance to his authority, for fear that a "levelling spirit" begun in the civil realm would destroy what little order

---

authority in the people rather than their rulers. But the powers of pope and king were too great to allow any practical reversal, in the emerging nation-states, of the theory that political power and right descend from lord to subject. Walter Ullmann, *A History of Political Thought: The Middle Ages* (Baltimore, 1965), 200–228.

3. Jonathan Edwards, "Concerning God's Moral Government," in *Remarks on Important Theological Controversies*, vol. 2 of *The Works of President Edwards*, ed. Edward Hickman (London, 1834; reprint, Edinburgh, 1974), 512.

4. Breen, *The Character of the Good Ruler*, 206–8. For the English background, see J.G.A. Pocock, "Machiavelli, Harrington, and English Political Ideologies in the Eighteenth Century," *William and Mary Quarterly*, 3d ser., 22 (1965): 549–83, and Caroline Robbins, *The Eighteenth-Century Commonwealth Men: Studies in the Transmission, Development, and Circumstance of English Liberal Thought from the Restoration of Charles II until the War with the Thirteen Colonies* (Cambridge, Mass., 1961).

remained in the church. The magistrate should be wealthy, they held, because only then would he have time for the study that was requisite for such office; Timothy Breen adds that this requirement was probably intended to keep the magistracy out of the hands of the rabble.[5] If for Holbrook "medieval feudalism" means a tendency to see the integrity of a state as comprising chiefly the magistrate's prerogatives rather than the rights and participation of citizens, then the New England Court held a view of political society similar to such a conception.

In this chapter I will use Charles Chauncy (1705–87), liberal minister at Boston's First Church, as a representative member of the New England Court party. Comparing Chauncy's political views with Edwards's should help put to rest the old opinion that Boston's liberal clerical elite were more socially conscious than evangelical ministers like Edwards.[6]

If New England's Court wanted to strengthen the magistrate's hand, the New England Country party was nearly obsessed with the magistrate's potential to abuse his power. The best rulers, they believed, can become tyrants because of the corrupting nature of power and the human tendency to greed and pride. Therefore magistrates should be watched carefully for both moral and political failure, and citizens should participate in government. For virtue is greater in the populace as a whole than in one individual. Civil power is a threat to the character of an individual magistrate, but hardly dangerous when the mass of freemen are politically involved. Country politicians and publicists adopted Puritan political theory, which made civil leaders accountable to the people by annual elections. They dismissed the Court's idea that the wealthy were better suited for political office.[7]

Edwards was probably well acquainted with New England Country ideology. We know that he read *The Independent Whig*, a weekly newspaper from England that mediated England's Country ideology to the American colonies. According to Bernard Bailyn, *The Independent Whig*

---

5. Breen, *The Character of the Good Ruler*, 203–39, 218.

6. See, for example, Alice M. Baldwin, *The New England Clergy and the American Revolution* (New York, 1928), 169; Max Savelle, *Seeds of Liberty: The Genesis of the American Mind* (New York, 1948); and Bernard Bailyn, *Ideological Origins*, passim, and "Religion and Revolution."

7. Breen, *Character of a Good Ruler*, 240–69; Bailyn, *Ideological Origins*, 33–54.

and *Cato's Letters*, both written by Thomas Gordon and John Trenchard, were "referred to repeatedly in the [New England Country] pamphlet literature" and "ranked with the treatises of Locke as the most authoritative statement of the nature of political liberty and above Locke as an exposition of the social sources of the threats it faced." It seems that Edwards read *The Independent Whig* early in his career, for its title is entered on the first page of his "Catalogue" of private reading, and is crossed out. We also can assume that he read the *Monthly Review*, a scientific and literary magazine with Whig and Nonconformist leanings, since he made seven references to it between March 1751 and January 1754. In addition, we know that Edwards read a large variety of newspapers and magazines from both Boston and London.[8] Since political theory was widely discussed in eighteenth-century periodicals,[9] it seems likely that he had wide exposure to Country ideology.

There is no evidence, however, that Edwards was directly influenced by Country ideology. In fact, in several respects he differed from Country ideologists. They cared little about the magistrate's religious qualifications or duties;[10] Edwards wanted the magistrate to support (the Edwardsean version of) true religion. Country writers tended to see virtue in the people;[11] Edwards usually saw little but corruption. Country publicists were primarily concerned with the loss of political liberty;[12] his chief concern was that New Englanders find and follow true religion. These differences will be discussed in more detail below.

Yet in one important respect Edwards's view of the magistracy mirrored that of his fellow Country-men. He was as suspicious as they of political power. In the sermons that were later published as *The History of the Work of Redemption*, for instance, Edwards lamented that "for a great many ages, the civil authority was all on the side of Antichrist, and the church seemed to be in their hands" (*HWR*, 448). In a 1728 occasional sermon he observed that most nations were then "under absolute and despotick

---

8. Johnson, "Jonathan Edwards's Background of Reading," 202; Bailyn, *Ideological Origins*, 36; 202, 215.

9. Bailyn, *Ideological Origins*, 36.

10. Breen, *The Character of a Good Ruler*, 204–5, 250.

11. Ibid., 240–45, 251–55.

12. Bailyn, *Ideological Origins*, 48.

power." In *Some Thoughts* Edwards implicitly deplored the paucity of political support for the revivals when he urged magistrates to promote them and threatened that they might be "struck through" by Christ if they did not.[13]

In a July 1740 sermon on "Dishonesty; Or, the Sin of Theft and Injustice," Edwards complained that "the best laws may be abused and perverted to purposes contrary to the general design of laws."[14] Who can abuse and pervert laws? In *True Virtue* (1755) Edwards criticized rulers of imperialistic nations who abuse and pervert language when they seek to disguise their "bloody work" with deceptive rhetoric: "So a nation that prosecutes an ambitious design of universal empire, by subduing other nations with fire and sword, may affix terms that signify the highest degrees of virtue, to the conduct of such as show the most engaged, stable, resolute spirit in this affair, and do most of this bloody work. . . . They use these terms inconsistently, and abuse language in it" (*TV*, 627).

But it was not only world-historical tyrants whom Edwards chastised. He urged citizens to denounce the sins of local and regional politicos as well. There should be freedom for everyone, he declared, to criticize the "management of public affairs, and the duty of the legislature, and those that are at the head of the administration, though vastly his superiors" (*ST*, 291). Like New England's Country writers, Edwards seemed to believe that it was more important to keep watch over political authority than to support it.

Chauncy, in contrast, persistently defended Boston's politicians against criticism and forbade his parishioners to speak evil of their magistrates. He argued that the governor and his assistants must have handsome salaries to raise them above the "vulgar people," and warned that persons who openly criticized politicians were not "good Christians."[15]

Another Country theme that surfaced repeatedly in Edwards's commentary on magistrates was the frequency with which they turned their office to the pursuit of "private" gain rather than to seek the "Interest of

---

13. "Fragment Three," 8; *ST*, 371.

14. "Dishonesty," in *Works*, ed. Hickman, 2:222.

15. Charles Chauncy, "Civil Magistrates Must Be Just, Ruling in the Fear of God" (Boston, 1747), 30–31, 67. See also Chauncy, "A Discourse on the Good News from a Far Country" (Boston, 1766), 30, and *Seasonable Thoughts*, 368–69.

the Publick." This theme was not new, of course; it can be found through-out Puritan political theory.[16] It is worth mentioning here, however, because it is further evidence that Edwards's view of the magistracy was not feudal in the sense that the honor and prerogatives of the magistrate seem more important to the integrity of a state than the dignity and rights of citizens.

In a 1729 fast-day sermon Edwards scored rulers "who seek their own Private Interest more than the Interest of the Publick. when all their aim is to Enrich and advance themselves. when they will make the Publick weal Give Place to their own Private designs." On a day in 1743 when he was supposed to be celebrating the recent victory, the Northampton Jeremiah instead lamented that "many of those that are in power are governed by their Private Interests . . . places of publick trust are bought and sold . . . disposed of to service private designs & G[od] is visibly much neglected in the management of publick affairs." He voiced the same complaint the following year on the fast day, charging that their sinfulness makes rulers "unfaithfull & treacherous to the Publick & re-gardless of the Publick interest." Corruption in a political ruler is not a sometime thing, for the ruler "*oftentimes* neglects yea betrays & sells the Publick Interest."[17]

Edwards did not shrink from telling rulers how they ought to behave. In a 1738 sermon, the pastor-turned-political theorist lectured the hand-ful of magistrates in the congregation (and the voters who elected them) that good rulers would serve the public good, not their own private interests (CF, 260–62). Ten years later, facing local politicians seeking his ouster, he implicitly rebuked them.[18] First, he pointed out, somewhat

---

16. See, for example, "William Perkins on Callings," in *Puritan Political Ideas: 1558–1794*, ed. Edmund S. Morgan (Indianapolis, 1965), 39. See also Morgan, *Puritan Political Ideas*, 237–38, and Breen, *The Character of a Good Ruler*.

17. Sermon of Proverbs 14:24, 1729; sermon on Isaiah 47:4, 13 October 1743, 29; sermon on Joshua 7:12, 28 June 1744, 6. Emphasis added.

18. The audience for this address, the funeral sermon for Col. Stoddard, included Hatfield squire Israel Williams, Edwards's cousin, who was alleged by Edwards to have been a principal agent in the anti-Edwards agitation at Northampton, and selectmen and General Court representatives from the families who opposed him in his last years at Northampton. John and Jonathan Hunt, Ephraim and Joseph Wright, Josiah and Seth Pomeroy, and Jonathan Strong, for instance, signed in 1749 a petition opposing Edwards;

tactlessly, that Col. John Stoddard, their rival, had also been their superior "in these parts of the world." Then he hinted that they served their own interests, not the public good. For good rulers, he admonished, would be "watchful against public dangers, and forward to use their powers for the promotion of the public benefit; not being governed by selfish motives in their administration; not seeking only, or mainly, to enrich themselves, or to become great, and to advance themselves on the spoils of others, as wicked rulers *very often* do; but striving to act for the true welfare of all to whom their authority extends." The good magistrate would have a "publick spirit," not a "narrow, quiet spirit" willing to "grind the faces of the poor, and screw their neighbors" because he was eager for "filthy lucre." He would not be like unnamed other magistrates who are "eminent for nothing but gluttony and drunkenness." In a possible reference to his enemies in Northampton, he further warned that the virtuous ruler would not be a busybody, or a meddler, or engaged in fraud, extortion, bribe-taking, and lying. In short, political office was no place for a "mean spirit."[19]

Charles Chauncy believed that the greatest danger to a state comes from ambitious, discontented members of the citizenry. It is not the ruler whom the body politic must particularly beware, but those who "strike in with the *popular* cry of *liberty* and *priviledge*," who serve their own ends. Evil most commonly comes from below, not above; hence the best protection against "*all* evil" is for the masses to keep their place and not aspire to a higher station in life. Indeed, this is one of the magistrate's principal

---

all of these men held political office or came from families that controlled political offices in the first half of the eighteenth century. James R. Trumbull, *History of Northampton, Massachusetts, From its Settlement in 1654*, 2 vols. (Northampton, 1898), 2:206; Tracy, *Jonathan Edwards, Pastor*, 148, 18, 152, 184. My thanks to Kenneth P. Minkema for pointing out the reference in Trumbull's *History*.

19. "A Strong Rod Broken and Withered," in vol. 6 of *Works*, ed. Dwight, 220, 227; emphasis added. Thus Alexis strays widely when he claims that Edwards would not have the saints tell their rulers what to do. Edwards's delineation of the qualities of a good magistrate gave saints the ability and implicit sanction to do precisely that. See Alexis, "Jonathan Edwards and the Theocratic Ideal," 343. Edwards could give pointed advice to magistrates in times of crisis as well. In 1755 he wrote the colonel of the county militia, chiding him for leaving Stockbridge "so easy and open a prey to our enemies" when Indian attacks seemed imminent. Dwight, *The Life of President Edwards*, 549.

functions. He must defend the public order against the unruly mob and make sure "inferiours" pay their debts to their "superiours."[20]

If Chauncy feared that the public order was imperiled by covetous citizens, Edwards worried more about the danger of self-seeking politicians. Because of the magistrate's influence upon his subjects, Edwards considered his selfishness particularly heinous, more culpable than that of the people under his authority. In a 1729 fast-day sermon on the theme, "Righteousness exalteth a nation but sin is a Reproach to Any People," Edwards charged the magistrate with the greater burden of guilt when a people is consumed by wickedness. "It is among a People as it is in the human body," he reasoned. "There especially may a disease be said to Prevail in the body when it has seized the more noble & vital Parts so that they dont well do their office." So when rulers "wink at" wickedness and immorality and fail to make or execute laws against immorality, then "Lawmakers are also Law breakers." And since "Publick Rulers *they Represent the whole People*," wickedness can be said to "Prevail and be [the] Rule amongst them" when the magistrate is consumed by selfishness and indifference to evil. For Edwards, then, the magistrate is in some sense responsible for the immorality of his people. For he is a "Keeper of the City." If he is "treacherous & open the Gates to the Enemy," the enemy will rush in and corrupt the city's inhabitants.[21]

Edwards may have heaped greater abuse upon the ruler than the people in the event of a society's corruption, but he did not follow Country theorists in their faith in the wisdom and virtue of the common people. Jonathan Mayhew, for example, broke from the jeremiad tradition in his 1754 election sermon when he congratulated New England for its virtue and challenged the familiar apostasy theme. New England, he declared triumphantly, was *not* "degenerated from the laudable spirit of our ancestors . . . we fear God . . . [and so] God will still give us to see the good of his chosen."[22] As we have seen in the first chapter of this study, Edwards

20. Chauncy, "Civil Magistrates," 34–35, *Seasonable Thoughts*, 366, and "Civil Magistrates," 28–30, 42–44.

21. Sermon on Proverbs 14:24, 1729, 8, 7; sermon on Joshua 7:12, 28 June 1744, 6.

22. Jonathan Mayhew, "An Election Sermon," in *The Wall and the Garden*, ed. Plumstead, 286, 302. For more examples of Country's faith in public virtue, see Breen, *The Character of a Good Ruler*, 273–74, and Hatch, *The Sacred Cause of Liberty*.

was never so confident of New England's spirituality. The problem, as he saw it, was not to convince New England of God's beneficence toward the colony, but to persuade the colony of its degradation.

Beyond Country Ideology

If Edwards's political theory reflected New England Country ideology in its suspicion of political authority, he transcended conventional Country critique by probing political power more incisively. Country publicists attacked magistrates for their tendency to encroach upon the political liberties of independent landholders for the sake of their own private interests. Edwards accepted that assessment of the magistrate's inclinations, but added two typically Puritan theological admonitions.[23] One concerned the religious status of the men who hold office; the other spoke to the ultimate importance of political office itself.

Edwards's first theological challenge amounted to a denigration of the spiritual worth of most magistrates. Like countless clerics and theologians before him, Edwards sought to deflate the pretensions of this world's eminences by appealing to a value system whose foundation lay in another world. Many, he charged, are spiritually worthless, contemptible in God's eyes. "There are many great men of the world, kings and princes, men of great power and policy, men of noble blood and honourable descent . . . that are honoured, and make a great figure, and great account is made of them in the world, *who are wicked men and reprobates.*" And wicked men, "however rich, learned and great, are of no account with [God]." They are fools and we fail to see through their pretensions when they "treat their inferiors . . . in a haughty and scornful manner, as vaunting themselves in their greatness." For the truth of the matter is that "they all are not of so great value in God's sight as one true Chris-

---

23. For an example of similar theological critiques in the Puritan tradition, see "Christopher Goodman on Resistance to Tyrants," in *Puritan Political Ideas*, ed. Morgan, 1–14. See also Quentin Skinner, *The Foundations of Modern Political Thought*, vol. 2, *The Age of Reformation* (London, 1978), 302–48, and Michael Walzer, *The Revolution of the Saints: A Study in the Origins of Radical Politics* (New York, 1973).

tian, however humble his birth and low his standing; however poor, or ignorant, or unknown." It was the humble Christian, not the arrogant politician, who is a "jewel" in God's eyes.[24]

Edwards's second strategy was to relativize the importance of the magistrate's *office* by measuring it against the vast drama of redemption. Such a measurement revealed, for Edwards, the relative insignificance of political power. Politicians have inflated ideas of what they can do to benefit humanity. But the "work of God in the conversion of one soul" produces more happiness, and a greater benefit to humanity, "than all the temporal good of the most happy revolution in a land or nation . . . or all that a people could gain by the conquest of the world" (*ST,* 344–45).[25]

In a day when politics was beginning to replace religion as the center of the intellectual universe,[26] Edwards was convinced that what went on in church was ultimately more relevant to world events than what transpired on election day. The mutual concerns of minister and people, he told his congregation in his Farewell Sermon, are of infinitely greater moment than the temporal concerns of human beings—more than the fates of the greatest monarchs, kingdoms, or empires. Politicians may have presumed that they could arbitrate right and wrong, but there would come a day when God would judge us "by his own laws and not by the laws of the commonwealth." On that day, whatever momentary glory was achieved by political machinations on this earth would "appear as it were infinitely less than nothing" in comparison with the heavenly glory that was to be revealed.[27]

Even magistrates' pretensions of pleasing God by favoring religion in their domains were illusory. For even if they did "much in many respects for religion" by building stately churches for the worship of God or encourag-

24. Sermon on 1 Peter 2:9, in *Works,* ed. Hickman, 2:946; sermon on Matthew 22:9–10, 1740, in Miller, "Jonathan Edwards's Sociology," 70; *CF,* 141; sermon on 1 Peter 2:9, 946; sermon on Matthew 22:9–10, 1740, 70.

25. By "revolution" Edwards did not limit himself to political transformations, but included religious, social, and economic changes.

26. See Tracy, *Jonathan Edwards, Pastor,* 188–89, and Hatch, *The Sacred Cause of Liberty.*

27. "Farewell Sermon," in vol. 1 of *Works,* ed. Dwight, 639; "Dishonesty," in *Works,* ed. Hickman, 2:222; *Images,* 57.

ing religion in their dominions "by their power and influence," as Cyrus did when he restored the Jews from captivity, they should have known that "God has a greater delight in the sincere worship and love of one poor, obscure Christian, than in all that is done throughout the globe by irreligious kings and princes." Edwards was too cynical to believe that Cyrus's intentions were strictly religious. In his view, history was full of occasions when political leaders thought they were serving God only to be advancing the designs of the Antichrist. And an enormous part of Christendom in his own day—that is, the Catholic countries of Europe—was still serving the Antichrist. For Edwards, then, civil religion—the political promotion of a religious cause—was highly ambiguous. History was too full of the cynical manipulation of religion by self-interested rulers. Honest and virtuous promotion of true religion by political power was certainly possible and to be encouraged, but Edwards viewed such attempts with a skeptical eye. [28]

Edwards may have been skeptical of political power, like many of his contemporaries, but his skepticism did not usually extend to the existing British government and kings. He condemned the royal court for graft and corruption, but praised the Hanoverian kings and proclaimed that the British constitution was the best on earth. [29] In this, too, Edwards simply reflected the views of contemporary political commentators. Opposition writers in Britain attacked the king's self-interested, deceitful courtiers or the financiers around the throne promoting a mercantilist economy, but not the king himself. John Trenchard and Thomas Gordon praised the liberality of the British system of government and advised obedience to it as long as the constitution was "preserved entire." [30] In 1756 Virginia's Samuel Davies rejoiced that the British constitution was the best in the world and hailed George II's protection of religious freedom. [31]

If Edwards was not ahead of his times in his political theory, neither was he behind them, as the attribution of "medieval feudalism" would suggest. His practice of keeping a wary eye on politicians was far closer to the

---

28. Sermon on 1 Peter 2:9, in *Works*, ed. Hickman, 947.

29. Sermon on Isaiah 47:4, 13 October 1743, 29; *AW*, 136; "Fragment Three," 7–8.

30. Pocock, "Machiavelli," 574; Patricia U. Bonomi, *Under the Cope of Heaven: Religion, Society, and Politics in Colonial America* (New York, 1986), 198.

31. Samuel Davies, "The Religious Improvement of the Late Earthquakes," 19 June 1756, in *Sermons by the Rev. Samuel Davies, A.M.*, 3 vols. (Philadelphia, 1864), 3:351–52.

principles of New England's Country party than to those of the Court party, which supported political authority in order to protect its own social position. His political views should therefore be seen as compatible with what amounted to the "progressive" party of the times, the party that laid the foundation for Revolutionary attitudes toward civil government.

The Importance and Functions of Public Authority

Despite his suspicion of rulers' propensity to self-interest, Edwards considered government to be of paramount importance. In this he was simply reiterating what was stock-in-trade for the Reformed tradition.[32] In his famous sermon given at the funeral of his cousin Col. John Stoddard, "God's awful Judgment in the breaking and withering of the Strong Rods of the Community," Edwards likened civil rulers, when they are at their best, to "the Son of the Most High." Good rulers are "vehicles of good to mankind, and . . . will be as the light of the morning, when the sun riseth, even a morning without clouds, as the tender grass springing out of the earth, by clear shining after the rain." Edwards did not stop there, but went on, piling superlative upon superlative. He reminded them that Scripture calls rulers "gods." Then he declared that good rulers are as the mainsprings or wheels in a machine, as the vitals in the body natural, or the pillars and foundations in a building. Upon them depend, in part, public morals, economic health, and the spiritual welfare of citizens.[33]

In time of war, rulers were especially important. Then they were "under God, the main strength of a people . . . and the chief instruments of their preservation, safety and rest." In general, the political head was to supply, animate, and direct the civil body. The office was so foundational that it would continue even in the millennium, even during the spiritual reign of Christ on the earth. God thought enough of the office that he

---

32. See, for example, Calvin, *Institutes*, 4.20.3–4, and Heinrich Bullinger, *Of The Holy Catholic Church*, in *The Library of Christian Classics*, vol. 24, ed. G. W. Bromiley (Philadelphia, 1953), 314.

33. "A Strong Rod Broken and Withered," in *Works*, ed. Williams and Parsons, 6:222, 223, 222.

helped even unregenerate magistrates do a good job. In sum, government was "great and important business."[34]

It may appear at this point that Edwards's estimation of the importance of the magistracy was inconsistent at best, and contradictory at worst. For, as we have seen, he seemed convinced that what happens in the church is far more important—ultimately—than what takes place in the throne room or on the battlefield. Yet he compared the good rulers to Christ, and claimed that a people's economic and spiritual prosperity partly depends on its ruler. How could he hold both convictions?

Like many of his Reformed predecessors, Edwards held a dialectical view of political power.[35] That is, he (and they) saw political power differently, sometimes in quite opposing ways, when viewing it from contrasting perspectives. His exaltation of the magistracy assumed that magistrates "are as they ought to be."[36] From the perspective of religious ideals, the magistracy took on immense importance. Yet in point of fact, few magistrates live up to those ideals. Colonel John Stoddard, Edwards's cousin, friend, and ecclesiastical ally, who was eulogized by Edwards as a "strong rod" exemplifying the good magistrate, was the exception rather than the rule. Because politicians more frequently abused their power, their importance in the work of redemption was more negative than positive. Not many rulers led their people in righteousness, but many were responsible for their nations' descent into corruption and idolatry. God would not be deterred from his purposes by their evil machinations,

---

34. Ibid., 224; *Images*, 128; *HA*, 339; *RA*, 207; "Strong Rod," in *Works*, ed. Williams and Parsons, 6:222. Edwards's conviction of the importance of the magistracy seemed to grow over the course of his career. For example, in his 1739 sermons on the history of the work of redemption, he said that the great work of God's Spirit [see Chapter 2] would come "not by the authority of princes . . . but by God's Holy Spirit." *HWR*, 393. Eight years later, however, he predicted that Christian magistrates would be used by God to overthrow the Antichrist. *HA*, 418. I am indebted to Thomas Schafer for this realization.

35. Calvin, for instance, called the magistracy "by far the most honourable of all callings in the whole life of mortal men," and in nearly the same breath mocked those rulers who thought "God had made over his right to mortal men, giving them the rule over mankind." He was as scornful as Edwards of wicked magistrates: "If they command anything against [God], let it go unesteemed. And here let us not be concerned about all the dignity which the magistrates possess." *Institutes*, 4.20.4, 4.20.32.

36. "Strong Rod," in *Works*, ed. Williams and Parsons, 6:222.

but he would work through their profanations rather than their acts of obedience. This was true even for England and New England. Some rulers were used by God positively, such as Henry VIII, Edward VI, Elizabeth, and the New England founders, but Edwards was generally more impressed with the system of English and colonial liberties than the persons who presided over the system.

This is not to say that Edwards's God circumvented the political realm except when Calvinist rulers held power. The Massachusetts theologian always considered the political realm, just like every other realm of human history, to be the arena in and through which the history of redemption would be worked out. God does not transcend human history to bring redemption, he was convinced, but works in and through the stuff of human history to build a kingdom for his Son. He superintends the machinations of every ruler, good and bad, to further his ultimate end. In that sense the political arena is as important as the church council to the workings of God's purposes. Because human beings are political as well as religious beings, their earthly and heavenly prosperities are partly dependent on their civil communities, just as they are dependent on the quality of life in their churches.

Yet Edwards also held that because the spiritual world is more truly real than the material world and God's purposes for history are not to be thwarted, the political realm is therefore ultimately relativized by "the mutual concern of minister and people." The magistracy is important, but only as it is used by God in his working out of the history of redemption. Political leaders can be instrumental in the temporal and spiritual prosperity of a people, but they seldom are. More often, their pretensions to importance are mocked by God and those (like Edwards) who are privy to his counsels.

When Edwards reflected on the *purpose* of civil government, he used the paternal image so familiar to Reformed thinkers from Calvin to his own day.[37] Magistrates, he preached, are to "act as the fathers of the commonwealth with that care and concern for the public good that the father of a

---

37. Calvin, *Institutes*, 4.20.5; Elisha Williams, "The Inalienable Rights of Conscience," in *Puritan Political Ideas*, ed. Morgan, 288. See Stout, *The New England Soul*, 168–69; Corrigan, *The Hidden Balance*, 65; and Breen, *The Character of a Good Ruler*.

family has for the family, watchful against public dangers, [and] forward to improve their power to promote the public benefit" (CF, 261–62).

Edwards's consideration of the *functions* of government was also conventional. In a list similar to ones made by Puritan stalwarts William Ames and Samuel Willard, the Northampton theologian detailed the proper duties of the good magistrate.[38] The first function of government, Edwards declared, is to secure property and protect citizens' rights: "The general design of laws is to maintain the rights and secure the properties of mankind."[39] From this initial purpose Edwards derived his second function, the maintenance of order. Without the strong arm of government to protect one citizen from the depredations of another, society would dissolve into horrifying chaos. In Edwards's graphic words, rulers keep "citizens from tearing one another apart." In a passage reminiscent of Hobbes, the Northampton divine warned that without the coercive power of the magistrate human existence would be constant strife, "going on in remediless and endless broils and jarring, until the society be utterly dissolved and broken in pieces, and life itself, in the neighborhood of our fellow creatures, becomes miserable and intolerable."[40] The demon inciting all this misery is the acquisitive quality of human nature, which, unrestrained, drives men to make "a prey of one another." The result— without government's restraint of human lusts—would be the "utmost deformity, confusion and ruin."[41]

Related to the first two functions of government—protecting property and keeping order—is a third, ensuring justice. For Edwards, justice is a proportional return of moral deserts. In principle, it consists "in the agreement of different things, that have relation to one another, in nature, manner, and measure." Applied to human society, it means that

---

38. William Ames, *Conscience with the Power and Cases Thereof* (n.p., 1639; reprint, Amsterdam, 1975), 4:165; Samuel Willard, *A Compleat Body of Divinity* (Boston, 1726), 620–30.

39. "Dishonesty," in *Works*, ed. Hickman, 2:222. Here again Edwards shows his affinities to Country ideology, which jealously guarded the liberties and property of citizens. Breen, *The Character of a Good Ruler*, 246–50.

40. "Miscellaneous Remarks," in *Works*, ed. Williams and Parsons, 6:335; "Strong Rod," in *Works*, ed. Williams and Parsons, 6:223.

41. "Miscellaneous Remarks," in *Works*, ed. Williams and Parsons, 6:335.

the evildoer will have evil returned to him in proportion to the evil of his
deeds. Similarly, justice prevails when the person who loves has the
proper returns of love (*TV*, 569).

Edwards understood justice principally in terms of the exchange of
property. The "mutual injustice" in economic exchange that Edwards
deemed it government's duty to prevent was more often than not the
oppression by which the strong take advantage of the weak. "Sellers," for
instance, "take advantage of their neighbor's poverty to extort unreason-
ably from him for those things that he is under a necessity of procuring for
himself or family." When merchants "raise the price of provisions, even
above the market," exploiting the plight of "poor people whose families
are in such necessity of bread," injustice triumphs. But the righteous
Governor of the world, Edwards warned, does not allow evil to go unpun-
ished, and the Bible demonstrates that this form of oppression causes him
(God) great displeasure. God will defend the cause of the poor, he
warned the oppressors in his auditory, "and you will be no gainers by such
oppression." Political rulers are therefore obligated to "restrain those who
would grind the faces of the poor, and screw their neighbors."[42]

The means that the strong utilize to oppress the weak is deception. In
the Stoddard funeral sermon Edwards inveighed against "the false colors
with which injustice is often disguised." In a sermon about the final day of
judgment he condemned the "oppression and extortion" that take place
under the cover of "deceit and fraud" and by means of "lying in trading."[43]

---

42. "Dishonesty," in *Works*, ed. Hickman, 2:222; ibid.; "Final Judgment," in *Works*,
ed. Williams and Parsons, 4:474; "Dishonesty," in *Works*, ed. Hickman, 2:222, 224;
"Strong Rod," in *Works*, ed. Williams and Parsons, 6:220. Edwards's economic ethics
were conventional, based on the traditionally Puritan notion that economic transactions
should be based on moral considerations, not the laws of the market. A market economy,
though it had always existed to some degree in New England and was beginning to be
accepted in principle, was still widely feared in Edwards's day as dangerous to morals and
corporate solidarity. For more on the moral and religious conflicts stirred by the rise of a
market economy, see J. E. Crowley, *This Sheba, Self: The Conceptualization of Economic
Life in Eighteenth-Century America* (Baltimore, 1974), 106–24, and Edwin J. Perkins, *The
Economy of Colonial America* (New York, 1980). For a fuller treatment of Edwards's
economics, see Valeri, "The Economic Thought of Jonathan Edwards."
43. "Strong Rod," in *Works*, ed. Williams and Parsons, 6:219; "Final Judgment," in
Works, ed. Williams and Parsons, 4:474.

Whereas Edwards was concerned about protecting the weak from the depredations of the strong, Chauncy, the pastor of Boston's wealthy First Church, took care to guard the interests of the commerical elite. Since the country's happiness was dependent on its "commercial interests," he insisted, the good ruler would do everything necessary to prosper commerce. Edwards defended the poor against merchants' duplicity and greed, but Chauncy worried that the poor would not pay their debts to their creditors or work hard enough to sustain Boston's economy. [44]

A fourth responsibility of government is national defense. Military force is justified, thought Edwards, when the "rights and privileges" of a people are threatened, or "when the preservation of the Community or publick society so requires it." If "injurious and bloody enemies" molest and endanger a society, it is the "duty" of government to undertake that society's defense by the use of force. This follows "from the Law of self-Preservation." [45]

The first four functions of government, for Edwards, are "negative" goods in the sense that they benefit society by preventing (or negating) an assortment of evils. They conserve the integrity of society in the face of forces that would tear it asunder. The next two confer "positive" goods by going beyond the maintenance of a just and peaceful exchange of property, and the enjoyment of civil and religious freedom, to the promotion of a common morality and a minimal level of material prosperity.

Edwards's fifth function of government was to "make good laws against Immorality." Rulers should be as concerned for public virtue and morality as they are that their coffers be kept full. For a people that fails in morality will also fail, eventually, in every other way. Rulers should therefore not "countenance vice and wickedness" by failing to enact legislation against it or enforcing what had been legislated. [46]

The sixth responsibility Edwards gave to government was to help the

---

44. Chauncy, "A Discourse," 8–9, and "Civil Magistrates," 19, 28–30, 44–45.

45. Sermon on 1 Kings 8:44–45, 4 April 1745, 10–11; sermon on Nehemiah 4:14, June 1746, 2; sermon on 1 Kings 8:44–45, 4 April 1745, 3. Another reason for going to war is fidelity to a "just alliance." Sermon on 1 Kings 8:44–45, 4 April 1745, 11. The defense of liberties was a common theme in Puritan political theory after the Glorious Revolution. See Breen, *The Character of a Good Ruler,* 164, 195, 198, 200.

46. Sermon on Proverbs 14:24, 1729, 7.

poor. The good magistrate "encourages and helps the people," particularly those unable to help themselves. A state welfare program is therefore required to assist those who are destitute for reasons other than their
own laziness or prodigality. Government welfare is necessary because
private charity (and here Edwards had in mind the charity of the church)
is unreliable: "In this corrupt world [private charity] is an uncertain
thing. Therefore the wisdom of the legislature did not think fit to leave
those who are so reduced upon such a precarious foundation for subsis-
tence." Because of the natural selfishness of all human beings, even the
regenerate, it is therefore incumbent upon the state to help provide for
the destitute.[47]

The seventh and final major item in Edwards's job description for the
magistrate was religious. The good ruler was expected to give friendly, but
distanced, support to true religion. By true religion, of course, Edwards
meant the evangelical religion of the Awakenings, in general, and the
sort outlined in his treatises, in particular. During a revival the magistrate
should call a day of prayer or thanksgiving. But he should not try to do
much more than that. In Edwards's list of the magistrate's qualifications
in his "Strong Rod" sermon at John Stoddard's funeral, "piety" was only a
subordinate trait, not listed among the five chief qualifications; and in
the context it is mentioned only for the purpose of administering "justice
and judgement . . . to bear down vice and immorality." In his private
notebooks Edwards reminded himself that the civil authorities were to
have "*nothing* to do with matters ecclesiastical, with those things which
relate to conscience and eternal salvation or with any matter religious as
religious." He would not brook, in other words, any magistrate telling his
parishioners what church to attend or telling him what to preach. For "it
belongs to the people—not their legislators—to decide whether they are
bound to obey ecclesiastical laws."[48]

---

47. Sermon on 2 Chronicles 23:16, March 1737, 19–20; "Christian Charity," in
Works, ed. Dwight, 6:567.

48. *ST*, 370–73; "Strong Rod," in *Works*, ed. Williams and Parsons, 6:228. The other
qualities required of the good ruler by Edwards were "great ability for the management of
public affairs," and then a long list of natural abilities: understanding of the nature and
processes of human government, statecraft and war, insight into human nature, knowledge of the political and social character of the county, knowledge of the political and

On this score Edwards was no innovator. Puritan tradition held that church and state were to be separate in function, and by the end of the seventeenth century it was generally agreed that "the magisterial calling no longer included coercive power over man's consciences." Even Cotton Mather said that civil governments should stay out of ecclesiastical matters.[49] Both evangelicals and liberals in Edwards's era insisted that the magistrate support religion and morality, but none insisted, as had their seventeenth-century predecessors, that civil government enforce correct doctrine. Religious leaders in early and mid-eighteenth century only asked the magistrate to take care "that religion be upheld and that God is worshipped, and by suppressing all that tends to root out religion from among them." They had come a long way from Calvin, who suggested the magistrate interfere even in ecclesiastical matters to prevent idolatry and blasphemy, and ensure the teaching of orthodox doctrine.[50]

Yet not all heirs of the tradition understood religious freedom in the same way. Edwards understood ecclesiastical freedom primarily from the point of view of the person in the pew. With New Lights in mind, he defended the Christian's right to choose his or her own church. If one's current pastor was not providing spiritual food for the soul, the Christian ought to be free to sit under another pastor who would. Charles Chauncy, on the other hand, was more concerned with the freedom of the established clergy to preach without fear of criticism or loss of income because of New Light defections. The magistrate therefore should use "the civil arm" to prevent people from insulting ministers of the Standing Order.[51]

Edwards considered some entanglement with religion by government to be inevitable; in those circumstances, the magistrate was bound to favor the interests of religion. This was obligatory for civil as well as

---

cultural features of the surrounding colonies (British, French, and Spanish), the Indian tribes, and Canadian peoples. "Strong Rod," 228. *Miscellanies,* no. 14, in Townsend, ed., *Philosophy,* 198–99; *Miscellanies,* no. 11.

49. *Puritan Political Ideas,* ed. Morgan, xxv–xxxv; Breen, *The Character of a Good Ruler,* 201, 200.

50. Barnard, "The Throne Established by Righteousness," in *The Wall and the Garden,* ed. Plumstead, 264–65; Calvin, *Institutes,* 4.20.3, 4.12.16.

51. Edwards, *Miscellanies,* nos. 10, 11, 14, in Townsend, ed., *Philosophy,* 197–99; Chauncy, "Civil Magistrates," 60–61, and *Seasonable Thoughts,* 368–69.

religious reasons. "It is for the civil interest of a people not to be disturbed in their public assembly for divine worship, that is, it is for the general peace, profit, and pleasure of 'em in this world." Thus Edwards did not favor any strict separation of religion and state.[52] He would have considered such a position naïve and necessarily injurious to religion. The religious and civil interests of a society are woven together in a seamless garment so that the attempted separation of one from the other would damage both. Not only is religion necessary for morality, which in turn is essential for a healthy society, but the dynamics of the national covenant require the state to promote true religion. For a society's neglect of religion will bring the wrath of God. Hence it is only prudent for civil government to ensure the free practice of true religion, for thereby the civil prosperity of society is also promoted.

We have seen from this chapter that Edwards was not out of touch, as often has been alleged, with the political and social currents of eighteenth-century New England. He probably was well aware of contemporary political theory, and certainly showed affinities to it in his own preachments on society and politics. To its analysis of political power he added typically Puritan theological critiques that sharpened its critical power. The significance of Edwards's deliberations on political power can be seen when compared with Boston's most prominent liberal cleric, Charles Chauncy, who has sometimes been portrayed (mistakenly) as more socially conscious and progressive than Edwards. Not only were Edwards's deliberations on civil government as developed and thoughtful as Chauncy's, but the Northampton preacher took a position closer to the reformist movements of the period.

---

52. *Miscellanies*, no. 14, in Townsend, ed., *Philosophy*, 198–99. He attacked the view, even after a Council had recommended his dismissal, that denies "all authority of councils & all Powers of the Civil Magistrate in matters of religion." His argument was that "just because parents abuse their authority to teach religion to children doesn't mean their liberty should be removed." I owe this observation to a conversation with Thomas Schafer.

5 The Priviledges and Duties of Subjects: A Theology of Citizenship

Jonathan Edwards's formulation of Christian citizenship was consistent with his understanding of magistracy: the Christian citizen, he believed, is obligated to full and responsible participation in the civil community for the purpose of improving its quality of life. In this chapter I argue that Edwards stressed the communal nature of regenerate life at a time when social forces emanating from the Great Awakening were breaking down social cohesion in America and elevating the individual. I also contend that Edwards supported the notion of loyalty to nation, but considered most patriotism to be based in fact on self-love, and the phenomenon of patriotism itself peculiarly susceptible to self-deception. In the final part of this chapter I maintain that Edwards ennobled the Christian citizen by showing theological preference for those marginalized by traditional religious and social norms, thereby subverting eighteenth-century hierarchicalism. Thus Edwards combined his own version of classical republican (Country) ideology with a theological form of radical egalitarian republicanism, suggesting a way in which the two ideologies came to coexist in the Revolutionary generation in an "unstable pluralism."[1]

A Society Sweetly United

In the middle of the eighteenth century, particularly during and after the Great Awakening, many colonials were concerned more for their individual rights than for what others told them was necessary for the community's good. These "New Lights" did their best to ignore Old Light threats that evangelical "enthusiasm" disrupted the communal order. Yet the Old Lights rightly detected in the New a radical individualism that, in principle at least, would let the rest of society be damned so long as the individual's religious goals were secured. When New Light preachers exhorted colonials to evangelical conversion, individuals were told to ignore the demurral of neighbors. "Stand up and act for GOD against all opposers," Gilbert Tennent told thousands of colonists, though "your Neighbors growl against you, and reproach you." Ebenezer Frothingham lectured his audiences on the "absolute Necessity for every Person to act singly . . . as if there was not another human Creature upon Earth."[2]

Individualism as a principle of conversion became individualism as a principle of separation from the unregenerate. Presbyterian and Congregational separatists defended their schisms by appeals to the rights of minorities against majorities, and of individuals against the whole in

---

1. Michael Kammen, *People of Paradox: An Inquiry Concerning the Origins of American Civilization* (New York, 1972), 89–96, quoted in Harry S. Stout, "Religion, Communications, and the Ideological Origins of the American Revolution," *William and Mary Quarterly,* 3d ser., 34 (1977): 540. "Unstable" refers not to Edwards's fusion of the two (which was theoretically consistent) but to American society's adherence to the two during and after the American Revolution.

2. Gilbert Tennent, "The Danger of an Unconverted Ministry" (Boston, 1744), in *The Great Awakening,* ed. Heimert and Miller, 86, 98; Ebenezer Frothingham, "The Articles of Faith and Practice, with the Covenant that is Confessed by the Separate Churches" (Newport, R.I., 1750), in *The Great Awakening,* ed. Heimert and Miller, 457. On Old Light–New Light conflicts in the Great Awakening, see Gaustad, *The Great Awakening,* 80–140; Goen, *Revivalism and Separatism,* 33–35, 36–67; and Bonomi, *Under the Cope,* 139–60.

matters of conscience. The duty of the individual to decide for God regardless of community opinion also became the right of the individual to defy civil and ecclesiastical statutes. When the Connecticut General Assembly passed a 1742 law imposing heavy restrictions on itinerant preachers, Elisha Williams, Edwards's cousin and tutor at Yale's Weathersfield campus, attacked the statute as a violation of "every Christian['s] . . . *Right of judging for himself* what he is to believe and practice in Religion." Williams illustrated the potentially atomizing tendency of evangelical individualism in his description of the extent of individual rights. All persons in the congregation, he claimed, were "equally vested in the same Right, and hold it independent one of another, and each one independent of the whole, or of all the rest."[3]

To be sure, separatist Congregationalists and Presbyterians formed new societies that embodied, in part, communal values. But the Great Awakening introduced a "new spirit of defiant individualism" that marked a shift from the more communal outlook of the seventeenth century, when colonials had rarely thought of themselves separate from a larger community— family, church, or town. After the eighteenth-century revivals, in contrast, more and more Americans began to see themselves as individuals distinct from a community and to make decisions accordingly.[4]

If evangelical New Lights tended to lose sight of the old communalism, Old Lights held stubbornly to a reactionary form of community. Jonathan Mayhew's 1750 "Discourse concerning Unlimited Submission and Non-Resistance to the Higher Powers" has been regarded as the vanguard of the American Revolutionary spirit, a signal call for resistance against the colonial political order.[5] A careful reading of the sermon, however, reveals that the sermon *supported* the social and political status quo in colonial New England. The occasion for the address was the anniversary

3. Elisha Williams, "The Essential Rights and Liberties of Protestants," in *Puritan Political Ideas*, ed. Morgan, 268, 293.

4. On the new eighteenth-century spirit of individualism, see Bonomi, *Under the Cope*, 152–60; the quotation is from page 158. See also Goen, *Revivalism and Separatism*, 294–95, 299.

5. Bernard Bailyn calls it "a classic formulation of the necessity and virtue of resistance to oppression." Bailyn, ed., *Pamphlets of the American Revolution, 1750–1776* (Cambridge, Mass., 1965), 209.

of the execution of Charles I, on which day colonial Anglicans honored Charles as a saint and martyr. Such honor threatened, to Mayhew and many other colonials, the reimposition of "tyranny"[6] and high-church episcopacy that would encourage Antichristian papism. Mayhew was supporting the doctrine of resistance against tyrants, but the tyrant he had in mind was Charles I, not George II, whom he explicitly called in this sermon a "good prince."[7] His aim was to defend the existing political order against Anglicans who, it seemed, would change it: "It becomes us, therefore, to be contented, and dutiful subjects. Let us prize our freedom; but not *use our liberty for a cloak of maliciousness*. . . . I would exhort you to pay all due regard to the government over us; to the *king* and all in due authority; and to *lead a quiet and peaceable life.*"[8]

Mayhew's support for the Hanoverian dynasty was typical in 1750, but his view of society was elitist. By his lights, the gentle classes had a better chance of perceiving ultimate truths: "It is not intended in this assertion, that all men have *equal abilities* for judging what is true and right. . . . Those of the lower class can get but a little ways in their inquiries into the natural and moral constitution of the world."[9]

Charles Chauncy, similarly, "sometimes implied that a Harvard degree was a means of grace." Chauncy feared that social chaos would result from the Awakening precept that the laity should control their own religious lives, so he reiterated in his preaching and writing that "Good Order is the Strength and Beauty of the World. The Prosperity of both the Church and State depends very much on it." For these liberals, community meant traditional, patriarchalist hierarchicalism, where the lower classes meekly defer to their political and religious superiors, whose positions in society inherently possess access to wisdom and grace.[10]

---

6. Jonathan Mayhew, "A Discourse concerning Unlimited Submission and Non-Resistance to the Higher Powers: With some Reflections on the Resistance made to King Charles I," in *Puritan Political Ideas,* ed. Morgan, 318.

7. Ibid., 330.

8. Ibid., Mayhew's emphases.

9. Jonathan Mayhew, "*Seven Sermons Upon The Following Subjects*" (Boston, 1749), 29–32.

10. James W. Jones, *The Shattered Synthesis: New England Puritanism before the Great Awakening* (New Haven, 1973), 185; Chauncy, *Seasonable Thoughts,* in *The Great Awaken-*

Like his fellow New Light evangelicals, Jonathan Edwards believed that the individual must pursue religious conversion even if that means social ostracism. He also was concerned, as we shall see, about individual political rights. But Edwards placed far more stress than his New Light cohorts did on the communal dimension of regenerate life. In his ontology, aesthetics, and philosophical ethics the good community was always the terminus on the edge of the horizon, toward which all is progressing. Existence, he proposed, is inherently relational, so life outside of community is unthinkable. Civil and ecclesiastical community is simply an actualization of what is already ontologically real. Had Edwards reflected on it, he would have agreed that John Donne was expressing an ontological as well as a sociological truth when he wrote, "No man is an island."

Edwards's aesthetics also pointed to community. All earthly beauty, he said, is based on the concept of "union," and is thereby an "image" of the union of spiritual beings in the "spiritual world." "That uniformity [whereby] diverse things become as it were one . . . is an image [of] . . . the union of spiritual beings in a mutual propensity and affection of heart" (*TV*, 564). This union of spiritual beings in the spiritual world, to which all earthly beauty is an "analogy," consists in "the consent of mind, of the different members of a society or system of intelligent beings, sweetly united in a benevolent agreement of heart" (565).

If all earthly beauty, for Edwards, is a natural image of a community of minds, all true virtue on this earth (and beyond) creates community. This was the basis, as we have seen above, for Edwards's social ethic. The essence of virtue is love, and the nature of truly virtuous love is to reach out to being in general. In the reaching out one enlarges oneself because one then "in some sort comprehends Being in general (*TV*, 546). Love's nature, then, is to create community by seeking union with others: "In

---

ing, ed. Heimert and Miller, 298. Corrigan notes, "Mayhew and Chauncy often wrote in defense of social deference and of the static character of the social order," and admits that they were "finally, taxonomic and therefore essentially conservative." Corrigan, *The Hidden Balance*, 88, 146 n. 5. As Stout puts it, "By 'obedience,' Chauncy meant not only personal piety but submission to social and ecclesiastical order and hierarchy." Stout, *The New England Soul*, 204. See also Jones, *The Shattered Synthesis*, 166–67.

pure love to others (i.e. love not arising from self-love) there's a union of the heart with others; a kind of enlargement of the mind, whereby it so extends itself as to take others into a man's self: and therefore it implies a disposition to feel, to desire, and to act as though others were one with ourselves" (TV, 589).

Significantly, Edwards commended true virtue precisely on the grounds of its "publick" interests, that is, its disposition to create community by reaching out to others beyond itself. In contrast, he described natural moral sense and conscience as ultimately "private," tending to restrict the self to "narrow" concerns in a limited circle of beings.[11] Thus community for Edwards was a positive good; and the enlargement or diminution of community were, respectively, positive and negative criteria that he used to evaluate competing ethical systems. Furthermore, Edwards was very concerned about the proper ordering of the human community beyond the confines of the church. As we saw in the previous chapter, he had definite ideas about what civil government should do, and was not bashful about presenting his ideas to those who were in a position to feel threatened by them.

But if Edwards retained a communal vision when many New Lights were more concerned with individual rights and experience, he did not revert to the elitist communalism of Chauncy and Mayhew. Edwards himself was a hierarchicalist of sorts, but his radical theological critique of all earthly structures of authority, coupled with his extraordinary ennoblement of the humble Christian citizen, gave to the dispossessed and marginalized the confidence to challenge the traditional hierarchical system and assume positions from which Chauncy and Mayhew would have barred them. Before we explore Edwards's "subversion" of traditional hierarchicalism, however, it is first necessary to understand his sense of community as it applied to the Christian's participation as a citizen in the *civil* community. For it is necessary to discern how Edwards construed the relative importance of the Christian's commitment to civil society in general before it can be discerned properly how that construal challenged the particular society of which he was a member.

---

11. *TV*, 590, 611.

Men May Love Their Country

Edwards was able to think of many reasons why the Christian ought to devote himself fully and responsibly to the welfare of his civil community. First, it is in his own interest. If the nation flourishes, it will benefit him.[12] Second, it is the just thing to do. The "duties of subjects" and "good neighborhood" partake of the nature of justice because the good of the community and the good citizenship of the Christian naturally agree with one another. And justice is based on "some natural agreement of one thing to another" (*TV*, 569).

Third, good citizenship is the beautiful thing to do. It is a manifestation of love to being in general, which is true beauty. To this, Edwards added the interesting corollary that the larger the polity, the greater the beauty. Since beauty in things "of considerable importance" is greater than beauty "in little trivial matters," truly virtuous commitment to one's nation is more beautiful than truly virtuous commitment to one's neighborhood.[13]

Fourth, good citizenship is the loving thing to do. It is the tendency of the spirit of Christian charity to be "publick-spirited." Christian love will dispose a person not only to be "greatly concerned for the good of the public community to which he belongs, and particularly of the town where he dwells," but also "to lay himself out for [its improvement]." For love is active, love reaches out, and love is possessed with concern for the good of all beings, but more particularly for those within one's own society (*CF*, 260–61).

It is particularly concerned for those because, fifth, commitment to one's civil society is natural. Affection for our land or nation is an instinct "the Creator of the world has put within mankind, for the good of mankind." So when a person is motivated to act for the good of his own civil society, the person is following a natural, God-given instinct. Therefore, in a strict sense, there is nothing wrong with loving one's own country more than others, for God has given us a greater responsibility

---

12. Sermon on 1 Peter 2:9, in *Works*, ed. Dwight, 8:406.

13. *TV*, 567. This assumes, of course, that the citizenship described is of the nature of true virtue. When it is of natural virtue, citizenship to a larger polity has a greater tendency to self-deception.

for it than for the people of other nations: "The people of our land and nation are more in some sense, committed to our care than the people of China, and we ought to pray more for them, and to be more concerned that the kingdom of Christ should flourish among them, than in another country, where it would be as much and no more for the glory of God."[14]

Commitment to one's nation also meant, for Edwards, willingness to go to war to defend that nation. "To exert and expose themselves in a war tending to their defence and safety is a good work and a duty [citizens] owe to their country." As long as the war is just, which for Edwards meant defense of property and liberty (both civil and religious), the Christian citizen is bound to obey "those that are in authority" and go to war. But Edwards left the door open for conscientious objection. The Christian is free of military obligation if it "be notoriously manifest that the war is unjust."[15]

Edwards demonstrated his patriotism by supporting colonial military expeditions against Cape Breton in 1745 and Crown Point in 1755. The first expedition was launched in the face of what seemed to be an ominous threat to New England society. France, which had declared war against England the previous year, could have disrupted New England shipping and fishing, and (worse yet) imposed Antichristian papism on the colony, thus threatening eternal perdition for the younger generation. New England's assault on the French fortress at Louisbourg, on the other hand, would, if successful, cut off French communication with Canada and prepare the way for assaults on Quebec and

---

14. *ST,* 470–71. Edwards's point here was not that we should love our country to the detriment of others, but that we should not suppose it selfish to work harder for the civil welfare of our country than for that of other nations. The context of this statement is his attempt to help those who "have doubted whether they might pray for the conversion and salvation of the souls of their children, any more than for the souls of others" for fear that that would be a "selfish disposition." *ST,* 470. So he could exhort his parishioners in his Farewell Sermon to "by all means in your power, seek the prosperity of this town." "Farewell Sermon," in *Works,* ed. Williams and Parsons, 379.

15. Sermon on Nehemiah 4:14, June 1746, 2; sermon on 1 Kings 8:44–45, 4 April 1745, 12; ibid. Edwards's openness to conscientious objection was not uncommon in eighteenth-century New England. Both Cotton Mather and William Williams had written similarly. See Arthur H. Buffinton, "The Puritan View of War," *Publications of the Colonial Society of Massachusetts* 28 (1935): 67–86.

Montreal.[16] Edwards delivered a special sermon on the eve of the expedition, and sounded every bit the patriotic chaplain inspiring his men to
fight for God and country. The twenty Northampton men must be
courageous, he urged, and warned that cowardice would show a "want
of trust in God . . . and will be offensive to him." Then, like an army
recruiter promising teenagers they would see the world, he promised,
"you will have opp[ortunity] to see Gods wonders in the Great deep."
On a more sober note, Edwards instructed the Northampton troops that
the deprivation they suffered would teach them "how [they] must behave [them]selves in order to take the Kingdom of H[eaven] . . . [For] a
soldier when he goes forth leaves all."[17]

In 1755 war was on again.[18] The British and colonials had suffered a
disastrous loss in July when General Edward Braddock lost 976 men
killed or wounded (of 1373 enlisted men) on the banks of the Monon-
gahela River near Fort Duquesne. After the news of the battle "spread
throughout the colonies like the shock wave from an earthquake,"[19]
Governor William Shirley of Massachusetts decided to launch another
expedition north to Crown Point in an attempt to regain momentum
from the French. Edwards bade the soldiers from Northampton to trust
in God, not themselves, as they set off on their expedition.[20] Unfortunately, the army only made it as far as Lake George, the Massachusetts
regiment, under Ephraim Williams, suffered severe losses, and the battle
was indecisive.[21]

Patriotism to one's nation was thus a positive good for Edwards. He
considered even the patriotism of the unregenerate an inferior virtue, but
a virtue nonetheless, for it tends to "the preservation of mankind, and
their comfortably subsisting in the world." It has something of love in it,

---

16. This was the War of the Austrian Succession (1739–49), fought on the North
American continent as King George's War (1744–49). See Leach, *Arms for Empire*,
206–61.

17. Sermon on Leviticus 26:3–13, 28 February 1745, 97, 99, 99.

18. This was the French and Indian War (in Europe, the "Seven Years' War"). The
European phase did not begin until 1756, but fighting had started in America in 1754.
See Leach, *Arms For Empire*, 307–414.

19. Ibid., 368.

20. Sermon on 1 Samuel 17:45–46, January 1755.

21. Leach, *Arms for Empire*, 371–78.

is "beautiful within [its] own private sphere," and shares common moral goals with the regenerate.[22] This is the condition of the possibility of Christian participation in a mixed community of regenerate and unregenerate, and one reason why Edwards could be an enthusiastic chaplain for New England's wars against the French.[23] It also demonstrates that for Edwards self-love was not necessarily bad. Although it is "the source of all the wickedness that is in the world," it nevertheless "is exceeding useful and necessary" because it both "restrain[s] from acts of true wickedness" and even "puts men upon seeking true virtue." So it can inspire virtue as well as vice (TV, 616).

Yet when Edwards compared patriotism rooted in self-love to patriotism inspired by true virtue, the former lost most of its luster. And most patriotism, he believed, is based on narrowly circumscribed self-love rather than genuine benevolence. In 1746, after observing his fellow colonials' participation in King George's War, Edwards observed somewhat cynically, "A natural principle of self-love, without any other principle, may be sufficient to make a man concerned for the interest of the nation to which he belongs: as for instance, in the present war, self-love may make natural men rejoice at the successes of our nation, and sorry for their disadvantages, they being concerned as members of the body." By 1755 Edwards was using his derogatory label "private" to describe this sort of self-love, and saying it falls "infinitely short" of true virtue. It does not have the power to unite created beings one with another, he claimed. Though it is "exceeding necessary to society," it makes a man an enemy to general existence if it is not subordinated to love for universal being. And no unregenerate patriotism has such love. So even if a person is patriotic to a society of "millions of individuals" like the Roman empire, that person can still be an enemy to humanity in general.[24]

Such patriotism boils down to natural instincts such as a sense of personal inconsistency, a sense of moral deserts, or a common sense of moral good and evil that comes from the human conscience. This is the

---

22. TV, 600 (see also 601, 608), 609, 610, 612–13, 623.

23. Other reasons, of course, include the papist religion of the French, the fact that they represented one of the political and military arms of the Antichrist, and the civil liberties that Edwards feared would be lost in the event of British defeat.

24. RA, 246–47; TV, 554–55, 621, 612, 612, 602–3.

origin of the sense for justice that many possess. It is merely "a relish of [moral] uniformity and proportion that determines the mind to approve these things. And if this be all, there is no need of anything higher, or of any thing in any respect diverse, to determine the mind to approve and be pleased with equal uniformity and proportion among spiritual things which are equally discerned." So even a concern for justice in the world is no sure sign of virtuous patriotism.[25]

Neither is gratitude. "Men may love . . . their country" out of gratitude for what their country has done for them, but loves like these are private in nature and therefore not truly virtuous because of the "narrowness of their views."[26] Edwards was saying that all patriotism, short of the universal benevolence that only the regenerate possess, is simply an enlarged version of love for self. It lacks true benevolence, an altruistic regard for the well-being of others regardless of the effects on self. Patriotism is generally a mélange of subtle calculations in ultimate—if unwitting—service to the self.[27]

Edwards's skeptical view of most patriotism was nearly unique in the middle of the eighteenth century. Far more prevalent was the "benevolist gospel" of such thinkers as the third earl of Shaftesbury and Francis Hutcheson, who taught that human nature is inherently benevolent and opposed to selfish egoism.[28] As Hutcheson put it, there is a "determination of our nature to study the good of others; or some instinct, antecedent to all reason from interest, which influences us to the love of others."[29] Shaftesbury wrote that "mutual succour, and the rest of this kind" are naturally altruistic. "This we know for certain, that all social love, friendship, gratitude, or whatever else is of this generous kind, does by its nature take place of the self-interesting passions, draws us out of our-

---

25. TV, 592–94, 596–97, 572–73, 573.

26. TV, 610. Here Edwards probably had in mind the third earl of Shaftesbury, who said gratitude is proof of a moral sense. Fiering, *Jonathan Edwards's Moral Thought*, 186.

27. "True virtue stands against the parochiality of the world, the comforting alliances of like souls and common blood." Fiering, *Jonathan Edwards's Moral Thought*, 196.

28. Ibid., 8. The benevolists taught that benevolence is rooted in natural feeling. On Shaftesbury and Hutcheson and benevolence theories, see ibid., 8, 128–31, 148, 159n, 162, 164, 166, 195–96, 356.

29. Hutcheson, *Inquiry into the Original of Our Ideas of Beauty and Virtue* (London, 1725), cited in Fiering, *Jonathan Edwards's Moral Thought*, 249.

selves, *and makes us disregardful of our own convenience and safety.*"[30] The logical implication of their position was that patriotism is also based on a benevolent altruism inherent to human nature.[31]

This view of human nature was shared by many eighteenth-century New England ministers. Edwards's fellow Congregationalist John Wise, for instance, held that "in every Mans Being [is] An Affection or Love to Man-kind in General."[32] Chauncy and Mayhew, similarly, believed that self-love cooperated with natural benevolence to bring about good. Moral perfection, they preached, comes by the cultivation of one's natural potential.[33] Edwards combated the premise underlying all these positions, that human nature has an inherent inclination to disinterested benevolence. He argued that true universal benevolence is discontinuous with natural affection or potential, and objected that no natural affections are extensive enough. All fall short of love for universal being and are therefore enemies to universal being (*TV*, 550–608).

But Edwards's critique of conventional patriotism cut even deeper. First, he surmised that patriotism is peculiarly susceptible to self-deception. Because it is a commitment to a "considerable number" of persons, it is easily mistaken for true virtue, and so we "applaud [the patriot] highly." For, because of the "contracted limits" and "narrowness" of our minds, we too easily allow a large number—though but a "small part even of the world of mankind . . . to seem as if they were *all*" (*TV*, 611).

---

30. Shaftesbury, *Characteristics* (1711), ed. Robertson, cited in Fiering, *Jonathan Edwards's Moral Thought*, 192.

31. Shaftesbury acknowledged that the cause of war and social conflict was group egoism, but still insisted that most affection for one's social group was rooted in natural benevolence. Fiering, *Jonathan Edwards's Moral Thought*, 195.

32. John Wise, "A Vindication of the Government of New England Churches," in *Puritan Political Ideas*, ed. Morgan, 255. Wise had been influenced by Samuel Pufendorf's treatises on natural law and by Commonwealthmen such as Trenchard and Gordon. James W. Jones argues that Wise came near the end of a gradual development in New England Puritanism—from Giles Firmin through Samuel Willard to Cotton Mather—toward moralism and acceptance of self-love as the spring of virtue. At the turn of the century, for instance, Willard was struggling to identify self-love with God's glory. As we have seen, Edwards took a more negative view of self-love and repudiated any tendency to see natural motivation as the seat of true virtue. Jones, *The Shattered Synthesis*, 125.

33. Corrigan, *The Hidden Balance*, 84, 91.

Edwards turned to an irony of history to illustrate his point. The Romans, he pointed out, considered love to their country to be the highest of all the virtues, yet this affection—though "so much extolled"—"was employed as it were for the destruction of the rest of mankind." Edwards found it to be a rule that "the larger the number is that private affection extends to, the more apt men are, through the narrowness of their sight, to mistake it for true virtue; because then the private system appears to have more of the image of the universal" (*TV*, 611). Edwards therefore thought patriotism to be more prone to self-deception than love for family or local society. For he concluded that the wider the gaze with which one looks to the prosperity of a society, the greater the danger of pretentiousness.

Second, Edwards used both philosophical and theological arguments to remind his audiences that all patriotisms to a single polity are penultimate. Drawing from his philosophy of being, he argued that all patriotisms restricted to a single polity fall infinitely short of devotion to universal existence. And because *infinitely* short, the moral weight of a patriotism restricted to a single polity is no greater than the moral weight of a devotion to a single person among a universe of an infinite number of persons. "For notwithstanding it extends to a number of persons, which taken together are more than a single person, yet the whole falls infinitely short of the universality of existence; and if put in the scales with it, has no greater proportion to it than a single person" (*TV*, 554).

Theologically,[34] Edwards compared the earthly nation with the heavenly. Earthly commitments are provisional, Edwards estimated, because Christians hold dual citizenship, a temporary one in the nation they inhabit in this world, and a permanent one in heaven. Even on earth Christians live by the principles of their heavenly, permanent citizenship, to the degree that their citizenship in their earthly country is less enjoyable and less real.

> Heaven is the native country of the church. They are born from above; their Father, of whom they are begotten, is in heaven. The principles that govern their hearts are drawn from heaven, since

---

34. In a broad sense, of course, all Edwardsean ethics are theological. But a theological ethic, for Edwards, includes both philosophical and (explicitly) Christian claims.

the Holy Ghost, whose immediate fruits those principles are, is from heaven. . . . The saints in this world are not in their native country, but are pilgrims and strangers on the earth, they are near akin to the inhabitants of the heavenly world, and are properly of that society. . . . Heaven is a country that much better suits their natures than this earth, because it is their native climate. When they are in heaven, they breathe their native air; in heaven is their inheritance.[35]

Therefore, Edwards judged, since their ultimate commitment is to another polity, Christians must conduct all their civil affairs in subordination to the principles of their heavenly citizenship. For an earthly polity to claim their ultimate allegiance would be idolatrous. All earthly patriotisms must come under constant scrutiny, to be judged by the norms of their more permanent citizenship in the heavenly nation. "Civil affairs . . . are designed and ordered in subordination to a future world, by the maker and disposer of all things. To this therefore they ought to be subordinated by us."[36]

This theme of heaven as the Christian's true home and earthly existence as a pilgrimage was nothing new in Reformed theology. Yet in Edwards it assumed considerable force because of his preoccupation with the millennium and the final, heavenly polity. That preoccupation helped check the temptation to identify earthly kingdoms with heavenly ideals. Perhaps his bitter quarrels with the Northampton congregation, many of whom were colonial patriots, and his own firsthand observations of the ironies and cruelties or war, sharpened his ability to distinguish earthly patriotism from benevolence to universal community. We will probably never know the motivations that led him to articulate such a distinction in *The Nature of True Virtue*. But we do know that at the end of his Northampton sojourn Edwards was willing to move his family to (presumably) permanent residence in another country: "My own country is not so dear to me, but that, if there were an evident prospect of being more serviceable to Zion's interests elsewhere, I could forsake it. And I

---

35. Sermon on 1 Peter 2:9, in *Works*, ed. Dwight, 8:404.
36. "The Christian Pilgrim," in *Works*, ed. Dwight, 7:141.

think my wife is fully of this disposition." The last sermon which he ever preached in Stockbridge, less than two months before his death, was on the theme (perhaps fittingly), "We have no continuing city, therefore let us seek one to come."[37]

You That Are . . . Not Much Accounted Of

We saw in the last chapter that Jonathan Edwards's view of the magistracy was similar to Country political theory. Now we shall see that his theology undermined the predominant social theory of his day.

The prevailing social ideal of pre-Revolutionary America was the deferential society. This view of society was founded on both political theory and metaphysics. Its foundation in political theory lay in seventeenth-century theories of compact developed by James Harrington, Algernon Sidney, and John Locke. These thinkers said that government originated from the mutual consent of members of a society that had organized for the purpose of protecting property. Those with more property naturally deserved more representation in the governance of the society.[38]

The metaphysical basis for the deferential society was commonly conceptualized as the "Great Chain of Being." Eighteenth-century thinkers assumed that reality consists of an ascending ladder of beings, from the tiniest amoeba, to plants, animals, humans, angels, and, finally, God. It was thought that the laddered structure of existence, with all of its steps, was perfect and therefore the best of all possible worlds. Applied to human society, this metaphysics legitimated the status quo. Goodness and beauty were identified not with material and social plenty for all human beings, but with fullness and diversity in the social order. Every level of social existence, including the most abject poverty, was necessary in order for the fullest beauty and goodness to be manifested. Hence

---

37. Letter to John Erskine, 5 July 1750, in Dwight, *The Life of President Edwards*, 412; ibid., 581.

38. Pocock, "Machiavelli," 551–71; John B. Kirby, "Early American Politics—The Search for Ideology: An Historiographical Analysis and Critique of the Concept of Deference," *Journal of Politics* 32 (1970): 821.

inequality and even evil were necessary components of a system that was, seen from the broadest perspective, perfect.[39]

Thus a hierarchical society was simply the manifestation of the Great Chain of Being in human history. Educated, propertied elites controlled church and civil government because they had been divinely fitted to govern their "inferiours." Their position in society, made secure by the possession of wealth, implied the possession of wisdom.

> Americans of 1760 continued to assume, as had their predecessors for generations before, that a healthy society was a hierarchical society, in which it was natural for some to be rich and some poor, some honored and some obscure, some powerful and some weak. And it was believed that superiority was unitary, that the attributes of the favored—wealth, wisdom, power—had a natural affinity to each other, and hence that political leadership would naturally rest in the hands of the social leaders. Movement, of course, there would be: some would fall and some would rise; but manifest, external differences among men, reflecting the principle of hierarchical order, were necessary and proper, and would remain; they were intrinsic to the nature of things.[40]

The lower classes of colonial America apparently agreed with this assessment of the social order, for they repeatedly elected their "betters" to public office. Many of their pastors had read Puritan theologian William Perkins, who instructed social inferiors to show their respect by standing when their superiors rode by, bowing the knee to them, offering them the best seat, allowing them to speak first, addressing them by their titles, and obeying them "because every higher power is the ordinance of God." Until 1760 this confidence in the metaphysical justice of the social order provided the "unifying spirit that bound the society to-

---

39. Toward the end of the century some thinkers began to see the Great Chain as a ladder of continual progress, but this interpretation was a minority report and too late to affect the principals in our story. Arthur O. Lovejoy, *The Great Chain of Being: A Study of the History of an Idea* (Cambridge, Mass., 1964), 242–87.

40. Bailyn, *Ideological Origins*, 302.

gether."[41] But soon thereafter the social fabric began to unravel when significant portions of society began to question social hierarchicalism.

What influenced them to change generations—centuries—of thinking? There were many factors, of course. Massive shifts in world view rarely occur without the confluence of diverse social, religious, and political influences. But Edwards illustrates the important role that New Light preaching played. Decades before the shift started to register in 1760, Edwards was promulgating a theology of Christian citizenship that undermined traditional hierarchicalism.

To be sure, Edwards was a hierarchicalist of sorts. He believed that God's original design was for there to be "heads, princes or governors, to whom honour, subjection and obedience should be paid."[42] Yet he never elaborated on the gradations among humans as liberal parsons often did, and waxed eloquent instead on the beauty of equality. His heavenly hierarchy was based on holiness and fairly inverted New England's social hierarchy. To his liberal contemporaries, the fact that the poor were on the bottom of the social hierarchy was evidence that God had placed them there, either as a punishment for their sins or simply for his own inscrutable purposes. Edwards's belief in a hierarchical structure for society, on the other hand, did not prevent him from pleading on behalf of those marginalized by the structure and exposing the moral corruption of society's elite.[43]

Yet Edwards did more than just bypass traditional hierarchical theory to defend those marginalized by it. He struck at the hierarchicalist structure itself by shifting the locus of religious authority from the external social structure to the internal place of the regenerate heart. To be sure, New England Congregationalists before the Great Awakening knew that a minister's office alone did not guarantee access to religious truth. But the clergyman's place atop the socio-religious hierarchy lent to his words a powerful presumption that God was speaking through him. Edwards's

---

41. Kirby, "Early American Politics," 827; William Perkins, A Golden Chaine; or, The Description of Theologie (London, 1635), 50.

42. Miscellanies, no. 336.

43. Works, ed. Hickman, 1:ccxxviii–ccxxix; "Heaven is a World of Love," 374–80. For an example of liberal celebration of the Great Chain of Being, see Charles Chauncy, The Benevolence of the Deity (Boston, 1784), 110–11, 188–201.

emphasis upon the sense of the heart, however, helped undermine that
presumption by creating theological space for what amounted to a fairly
consistent theological preference for those marginalized by traditional
social and religious norms. Edwards never said God preferred the marginalized, but he implied that God more often called saints from their
ranks than from the castes of the privileged.[44]

Edwards shifted the center of religious authority by his definition of the
nature of true religion. That is, his explication of the difference between
genuine and spurious religion identified what for him was the source of
religious truth. From his first sermons and treatises to the very last work
he prepared for publication before his death, Edwards kept refining and
developing his conviction that the essence of true religion is a "sense of
the heart." This sense, experienced in regeneration and nurtured by
obedience and Christian fellowship, is the source of authentic religious
truth and experience, which for Edwards constituted religious authority.
Religious experience as defined by the Northampton theologian, not a
clerical collar, gives one access to ultimate truths, which is true religious
authority. This meant that spiritual attainment was not dependent on
learning or social position but open to anyone. Mayhew's contempt for
the spiritual perception of the untutored masses gave epistemological
privilege to those favored by a liberal education. But Edwards explicitly
appealed to those who were "weak in understanding and comparatively
ignorant" and assured them that Christ was just as interested in their
salvation as those who were better instructed.

> Christ does as much invite you as any of the politicians, philoso-
> phers, or divines of the world. Christ is able savingly to en-
> lighten you; he does not stand in need of great abilities or
> acquired knowledge in order to his imparting that knowledge
> that is saving; he has chosen the foolish things of the world to
> confound the mighty, and things which are despised, hath God
> chosen, yea, and things which are not, to bring to nought things
> which are.[45]

---

44. Sermon on Romans 9:18, in *Works*, ed. Hickman, 2:852.
45. Sermon on Matthew 22:9–10, in Miller, "Jonathan Edwards's Sociology," 70.

In fact, the spiritual knowledge that they could gain by a sense of the heart, he told them, is infinitely more valuable than all the knowledge of which the privileged are so proud: "The last beam of the light of the knowledge of the glory of God in the face of Jesus Christ is worth more than all the human knowledge that is taught in all the most famous colleges and universities in the world."[46] By this claim Edwards signaled to all regenerate social inferiors that true authority depended not on education or political office, but the spiritual awareness which they themselves had attained.[47]

Edwards informed the social "inferiours" in his auditory that he was well aware of how they were snubbed in the social and political arenas. "You that are . . . not much accounted of, you see that your judgment of things is not much regarded, what you say in conversation is not so much taken notice of, your voice is not so much heard as others in publick affairs."[48] Do not be dismayed, Edwards assured them, for Christ was of lowly social rank like them: "Christ himself, when he was upon earth, confined himself to your condition. He did not appear in the world in the circumstances of a man of note, but *in the state of the poor and despised.* He was of low parentage; his mother was a woman of low degree, her husband Joseph was not one of their men of influence, but an obscure person."[49]

Here, perhaps, was where Edwards's social theory most powerfully challenged eighteenth-century hierarchicalism. Edwards likened the so-

---

46. Ibid. For more on Edwards's sense of the heart, see *RA,* 5, 9, 32–33, 41, 43, 50, 56, 272–73, and 286, and Cherry, *The Theology of Jonathan Edwards,* 14, 19–30, 51, 127, 167, 192–94.

47. Alan Heimert's much-maligned *Religion and the American Mind: From the Great Awakening to the Revolution* is correct in its assertion that Edwardsean social theory was democratic in its implications, in contrast to the elitist social theory of liberals (17–20, 302–3). Unfortunately, Heimert goes on to claim that Jacksonian democratic republicanism was a direct legacy of Edwards (510–52). A chief problem with that claim is that the New Divinity, the school of Edwards's disciples, was largely Federalist. Heimert also mistakenly asserts that Edwards rejected New England's national covenant (126–27) and predicted an imminent millennium that could be brought on by human will (60–61, 80–81). But Heimert accurately portrays Edwards's interest in community (34, 95, 103, 351–412), and the implications of his thought for social reform (58, 99, 102, passim).

48. Ibid.

49. Ibid., 69–70; emphasis added.

cial status of the poor, humble Christian to the mean status of the earthly
Christ. Christ was not regarded by the social leaders of his world, just as
many of Edwards's auditors had no standing in Northampton society. But
Christ surely *deserved* respect and power. All that prevented his getting
those things was the spiritual blindness of the influential men of his day.
In the same way, the lowly (in social status) members of Edwards's congregation who were nevertheless regenerate could justly conclude, from the
logic of Edwards's appeals, that the hierarchical social structure of their
day was a sham. By it, those deserving of power were excluded from
positions of influence. And those holding power were not worthy of it.

> There are many great men of the world, kings and princes, men of
> great power and policy, men of noble blood and honourable de-
> scent, men of great wealth, men of vast learning and knowledge
> in the world, that are honoured, and make a great figure, and
> great account is made of them in the world, *who are wicked men
> and reprobates,* and they all are not of so great value in God's sight
> as one true Christian, however humble his birth and low his
> standing; however poor, or ignorant, or unknown.[50]

Of course, Edwards's displacement of traditional social theory was not
new to the Christian tradition. His attempt to shift attention from one
hierarchicalism (the traditional social one) to what was really another
hierarchicalist structure (the Christian distinction between regenerate
and unregenerate) was the latest in many similar attempts throughout the
history of Christian thought. But a shift in emphasis can be very important nonetheless. As Edmund Morgan has observed, "Change in Christian thought, even so radical a change as the Reformation, has usually
been a matter of emphasis, of giving certain ideas a greater weight than
was previously accorded them or of carrying one idea to its logical conclusion at the expense of another. In this way one age slides into the next,

---

50. Sermon on 1 Peter 2:9, in *Works,* ed. Dwight, 8:410. For other examples of this
theme, see sermon on Matthew 22:9–10, 1740, in Miller, "Jonathan Edwards's Sociology
of The Great Awakening," 69–72, sermon on John 14:2, in H. Norman Gardiner, ed.,
Selected Sermons of Jonathan Edwards (New York, 1904), 64–77, *ST,* 513–14, and sermon
on Jeremiah 8:11, October 1733, 29.

and an intellectual revolution may be achieved by the expression of ideas that everyone had always professed to accept."[51]

Edwards was by no means the only religious leader whose theology undermined traditional hierarchicalism, and religion was not the only factor producing this change in thinking. Yet Edwards is an illustration of how this intellectual shift was prefigured and perhaps even set into motion by changes of emphasis in religious discourse. Whereas his liberal contemporaries continued to celebrate the Great Chain of Being, Edwards filled the ears of the regenerate marginalized with notions of their spiritual superiority to the unregenerate elite. Under his preaching, and through the influence of his published works, segments of colonial society that had long been deprived of social and political influence were given theological legitimacy to begin or continue struggles to be heard. Thus, no doubt without being aware of it, Edwards may have helped prepare the way in colonial society for the egalitarian republicanism that came to mean "nothing less than a reordering of eighteenth-century society and politics."[52]

Edwards never would have countenanced a social reordering based on secular egalitarian principles. For he was as skeptical of plebeian wisdom as any: "Common people, whose judgments, in all nations and ages, are exceedingly led and swayed. They are not very capable of viewing things in the extent of their consequences, and of estimating things in their true weight and importance."[53] But he was stubbornly confident that the sense of the heart would give supernatural insight and wisdom to any "common" person.

To understand better the possible connection between Edwards's theology of Christian citizenship and egalitarian republicanism, it is necessary to see the ways in which Edwards provided several groups marginalized by American social and religious norms with a perspective that, if applied, could lend them dignity and self-respect. Let us first look at the consideration Edwards gave to the poor, a class whose welfare, as we have already seen, he vigorously championed.

---

51. *Puritan Political Ideas*, ed. Morgan, xiii.
52. Gordon S. Wood, *The Creation of the American Republic, 1776–1787* (Chapel Hill, N.C., 1969), 48.
53. Dwight, *The Life of President Edwards*, 206.

While Charles Chauncy was intimating to Boston's elite that the poor
were undeserving and greedy, Edwards was exhorting the middle and
upper classes at Northampton to empty their pockets and give. But more
important, he told them that, if unregenerate, they were " contemptible
in God's eyes" despite the esteem society lavished upon them. At the
same time he assured the poor members of his church that when Christ
came into the world, he chose to appear "in the state of the poor and
despised," not as a wealthy nobleman, and that a poor man with a godly
sense of the heart was infinitely more valuable than all the rich men of
the world put together. In fact, Edwards told the group of "inferiours" at
Northampton, most members of the true church of God are poor, and
Christ himself has designated their persons as his receivers in the world.[54]

Edwards's message probably struck a responsive chord at Northampton.
Since just before the beginning of the eighteenth century there had been
"increasing psychological distance" between rich and poor in Hampshire
County. In 1692, for instance, some wealthy citizens had dissented when
it was proposed (and passed) that the education of all Northampton
children, rich and poor, be paid for out of a common fund. The community's provision for the poor betrayed a similar polarization. In the seventeenth century, town funds or private charity had boarded the poor in
wealthier homes. But this practice came to a halt when, in 1705, the
Northampton town meeting decided to build a poorhouse. For unex-
plained reasons, the poorhouse was never built; yet there was no return to
seventeenth-century practice. A similar pattern could be observed in
Northampton's road maintenance. Before the turn of the century all
able-bodied men had been required to donate time each year to help keep
the roads in good repair; but in Edwards's time a constable and permanent
detachment of road workers were paid out of town funds. In 1715, preex-
isting land divisions were confirmed but this time without any mention of
public rights to wood on common fields; the access of less advantaged

---

54. Chauncy, *Seasonable Thoughts*, 63. "[Some New Lights have pleaded for] a Liberty
hereupon taken to have Communion, not only with other Men's *Goods*, but *Wives* also."
Seasonable Thoughts, 372–74, and "Enthusiasm Described and Cautioned Against" (Boston, 1742), 15; "Christian Charity," in vol. 6 of *Works*, ed. Dwight; sermon on Matthew
22:9–10, in Miller, "Jonathan Edwards's Sociology," 72, 70; sermon on 1 Peter 2:9, in
Works, ed. Dwight, 8:410; *ST*, 514, 526.

townspeople to a public source of firewood became a continual cause for
dispute. As time passed, therefore, economic classes were solidifying and
growing increasingly distinct.[55]

Jonathan Mayhew responded to similar economic stratification by
telling the impoverished that their hunger was probably their own fault:
"Most of the pains, both mental and corporal, which mankind suffer in
this world are of their own creating. They are the natural effects on
intemperance and other vices. . . . [They are] brought upon us by the
providence of God for our own sins, to chastize and thereby to reform
us, in order to our present and future good."[56] Social betters in his
congregation were thereby conveniently relieved of responsibility to
help the poor, and comforted with the thought of how much they had
achieved.

Edwards, however, did not let the prosperous of his congregation gloat
over their social success. He reminded them that their social position was
a gift of undeserved grace: "Let us remember, that it is owing only to the
distinguishing goodness of God to us, that we are not in their [the poor's]
circumstances." Neither did he let them escape their responsibility to
give to the poor. If they suspected that people were poor because of their
own irresponsibility, the prosperous should nevertheless express their
gratitude for their own gifts by helping the poor who repent of their
laziness. Even if indigent fathers do not repent, their innocent families
should be helped. Lest some dodge responsibility by pointing to civil
welfare programs, Edwards, while affirming the absolute necessity for
public welfare, pointed out that the Christian's goal should be the total
eradication of poverty. Public welfare alone would never meet that goal,
so supplementary Christian giving is imperative.[57]

In the 1740s Edwards implemented this conviction by making it "the
principal business of Deacons" to take care of the poor, and called on his
wealthier parishioners for "frequent and liberal Contributions, to maintain a public Stock, that might be ready for the poor and necessitious

---

55. Tracy, *Jonathan Edwards, Pastor*, 42–43, 148.

56. Jonathan Mayhew, "Two Sermons on the Nature, Extent and Perfection of the
Divine Goodness" (Boston, 1763), 61–62.

57. "Dishonesty," in *Works*, ed. Hickman, 2:222; "Christian Charity," in *Works*, ed.
Dwight, 6:565, 566–67.

members of the Church." In contrast, Chauncy did not set up such a deacon's fund until the 1770s.[58]

Edwards used his social position to defend the poor against those who would exploit them. In an address on the qualities of the good ruler, Edwards excoriated those rulers who use their office to oppress the poor. In a sermon on dishonesty, he attacked businessmen who take advantage of market conditions to gain exorbitant profits at the expense of the poor, and then threatened that "God will defend their cause." He also warned those who purposely used depreciated currency in public collections for the poor that they were lying to God as Ananias and Sapphira did; all who heard knew that Ananias and Sapphira were struck dead by divine wrath for their dishonesty. When a new meetinghouse was built between 1736 and 1738, church elders departed from previous custom by basing the new seating plan primarily on wealth, and only secondarily on age. On 25 December 1737, "the Sabbath after seating the new meetinghouse," Edwards, while describing the delights of heaven, temporarily took his sights off heaven and commented acidly on the seating below him. "You that are pleased with your seats in this house because you are seated high in a place that is looked upon hungrily by those that sit round about . . . consider it is but a very little while before it will [be] all one to you whether you have sat high or low here." Three years later he was still criticizing the church's seating plan, but this time he was even more caustic. Those with the best seats may have no seat at all in heaven: "Those that possess a greater measure of this world's goods, and are in higher circumstances in the world. . . . though you now sit forward in the meetinghouse, and have a higher seat than your poor, inferiour neighbours, yet *hereafter you shall have no place at all in heaven.*"[59]

Edwards also defended the rights and dignity of women. In a time when women's testimony in religious meetings was excoriated, Edwards used the Hebrew prophetess Deborah's leadership of a religio-political revolution as an illustration of revivals (like Northampton's) that ought

---

58. Samuel Hopkins, *The Life of the Late Reverend, Learned and Pious Mr. Jonathan Edwards* (Boston, 1765), cited in Heimert, *Religion and the American Mind*, 250.

59. "Strong Rod," in *Works*, ed. Williams and Parsons, 6:220; "Dishonesty," in *Works*, ed, Hickman, 2:222, 224–25; sermon on John 14:2, cited in Tracy, *Jonathan Edwards, Pastor*, 129; sermon on Matthew 22:9–10, in Miller, "Jonathan Edwards's Sociology," 73.

to be supported.[60] When pleading for his Native American child scholars at Stockbridge, Edwards urged that Indian girls be given the same educational privileges as boys. This was somewhat novel for the time. Girls had been educated in Northampton, for instance, but separately from boys and not systematically. Generally, the attitude of Puritan New England toward women's education was "decidedly unfavorable." Even as late as the Revolutionary period, Abigail Adams lamented that it was fashionable to ridicule "female learning."[61]

When illustrating true religion by means of personal examples in his two major accounts of the revival (*Faithful Narrative* and *Some Thoughts Concerning the Revival*), Edwards restricted himself to women.[62] This is particularly significant. Chauncy opposed women's testimonies in church meetings and pronounced women—like children—more inclined to religious delusion because of the "Weakness of their Nerves." But Edwards's use of women's experiences in an apology for the Awakening suggested that in the final estimation of things, the standard of which is the sense of the heart, women are at least equal to men.

In fact, there are hints that Edwards considered women to be more spiritually sensitive than men. The use of women as illustrations of piety could give readers of the revival treatises the impression that women have an easier time making it into the kingdom of heaven than men.[63] In addition, Edwards wrote in his private notebooks that men are stronger in mind, but women are more "affectionate." Considering Edwards's convic-

---

60. *ST,* 363. Edwards was hardly a twentieth-century feminist, but his use of this story is not insignificant. Chauncy denounced the use of women's testimonies during the Great Awakening. See Chauncy, "Enthusiasm Described."

61. Jonathan Edwards, letter to Sir William Pepperell, 28 November 1751, in Dwight, *The Life of President Edwards,* 478; Thomas Woody, *A History of Women's Education in the United States* (New York, 1929), 128, 129; Trumbull, *History of Northampton,* 2:182.

62. Edwards reserved a separate postrevival work for David Brainerd's model of piety. *Life of David Brainerd,* ed. Pettit.

63. It was rather unusual to use women as models of normative religious experience. Thomas Prince's *Christian History* (1743–44), "which publicized virtually every revival in the Awakening, scarcely mentions women." Martha Tomhave Blauvelt and Rosemary Skinner Keller, "Women and Revivalism: The Puritan and Wesleyan Traditions," in *Women and Religion in America,* vol. 2, *The Colonial and Revolutionary Periods,* ed. Rosemary Radford Ruether and Rosemary Skinner Keller (San Francisco, 1983), 321.

tion that the affections are the seat of true religion, this could be an indication that Edwards thought of women as more religious by nature.[64]

Edwards intimated the same in a sermon delivered during the 1740 Awakening. He condemned the male sex as being "more ready to stand out against what is affecting and awakening," more given to pride, more exposed to temptation, and more likely to fall into the sin Edwards so particularly despised, "publick contention." Men are therefore more guilty; for God has given them more—greater strength and a larger "sphere of action"—but they have produced less. After addressing the men with nothing but criticism, Edwards turned to the women and praised them. Despite woman's role in the fall, he said, "this sex has peculiar honour in the affair of the redemption of the second [Adam] . . . and all you, if you are converted, will become mothers of Christ in a more honourable and blessed sense than the virgin Mary was, for it is more blessed to have Christ conceived in the heart than in the womb." Edwards conceded that woman is more easily deceived, but then proceeded to regale her with a description of the gifts her "lover" Christ holds out to her. He concluded by reassuring busy homemakers without time for religious pursuits that they could still find conversion.[65] Edwards's appreciation for female religious sensibility could help explain why women "especially" supported him at the time of his ejection from the Northampton pulpit.[66]

Edwards accorded attention and esteem to the young as well. He used young people as religious models from which adults could learn. Four-year-old Phebe Bartlet was one of his three living illustrations of true piety in Faithful Narrative; Edwards related how she exhorted even her parents to greater religious zeal, perhaps to their chagrin. In the same

---

64. Miscellanies, no. 37, excerpted in Blauvelt and Keller, "Women and Revivalism," 365–66. If this interpretation is correct (that Edwards considered women more disposed to religion), then Edwards anticipated the nineteenth century. It must also be noted, however, that this kind of character definition of the two sexes "became the primary justification for the separation of men's and women's functions into public and private spheres during the nineteenth century." Blauvelt and Keller, 319, 327.

65. Edwards, sermon on Matthew 22:9–10; in Miller, "Jonathan Edwards's Sociology," 66–69.

66. Dwight, The Life of President Edwards, 467; the quotation is reproduced below.

treatise he commended the young people's prayer meeting as an example to be "imitated by elder people." In addition, Edwards's relationship with teenagers was a departure from customary pastoral practice. Instead of returning them to their parents for instruction, as most New England pastors had done, Edwards divided children and parents by gathering teens into groups for study and prayer under his supervision. He further defied convention by strenuously advocating their participation in congregational singing.[67]

Older teens and even young unmarried men in their twenties must have appreciated Edwards's defiance of traditional bias against youth. In mid-eighteenth-century western Massachusetts, men without land and wife were considered less than full and independent members of society. Many otherwise able men were frustrated by the near-impossibility of getting either. Generally it was impossible for a man to get married until he had land, and land was obtainable only by inheritance or purchase— at very high prices. Most would be too old to marry before they could save enough to buy land. For the few who inherited land, even what they received was devalued by the land's decreasing productivity. It is no surprise, then, that a high percentage of Edwards's converts were young men. Conversion provided a measure of social status otherwise denied them for lack of property, and Edwards's unconventional invitation to fuller participation may have made conversion all the more attractive.[68]

Edwards's theology provided theoretical religious equality for minorities as well. To be sure, Edwards practiced a form of racism common to his age. The Edwards family employed several black "servants," at least one of whom they purchased for money in 1747. But it is not accurate to say that Edwards "opened the ranks of the American army [i.e., the Ameri-

---

67. *FN*, 199–205, 148. The Hampshire Association of Ministers voted in 1731 that although "personal [pastoral] visitation may in some cases be very expedient or beneficial," it was better to have families catechize their own young; quoted in Tracy, *Jonathan Edwards, Pastor*, 112. For attitudes of early American evangelicals toward children, see Philip Greven, *The Protestant Temperament: Patterns of Child-Rearing, Religious Experience, and the Self in Early America* (New York, 1980), 21–148.

68. Tracy, *Jonathan Edwards, Pastor*, 96–99; Cedric B. Cowing, "Sex and Preaching in the Great Awakening," *American Quarterly* 20 (1968): 635–40. This study demonstrates that, when compared with other New England towns affected by the Great Awakening, Northampton's proportion of male converts was higher than average.

can Christian church] to every white Protestant believer," as if to imply that Edwards would have closed it to blacks. Edwards in fact denied any metaphysical distinction between black and white when he preached, "You that are servants and poor negroes. . . . Though you are a servant, yet if you will come to Christ, and heartily give up your life to his service, you shall be the Lord's freeman," and when he exhorted *all* to "hearken to the call of Christ . . . young men and maids, old men, middle aged and little children, both male and female, *both black and white,* high and low, rich and poor together."[69]

Although Edwards never wrote, as far as I know, about the relative spiritual worth of native Americans, his heroic efforts on their behalf testify to a conviction that "whites and Indians were part of the human community, and neither were inherently inferior to the other."[70] Throughout his seven years at Stockbridge (1751–58) he defended Native Americans against greedy whites who were manipulating the Indian Mission for their own aggrandizement. Despite recurrent physical distress and public vilification of his efforts, Edwards wrote numerous letters to Boston and London pleading their (his Housatonnuk parishioners') rights to education and true religion. In 1751, for example, Edwards wrote to the Speaker of the Massachusetts Assembly to influence that body to honor its treaty obligations to the Housatonnuks. When a friend of one of the whites seeking to exploit the mission struck an Indian child on the head with a cane, it was Edwards who managed to convince the offender to pay damages. Edwards spent hours patiently listening to the broken English and sign language of Indian children and asking questions in broken native language, so that he could accurately report to Boston Commissioners[71] that his Indian scholars did not have enough blankets or food, that some

---

69. Murray, *Jonathan Edwards: A New Biography,* 180. In 1747 they purchased the slave girl, "Venus," for eighty pounds. Winslow, *Jonathan Edwards 1703–1758,* 216. "Mercy" was a favorite of the children, and may have "belonged" to the family from birth. Murray, 180. Bercovitch, *The American Jeremiad,* 106; sermon on Matthew 22:9–10, 1740, in Miller, "Jonathan Edwards's Sociology," 72, 77.

70. Patricia Wilson-Kastner, *Coherence in a Fragmented World: Jonathan Edwards' Theology of the Holy Spirit* (Washington, D.C., 1978), 53–54.

71. These men were Commissioners of the "Society in London, for Propagating the Gospel in New England, and the Parts Adjacent." Dwight, *The Life of President Edwards,* 449.

boys had no breeches and many were going ragged to meetings, and that all the boys were being forced to work six days per week.[72] In a 1738 sermon Edwards berated New England for having "debauched em [the Indians] with strong drink" instead of seeking their spiritual welfare.[73] It is of little surprise that some of the most distinguished religious and charitable work done among Native Americans in the eighteenth century was conducted by Edwardseans (David Brainerd, John Sergeant, Eleazer Wheelock, Samuel Hopkins, Gideon Hawley, and Samuel Suell).[74]

Not only did Edwards enhance the religious worth, and thereby boost the religious and social confidence, of minorities, women, young people, and the poor, but he defended the rights of lay persons in general. Unlike many of his clerical contemporaries, the Northampton theologian endorsed lay testimony about revival experience. Charles Chauncy decried popular exhortation as a threat to the public order. Although, as John Butler rightly points out, Edwards guarded the minister's prerogative, Edwards allowed laypersons to speak as long as they did not assume the "authoritative manner" of ministers. He defended the testimonies of women and young people on the grounds that their "extraordinary" experiences sometimes require them to disregard the customary rule of silence.[75] And whereas liberals understood liberty as the freedom of clergy

---

72. This is another piece of evidence that belies the stereotype of an Edwards "so wrapped in a vision of the otherworld" that he could not comprehend this-worldly needs. Miller, "Jonathan Edwards's Sociology," 52.

73. Dwight, *The Life of President Edwards*, 449–541; sermon on Jeremiah 2:5, April 1738, 35.

74. Cedric B. Cowing, *The Great Awakening and the American Revolution: Colonial Thought in the Eighteenth Century* (Chicago, 1971), 83. See R. Pierce Beaver, "American Missionary Motivation before the Revolution," *Church History* 31 (1962): 216–26, and "Methods in American Missions to the Indians in the 17th and 18th Centuries," *Journal of Presbyterian History* 47 (1969): 124–48.

75. Jon Butler, "Enthusiasm Described and Decried: The Great Awakening as Interpretative Fiction," *Journal of American History* 69, no. 2 (September 1982): 314; Chauncy, *Seasonable Thoughts*, 226; *ST*, 484, 486. Patricia Tracy accuses Edwards of enhancing "ministerial power" by inferring from some ambiguous statements, not any direct assertion by Edwards, that he allowed only a minister to interpret the signs of grace. Edwards certainly had a high view of the ministry, but he openly published his signs of grace in his treatises, for all (including laymen) to read, thus removing the process of discernment from the occult science of clergy and putting it within the capability of any who can read

from the laity and Calvinist associations, Edwards adamantly defended
the freedom of the laity to choose their own ministers.[76] It is not unlikely
that Edwards's descriptions of the revivals, with laypersons serving as
models of true religion, helped open the door for the popular enthusiasm
and "assertive lay piety" of the post-Awakening years.[77]

In this chapter I have argued that Edwards's theology of citizenship
undermined—at least in theory—traditional hierarchicalism by enno-
bling the religious and (therefore) social worth of those traditionally on
the underside of society. I shall now propose that Edwards's ejection from
his Northampton pulpit may have been prompted in part by the subver-
sive nature of his teaching. Therefore the ejection may be further evidence that Edwards's understanding of citizenship was nontraditional and
threatened social and political elites.

Edwards's 1750 dismissal from the Northampton pulpit followed a
protracted controversy over his departure from Solomon Stoddard's policy of open admission to communion. Stoddard required only that the
applicant for communion believe the Scriptures and Congregational
doctrine, and desire grace, whereas Edwards, after following Stoddard's
practice for nineteen years, in 1748 began to insist on a profession to
undertake the covenant. The heart of the issue was regeneration. Stoddard admitted those who conceded they were unregenerate, but Edwards
required that applicants have visible evidence, by profession and conduct, that they were regenerate.[78] Historians have rightly sensed that

---

and have a sense of the heart. Tracy even admits that "in the Inquiry [Concerning Qualifications for Communion] and in his letters to his opponents, Edwards explicitly denied any
special skill in judging hearts." His statement before the ministerial council in December
1749, that he wanted a veto over church membership contradicted, as Tracy concedes,
what he had always previously said and written. Tracy, Jonathan Edwards, Pastor, 144–45,
177.

76. Edwards, Miscellanies, no. 10, in Townsend, ed., Philosophy, 197–98.

77. Faithful Narrative, which contains "in rich detail the spiritual travails he observed
in more than three hundred parishioners" and two individual case histories, was the most
popular of all Edwards's works. Hence his account of lay religious experience had wide
circulation. See GA, 30.

78. For an early account of the affair, with selections written by Edwards himself, see
Dwight's Life of President Edwards, vol. 1 of Works, ed. Dwight. For Edwards's mature
views on communion, see Edwards, An Humble Inquiry into the Rules of the Word of God,
Concerning the Qualifications Requisite to a Compleat Standing and Full Communion in the

the communion controversy was the formal rather than the material cause of dismissal.

But while many fascinating insights have emerged from their efforts, too many interpreters have tried to attribute Edwards's expulsion from Northampton to a single factor or cause. Ola Winslow reduced it all to Edwards's opposition to the rising tide of democracy in his parish and in the colonies as a whole. But this does not account for Edwards's defense of the rights and dignity of the godly Christian citizen against both religious and civil authority. Sereno Dwight attributed the ejection primarily to opposition from the "evil Williams clan." Yet this does not account for Edwards's being invited to preach the sermon at William Williams's funeral. Neither does it seem to have been a quarrel about Arminianism, as Miller suggested, since Northampton was generally Calvinist.[79]

Patricia J. Tracy insightfully suggests that fear of pastoral authoritarianism was a significant factor. New England, and Northampton in particular, had changed its idea of what role a pastor should play. The days of Solomon Stoddard, who was called "pope" because of his domineering, paternalistic pastoral style, were over. People now turned to lawyers such as Joseph Hawley for advice they formerly sought from pastors. Unfortunately, Edwards's leadership style resembled his grandfather's (Stoddard's).[80]

Ironically, it was the use of the very principles which Edwards himself promoted that led some to consider him a dictator. Edwards had taught that every person with a sense of the heart has spiritual authority to judge basic spiritual questions, and does not need to rely on the authority of a minister, particularly if that minister is of a different spirit. Solomon Williams's written reply to Edwards's work on communion qualifications accused Edwards of making judgments for individuals that only those

Visible Christian Church (Boston, 1749), and Misrepresentations Corrected, and Truth Vindicated, in a Reply to the Rev. Mr. Solomon Williams's Book (Boston, 1752). Both of these works can be found in most nineteenth-century editions of Edwards's collected works.

79. Winslow, Jonathan Edwards 1703–1758, 241–67; Dwight, The Life of President Edwards, 288–449; Miller, Jonathan Edwards, 125–26, 205–29, 230–32, 249–50; Jonathan Edwards, "Resort and Remedy of those that are Bereaved by the Death of an Eminent Minister" (Boston, 1741); Tracy, Jonathan Edwards, Pastor, 185.

80. Tracy, Jonathan Edwards, Pastor, 188–89.

individuals could make. Does not the law of Christ specifically forbid people "to judge one another?" asked Williams.[81]

In her reduction of the entire affair to opposition to Edwards's pastoral style (her book, after all, is entitled *Jonathan Edwards, Pastor*), Patricia Tracy discounts the opposition of the social elite. Yet, although one of Edwards's supporters (Timothy Dwight) was wealthy, other supporters were, by Tracy's own admission, "much poorer." The anti-Edwards faction, on the other hand, included three of the four richest men in town.[82] Edwards himself noted that his opposition was led by "the leading men" who were "assisted and edged [sic] on" by "persons of note" and "some great men in civil authority." Northampton's social inferiors, Edwards claimed, "came slowly into" the imbroglio, only after the social elite had "taken vast pains to stir [them up]."[83]

Tracy claims that the town was united in its opposition to Edwards. Yet the vote was not unanimous: two hundred thirty for dismissal, twenty-three against, with the rest abstaining.[84] Although there seems no way to determine the number of abstainers (Edwards said only that "others staid away, choosing not to act either way"[85]) there is evidence that majority sentiment against the pastor may not have hardened. According to a group of his supporters who withdrew from communion services in protest of the majority decision, most of those who voted against Edwards were coerced. These supporters cited a statement reportedly made by Colonel Timothy Dwight that "the greatest part of the Church & parish could be content, & really chose to have Mr. Edwards for their pastor, his late principles notwithstanding, & that the church & Parish were nosed & forced from their true inclination, by a few particular rash & hot headed men."[86] If this report is accurate, one

---

81. Solomon Williams, "The True State of the Question Concerning the Qualifications Necessary to Lawful Communion" (Boston, 1751), 142.

82. Tracy, *Jonathan Edwards, Pastor*, 186–87, 263n. Tracy uses Trumbull's *History of Northampton* and a 1749 tax list to reach these conclusions.

83. Dwight, *The Life of President Edwards*, 466–67.

84. Ibid., 410.

85. Ibid.

86. "We the subscribers members of the First Church in Northampton offer what follows for our vindication in absenting from the Communion at the Lords Table," 1750/n.d., Franklin Trask Library, Andover Newton Theological School, Newton Center, Mass.

could hardly conclude that the town was united in its opposition to Edwards.

But more interesting, and generally unnoticed, are those who were not allowed to vote. Edwards reported in 1735 that the Northampton church contained "about six hundred and twenty communicants" (FN, 157). The number was most likely no smaller in 1750 at his expulsion, when it appears that fewer than half of these were voting males.[87] Hence communicating women, servants, and young people who did not vote must have made up a considerable number—perhaps two to three hundred. By Edwards's own admission (and this admission did not increase his credibility in the eyes of eighteenth-century men[88]), most of his supporters were women and young people.

> There are about twenty heads of families, besides others, women and young people, who ever appeared openly against the proceedings of the town, and many others have appeared friendly to me. And there is not a little reason to think, that there are many more, *especially women and youths,* that would appear so, if they dare. For a person, by appearing my friend at Northampton, even so much so as openly to discountenance my being turned out of the pulpit, exposes himself to the immediate persecution of his neighbours, and perhaps of his nearest friends. I mean, he falls under their great resentment, loses all their friendship, and is every where the object of reproach.[89]

---

87. By Edwards's account, "the generality of the church, which consists of about 230 male members, voted for my dismission"; Hopkins reported that there were "above two hundred against twenty." Dwight, *The Life of President Edwards,* 410, 399. Combining these two accounts suggests that the total number of male members was roughly between 230 and 250.

88. An opponent of the awakening decried most conversions as of "an epidemical distemper . . . especially [among] the younger women and children." John Caldwell, "An Impartial Trial of the Spiritual Operations in this Part of the World" (Boston, 1743), 23, cited in Goen, *Revivalism and Separatism,* 57–58. Charles Chauncy sought to dampen excitement over the 1740 revivals by reminders that many participants were women. *Seasonable Thoughts,* 105.

89. Dwight, *The Life of President Edwards,* 467.

Two observations may be made. First, if the franchise had been open to
the whole town—that is, to include women, servants, and young people
admitted to communion but unable to vote—the vote against Edwards
would probably not have been so lopsided. For the majority of Edwards's
most fervent supporters (women and young people) were barred from
voting. Second, all those groups that were excluded from the decision
had the most to gain from his retention. For he had consistently defended
their dignity from the pulpit and in his treatises. This suggests that other
groups besides women may also have supported him, if given the chance.
The point of all this is not to speculate about something that never did
happen, but to suggest that the town was not united in its opposition to
Edwards, as has been alleged. That leaves open the possibility of a factional, rather than united, opposition to the pastor.

There is more evidence that factional opposition may have cohered
along social, hierarchical lines. This study has noted Edwards's repeated
sniping at businessmen and the landed elite. In his sermon at Colonel
John Stoddard's funeral, for example, Edwards criticized businessmen
who took advantage of market conditions to gain exorbitant profits from
the poor. When the church elders decided to give the best seats in the
new meetinghouse to the wealthy, he denounced them from his pulpit.
His 1742 covenant requiring Northampton entrepreneurs not to cheat in
business dealings was not appreciated by town merchants and probably
created resentments that came home to roost in 1750. "Eager to make
their place in the world of commerce," Mark Valeri observes, "the town's
leaders would not have Edwards lecture them about the sins of covetousness." Perry Miller was probably right to locate part of the opposition in
"the oligarchy of business and real estate."[90]

That the traditional hierarchy was threatened is further suggested by
Gregory Nobles's conclusion that most of the other ministers in Hampshire
County were threatened by the democratic import of Edwards's public
theology. They supported the Northampton dismissal because they feared
that Edwards's principles, which would separate saved from unsaved and
level all the saved regardless of ministerial ordination, might lead to their

---

90. GA, 551–53; Valeri, "The Economic Thought of Jonathan Edwards," 51; Miller,
Jonathan Edwards, 219.

own ousters.[91] Tracy therefore misses the dynamic direction of Edwards's social theory when she calls Edwards a Tory who opposed the spirit of democracy. To be sure, he condemned "often changing the persons in whose hands is the administration of government," and favored the "old-fashioned ideal of a stable, unified community with 'natural' leaders, rather than the faction-oriented politics of the mid-eighteenth century." But the question for Edwards was, What makes for a natural leader? As these last two sections have shown, Edwards's answers to this question implicitly challenged existing authority. He denounced contention and political upheaval but preached the very principles that made those possible. That is, he provided society's inferiors with religious confidence to challenge their superiors and contemplate assuming their positions in society. As Tracy herself admits, Edwards "gave his children inner resources to rebel."[92]

Therefore it seems that while Edwards's dismissal may have been caused partly by the perception of some (the male elite) that his pastoral style was too heavy-handed and authoritarian, this perception might have been influenced in turn by the fear that Edwards's principles challenged their social and political authority.[93]

---

91. Five of eight of the Hampshire County ministers opposed Edwards. Dwight, *The Life of President Edwards*, 395–403; Nobles, *Divisions Throughout the Whole*, 73.

92. Tracy, *Jonathan Edwards, Pastor*, 149; Edwards, sermon on Proverbs 28:2, cited in Tracy, 149; ibid., 194. For Tracy to claim that Edwards "was no democrat" on the basis of a sermon doctrine that "a levelling spirit is a very evil and unchristian spirit" misses the point of the sermon. Edwards contested opposition to the *principle* of authority, not the discriminate criticism of those who are unworthy of authority. Edwards could hold to principles of political and religious authority with democratic implication while still opposing indiscriminate leveling. Tracy, 254 n. 11.

93. A third factor must be added. Edwards seems to have shared with older Edwards generations a determination to see grievances through to the very end, despite the consequences. "Back of it was a sense of justice to the letter, a pastoral urge toward the reproof and correction of others, and a lamentable lack of any sense of humor." Additionally, Edwards showed a notable lack of tact at times in relations with his church. One reason, for example, why the "Bad Book Affair" got out of control was Edwards's failure to deal first with the offenders privately. Instead, he announced from the pulpit the names of all those even remotely involved in the caper, without differentiating between leaders and relatively innocent followers. Winslow, *Jonathan Edwards 1703–1758*, 68–69, 221.

Edwards's Theology of the Christian Citizen and the New Nation

I have argued that Jonathan Edwards's theology of the Christian citizen helped undermine traditional views of society. By locating the citizen's authority in his own sense of the heart rather than his external attainments in society (such as wealth, political office or education), Edwards challenged all authority based on those attainments alone. His theology provided all social "inferiours" with theological legitimation for their challenges to religious, and then political, authority.

It is very difficult to ascertain how and to what extent the revolutionary implications of this theology were understood by his contemporaries. There are indications that he might have viewed the post-1760 Revolutionary movement with some sympathy. In 1755 he warned, in words repeated nearly verbatim twenty years later by colonists challenging England's authority, that "the civil & religious liberties & priviledges of the British Plantations in America & all that is dear to us . . . is so threatened[,] never as at this time."[94] In the same period he expressed pride in American military prowess and disdained British oversight of American forces: "Let New England men manage the business [fighting against French and Indians in 1755] in their own way, who alone understand it. To appoint British officers, over them, is nothing but a hindrance and discouragement to them."[95]

But Edwards was not the only American religious leader in the mid-eighteenth century to attack traditional authority and envision a new society founded on the New Birth. From the 1740s on, Congregationalists in the north joined Presbyterians in the middle colonies in open rebellion against the "spiritual tyranny" of traditional church authority.[96] Nor do his own parishioners seem to have acted on the democratic implications of his preaching. They were slow to join the Revolutionary movement.[97]

---

94. Sermon on Psalms 60:9–12, 28 August 1755, 21.

95. Dwight, *The Life of President Edwards*, 552.

96. See Bonomi, *Under the Cope*, 157–58; Stout, *The New England Soul*, 233–81; Heimert, *Religion and the American Mind*.

97. Robert J. Taylor, *Western Massachusetts in the Revolution* (Providence, R.I., 1954), 52–74.

The most vigorous patriot from Northampton was Joseph Hawley, the lawyer who helped oust Edwards from his pulpit. One of Edwards's most prominent supporters, Timothy Dwight, was a Tory.[98] Furthermore, much of Edwards's politically oriented thought lay buried in his unpublished sermons and private notebooks, hidden from New England's view.

This does not necessarily mean that Northampton was wholly untouched by the radical import of Edwards's social views. After all, the Northampton elite were disinclined to follow their former pastor's lead in any direction after the contention surrounding his departure; yet the majority of the town eventually did support the Revolution.[99] And Joseph Hawley repented of his role in Edwards's expulsion just five years after the affair.[100] Nevertheless, if Edwards's social and political theory had any influence on American thinking before and after his death, it was not primarily through his Northampton parish.

There is reason to believe that the American mind may have been affected by Edwards's social and political thinking through the mediation of the New Divinity, the school of theologian-pastors who called him their master. This movement's most important leaders (Samuel Hopkins, Joseph Bellamy, and Jonathan Edwards, Jr.), who had studied Edwards's unpublished sermons and private notebooks, advocated resistance against Britain and trained legions of pastors who "energetically promoted" the patriot cause.[101] A recent historian has characterized their work as a protest movement that appealed to the young and challenged existing social structures. "The New Divinity men were sharply critical of the established ministry, of the development of Puritan theology, and . . . the evolution of New England society."[102]

Of course, this is only circumstantial evidence for Edwards's influence on American political thinking. But we also know that Edwards's fame grew in the decades after his death and contributed to the growth of the

---

98. Trumbull, *History of Northampton*, 2:324, 372, 547–48; Taylor, *Western Massachusetts*, 61–62, 69–70.

99. Taylor, *Western Massachusetts*, 62–74.

100. His letter of repentance is in *Jonathan Edwards: Representative Selections*, ed. Faust and Johnson, 392.

101. Valeri, "Joseph Bellamy," 170, 172.

102. Conforti, *Samuel Hopkins*, 74, 5–6.

New Divinity. Even before his death Edwards was heralded by a religious leader from another colony as a man "whose praise for Superior acumen, Orthodoxy, Learning, Piety, & courage in the cause of God, *is in all the churches.*"[103] In the five decades after his death, hundreds of ministers dedicated to his theology held pulpits from north to south, preaching universal benevolence and the sense of the heart.[104] As a result, Edwards became a household name.

> The image of Edwards as an immensely popular figure from New England to the Carolinas and, eventually, Kentucky has been all but effaced by the nineteenth century Unitarian-drawn caricature of the cold logician threatening the resentful American populace with an eternity of hell torments. John Adams (writing to Jefferson in the "friendly" correspondence of their twilight years) insisted that Aaron Burr, "from the single circumstance of his descent," was always assured of one hundred thousand votes—more than enough, by any calculation, to have accounted for the Republican victory in 1800.[105]

It is not unlikely that many a radical Whig of the Revolutionary generation was schooled in Edwardsean theology by New Divinity preachers like Levi Hart, who, "completely saturated" in Edwards's writings, preached both universal benevolence and Real Whig politics from his Preston, Connecticut, pulpit.[106] Hence this confluence of factors— Revolutionary activity by disciples who were intimately acquainted with his social and political theory, the eminence in which Edwards was held, and the instrumentality of New Divinity preaching that reached tens of thousands of laypersons—makes it not implausible to suggest Edwardsean

---

103. Gilbert Tennent, letter to the Rev. Dr. Guise of London, Philadelphia, 15 November 1757, original in Princeton University Library; cited in Howard C. Rice, Jr., "Jonathan Edwards at Princeton: With a Survey of Edwards Materials in the Princeton University Library," *Princeton University Library Chronicle* 15 (1953–54): 70.

104. Conforti, *Samuel Hopkins,* 181–82.

105. Aaron Burr, Jr., was Edwards's grandson. Heimert, *Religion and the American Mind,* 194.

106. Weber, *Rhetoric and History,* 75, 74–90.

influence on American socio-political thinking in the last third of the eighteenth century. Edwards should therefore be included among those who contributed to the revolution in the American mind, of which John Adams spoke,[107] that produced the political revolution.

But it was neither his millennialism[108] nor a particular rhetorical form[109] that influenced American minds. Rather, whether Edwards intended it or not, his social theory may have helped pave the way for popular acceptance of both classical republicanism and radical egalitarian republicanism, two "ideological explosions" that found a home in American consciousness to produce an "unstable pluralism" in the early Republic.[110] Edwards's theological critique of the magistracy lent to Country ideology religious legitimation and prophetic power. He rejected social hierarchicalism, and taught an implicit egalitarianism based on the sense of the heart, a social model that had striking affinity to popular egalitarianism in the Revolutionary age.[111] Thus he may have helped some colonists make the transition from what Richard Bushman has called a "Puritan" to a "Yankee" mentality.

According to Bushman, the Puritan mind-set forbade resistance to

---

107. "What do we mean by the Revolution? The war? That was no part of the Revolution; it was only an effect and consequence of it. The Revolution was in the minds of the people, and this was effected, from 1760 to 1775, in the course of fifteen years before a drop of blood was shed at Lexington." John Adams to Jefferson, 1815, cited in Bailyn, *Ideological Origins*, 1.

108. Bercovitch, *The American Jeremiad*, 105; Hatch, *The Sacred Cause of Liberty*, 21–54; Bloch, *Visionary Republic*; Suzanne Geisler, *Jonathan Edwards to Aaron Burr, Jr.: From the Great Awakening to Democratic Politics* (New York, 1981), 238–39; Bryant, "America as God's Kingdom," 55.

109. Both Stout and Donald Weber claim that there was little connection between the awakening and the Revolution at the level of ideas. The connection, they claim, was only rhetorical. For Stout, the oral and itinerant nature of revival preaching showed colonists the possibility of a new social order beyond the printed discourses and settled positions of the religious elite. Stout, "Religion, Communications," 523, 525; Weber argues that religious vocabulary from the awakening "provided an enabling discourse that helped . . . make sense of revolutionary experience." Weber, *Rhetoric and History*, 12, 63.

110. Stout, "Religion, Communications," 538; Kammen, *People of Paradox*, 89–96.

111. I am not the first to notice Edwards's incipient egalitarianism and its connection with Revolutionary consciousness. Alan Heimert observed that "Calvinism and Edwards provided pre-Revolutionary America with a radical, even democratic, social and political ideology." Heimert, *Religion and the American Mind*, viii.

political and religious leaders, except in the most circumscribed of situations. Since those situations were so rare, most Puritan resistance turned
inward and produced guilt. The Yankee outlook, on the other hand,
could resist without guilt and pursue a course of rational, if somewhat
defensive, independence. The evidence proffered in these pages suggests
that Edwards's subtle undermining of traditional hierarchicalism may
have helped some colonists free themselves from "Puritan" guilt.[112] It also
suggests ways in which both classical republicanism (in the form of Country ideology) and a version of radical egalitarian republicanism were
mediated to the "social world of popular assembly"[113] where literacy was
limited. Edwards thus provides historians with a clue to how both ideologies could appeal to Americans with similar religious views.

---

112. Richard L. Bushman, *From Puritan to Yankee: Character and the Social Order in
Connecticut, 1690–1765* (Cambridge, 1967), 282ff. Thus Clyde Holbrook misplaces his
emphasis when he claims that for Edwards there was no systemic problem. To be sure,
Edwards professed allegiance to a hierarchical social structure. But the structure he had in
mind was animated by a spirit foreign to what he saw in New England society. Edwards
called for a social order based on public-spirited benevolence, not private cupidity. He
urged his fellow citizens to replace a social system oriented inwardly to protection of self
with a system that reaches outside of self to embrace the other. Holbrook, *The Ethics of
Jonathan Edwards*, 95.

113. Stout, "Religion, Communications," 533.

6 In Retrospect

The foregoing study of Edwards's public theology has suggested a new interpretation of the political and social views of "the American Augustine."[1] It has also demonstrated that Edwards may have played a role in the preparation of the New England mind for the American Revolution. This last chapter attempts to evaluate Edwards's public theology by, first, trying to identify its principal limitations and, second, assessing its contributions to the social and religious thinking of his day. It concludes with remarks on the implications of this study for American historiography.

---

1. Wilson, "Religion at the Core of American Culture," in *Altered Landscapes*, ed. Lotz et al., 373.

Limitations

Edwards's analysis of society and history was limited by his presumption that he could explain nearly every historical contingency and by his failure to recognize sufficiently his own capacity for self-deception. His reading of eighteenth-century history, for example, was ideological rather than empirical. In his private notebooks he compiled lists of commercial, political, social, and military setbacks for the Roman Catholic church in order to document what he was already convinced would take place, the downfall of the papacy. These Catholic reverses were noted along with signs of evangelical success, particularly the conversions of Native Americans, Jews, and Turks.[2] All of these events were, for Edwards, signs that the sixth vial was beginning to be poured out and (thus) that the world would soon see a general effusion of the Spirit and the destruction of the Antichrist before the coming of the millennium.

Edwards's interpretation of these events was apparent neither to the actors involved nor to most of his contemporaries. Rather than deriving the meaning of these events from a careful study of empirical data, Edwards brought to the data a preconceived interpretation derived from an eschatology that could not be falsified by contemporary history.

Furthermore, Edwards's eschatology was limited in its appeal, for, though cast in terms of a cosmopolitan theology, it evidenced a parochial knowledge of geography and politics. Edwards's historico-theological myopia was not atypical, however. His was the common mistake of religious interpreters of history who construe secular events as fulfillment of their own eschatological timetables.

Edwards used a similar method when construing God's administration of justice during the history of redemption. Again the meaning of events was derived not from the events themselves but from prior assumptions. Once more his interpretation was not falsifiable. If a righteous person prospered, it was because God had rewarded her righteousness or mercifully overlooked her sin. If she suffered, it was because of her sin. That her actions and fortune could have occurred independently of God's control was ruled out by Edwards's understanding of providence.

---

2. See AW, 46–47.

Alan Heimert has attributed Edwards's presumption that he alone understood history's blueprint to a certain "hubris." Certainly, Edwards was seldom self-critical in his public preaching and writing. Though ruthlessly critical of Northampton and New England, he rarely applied the same cynicism to himself. At times, in fact, he seemed to hold an exalted estimation of his own role in history. As we saw in Chapter 2, he viewed himself as an end-time prophet called by God to set his house in order.

Edwards's criticism of government was also limited by a certain myopia. He was suspicious of governmental attempts to use or control religion, but did not seem to imagine that a church could illegitimately interfere with government. Nor did he seem to consider deeply that ecclesiastical power of his own kind was predisposed to corruption. In his farewell sermon at Northampton he acknowledged that "ministers have no infallible discernment of the state of their people; and the most skillful of them are liable to mistakes, and often are mistaken in things of this nature." But this (tacit) admission of the possibility of his own error came at the end of his Northampton tenure, after months of (his) insisting that he was taking God's position. It also came after twenty-three years of sermons in which there were precious few admissions of error but numerous denunciations of his parishioners. Little wonder that Northampton sent him packing.

Edwards's attempts to chart the future work of redemption reveal his finitude. But they also illustrate the perils of any seer's attempt to pronounce with certitude what is to come. Edwards's prophecies are particularly interesting for the ironies they display. Though acutely aware of the corrosive power of sin, for instance, Edwards underestimated its intransigence in history. The Antichrist was not defeated by the end of the twentieth century, as he forecast, and the Spirit's effusions show no sign of bringing on the millennium. So while Edwards was pessimistic about New England's and America's future, he was too *optimistic* about the progress of redemption as a whole.

Conversely, Edwards underestimated humanity's natural capacities for promoting social welfare. Though convinced that unregenerate humanity sees the moral good and can cooperate with the regenerate for common moral ends, Edwards condemned the market economy because he thought that self-interest would only corrode the social fabric. But he failed to foresee (and here, of course, he was not alone) that the interest-driven market would be partly responsible for over two centuries of growth in wealth and economic opportunity.

Contributions

If Edwards's socio-religious vision was both myopic and presumptuous, it nevertheless charted with new sophistication a role for religion in the public square. Indeed, it was Edwards's singular achievement to have achieved a grand synthesis of social concern and private religious experience. The individual's religious sensibility, he determined, could not be understood apart from its (inevitably) public engagement. Hence Edwards's faith was not privatistic, but it was profoundly private. That is, he denounced religion devoid of social expression (privatistic) as false, but insisted that true religion emanated from a transformed heart (private).

Edwards's concern for religious feeling is widely recognized by historians. It was his passion for the inner realities of the spirit that helped give his preaching and writing the power for which they have been known. And he led and defended a religious movement that regarded inner religious experience as absolutely indispensable. But what is less well known is that for Edwards religious sensibility was never divorced from its social expression. Inner spiritual experience and outward religious action were movements of the same soul, pieces of the same cloth.

Yet just as he repudiated as spurious religious feeling that did not manifest public concern, Edwards denounced as empty social and religious acts that were not animated by Christian spirituality. In addition to insisting that faith must have social expression, Edwards reproved magistrates who thought their public duties were more important than private religious affection. Neither was more important than the other, he insisted. They were simply different aspects of one religious exercise. True religion was the proper synthesis of the two. Social action that did not spring from a heart captivated by God's beauty and love would be less than fully virtuous. Consequently, it would also be less than fully effective.

The good society, for Edwards, would be so animated by love that every social relation would be an expression of love. But the love he urged was possible, he claimed, only for a heart transformed by the sort of spiritual experience he preached. Thus the social duties urged by New England politicians who did not also urge religious transformation might have improved social conditions but were incapable of creating the beautiful society. Religious experience centered in the apprehension of God's beauty as described by Edwards was the necessary precondition for fully effective social transformation. This is not to say that Edwards frowned upon all social action unless performed by the converted. He favored his evangelicals cooperating with non-Christians for the sake of common moral objectives but insisted that those objectives would fall short of optimal benefit without the spiritual regeneration of all involved.

This study has shown that Edwards did not just draw pictures of visionary communities in the sky, but used his pulpit and study to subject eighteenth-century political powers to the judgment of transcendent ideals. He did this in a number of ways. First, he limited the pretensions of society's power brokers by shifting the locus of authority from the social hierarchy to the inner recesses of the heart. By such a move he exposed the spiritual poverty of New England's movers and shakers and pronounced God's esteem for the poor, God-fearing Christian. For that reason, he proclaimed, the poor, the blacks, the uneducated, the women, and the young people who had found salvation could hold their heads high, for they possessed greater personal worth than their worldly superiors. Edwards never contemplated or advocated a reordering of society, but his ennoblement of the common Christian may have given confidence to those colonials who tried to challenge society's elites.

Second, Edwards limited economic pretensions by teaching that God was found especially in the poor and that God called the poor into his Kingdom more often than he called the rich. The Christian served God, Edwards taught, by helping the poor. Both the church and the state were to actively assist the underprivileged.

Third, Edwards defended the poor by denouncing their exploitation in the marketplace. He attacked businessmen for taking advantage of the poor family's desperation in order to make an unreasonable profit. He warned merchants that God would defend the poor, and threatened that those who did not honestly contribute to the town's poor rates might be struck dead. He supported the town's welfare system, and attacked his own church for preferring the rich in its seating design.

Edwards, then, was no ivory-tower theologian, reluctant to engage the social realities of his day. He did not shrink from confronting what he considered to be social evil, whether in New England society or his own church. He was not fully aware of his own pride and presumption, but there was no shortage of "critical distance" between his own prophetic office and the institutions around him. Perhaps this is why he spent most of his last decade banished to the frontier.

Final Remarks

This study has attempted to counter charges that Jonathan Edwards's socio-political views were minimal, chauvinistic, and feudal by delineating his public theology. It has shown that Edwards's doctrine of the national covenant was neither tribalist nor provincial. Instead, he was a prophet in the tradition of the New England jeremiad who never consistently embraced the optimistic nationalism often attributed to him. God's judgment on a sinful people was the predominant message of his sermons on public and civil concerns. Rather than seeing New England or America as a redeemer nation, he threatened his countrymen with the possibility that they might lose their covenant to another, more faithful people.

Edwards's portrayal of the coming millennium did not highlight America, as has been claimed by some scholars. The preponderance of his eschatological reflection cast the coming eschaton in global, international terms, and placed it centuries in the future. America's role in end-time events was projected only at the height of the Great Awakening, and even then America was given a relatively inconsequential role. At most, America would *probably* be the site of the beginning of the centuries-long, troubled age of intermittent revival that would eventually usher in the millennium.

Therefore, Edwards could not have fathered the self-congratulatory civil religion that flavored much of the American Revolutionary experience, but he may have helped prepare colonial minds for Revolutionary political ideology. For Edwards's political theory was not feudal, as one scholar has suggested, but similar to "Country" ideology in its suspicion of political power. His theology of the Christian citizen, which imparted dignity and respect to those marginalized by traditional social and political norms and simultaneously questioned the religious authority of colonial elites, undermined the pre-Revolutionary concept of social deference. The preaching of his New Divinity disciples probably helped colonists reject a traditional hierarchical understanding of the social order.

This reading of Edwards's public theology has implications for historians' understanding of American religious history. In the last few decades scholars have written a plethora of books and articles chronicling the supposed American penchant for myths that tell of God's special favor on their nation.[3] Many of these myths, we have been told, enabled Americans to weather crises by holding out the promise of future national greatness. In Edwards's myth, New Englanders were a chosen people that nevertheless faced the threat of divine rejection. If there was an American myth of divine election and future glory, Edwards turned it into a frightening augury of future judgment.

That Edwards, who was arguably America's greatest religious thinker in the eighteenth century and perhaps this nation's greatest theologian to date, should have dissented from what has been depicted as a national predisposition may lead historians to reevaluate this tribalist motif in American religious history. Some historians have already noted that some of Edwards's most prominent disciples rejected the complacent nationalism so prevalent in the Revolutionary period.[4] Perhaps more attention needs to be given to this Edwardsean tradition in early America, which was at once influential and opposed to a prevailing zeitgeist. Further study may indicate that Christian views of America in the colonial and Revolutionary periods were more diverse than has been imagined.

Finally, Edwards's insights into the nature of political community and the role of the church within that community show that he gave considerable attention to the public square and developed a public theology

---

3. See, for instance, Tuveson, *Redeemer Nation*; Bercovitch, *The Puritan Origins*, and *The American Jeremiad*; Lowance, *The Language of Canaan*; and Stout, *The New England Soul*.

4. Conforti, *Samuel Hopkins*, and "Samuel Hopkins and the New Divinity"; Bryant, "From Edwards to Hopkins"; Valeri, "Joseph Bellamy."

whose sophistication had few rivals. His most important contribution was his painstaking unfolding of the relation of private to public religion. Like some of his clerical contemporaries, Edwards reflected on the public square from within a life given to the promotion and explication of personal spirituality. Yet Edwards was also the leader and promoter of revivals, a director of souls, and an acute analyst of private (but not privatistic) religious experience. None of his contemporaries, and few of his predecessors, took such pains to interpret the interface of public and private religion.

Edwards never discussed the public square without explicit attention to the private spirituality that he felt was required for proper public action. Private religious sensibility and its public expression were indivisible, two sides of a seamless garment. This was a truth that Edwards would not let go unstated. It was this unity of Christian experience, transcending all dichotomies of public and private, and the particularity with which he dissected various dimensions of that experience, that mark the singularity of his achievement.

Selected Bibliography

Primary Sources

Manuscripts

Edwards, Jonathan. Fast, Thanksgiving, and Election Day Sermons. Edwards Papers. Beinecke Rare Book and Manuscript Library, Yale University. New Haven, Connecticut.
———. *Miscellanies.* Typescript by Thomas A. Schafer. Beinecke Rare Book and Manuscript Library, Yale University. New Haven, Connecticut.
[Edwards, Jonathan.] "We the subscribers members of the First Church in Northampton offer what follows for our vindication in absenting from the Communion at the Lords Table." Franklin Trask Library, Andover Newton Theological School, Newton Center, Massachusetts.

Published Works

Ames, William. *Conscience with the Power and Cases Thereof.* N.p. 1639. Reprint. Amsterdam, 1975.
———. *The Marrow of Theology.* Edited by John Dykstra Eusden. Boston, 1968.

Aquinas, Thomas. *Nature and Grace: Selections from the Summa Theologica.* Translated by A. M. Fairweather. The Library of Christian Classics, vol. 11. Philadelphia, 1954.

Bailyn, Bernard. *Pamphlets of the American Revolution, 1750–1776.* Cambridge, Mass., 1965.

Baxter, Richard. *The Practical Works of Richard Baxter.* 4 vols. London, 1864.

Breward, Ian, ed. *The Work of William Perkins.* Appleford, England, 1970.

Calvin, John. *Institutes of the Christian Religion, 2 vols.* Translated by Ford Lewis Battles. Edited by John T. McNeill. Philadelphia, 1960.

Chauncy, Charles. *The Benevolence of the Deity.* Boston, 1784.

———. "Civil Magistrates Must Be Just, Ruling in the Fear of God." Boston, 1747.

———. "A Discourse on the Good News from a Far Country." Boston, 1766.

———. "Enthusiasm Described and Cautioned Against." Boston, 1742.

———. "The Idle Poor." Boston, 1752.

———. "Marvellous Things." Boston, 1745.

———. *Seasonable Thoughts on the State of Religion in New England.* Boston, 1743.

Danforth, John. "Vile Profanations." Boston, 1663.

Davenport, John. "A Sermon Preached at the Election of the Governour." Publications of the Colonial Society of Massachusetts, vol. 10. Boston, 1910.

Doddridge, Philip. *The Works of the Reverend Philip Doddridge, D.D.* London, 1803.

Edwards, Jonathan. *Charity and Its Fruits.* 1852. Reprint, edited by Tyron Edwards. Edinburgh, 1969.

———. *Images or Shadows of Divine Things.* Edited by Perry Miller. New Haven, 1947.

———. "Jonathan Edwards's Letter of Invitation to George Whitefield," [12 February 1740]. Edited by Henry Abelove. *William and Mary Quarterly,* 3d ser., 29 (1972): 487–89.

———. *The Nature of True Virtue.* 1765. Reprint, edited by William K. Frankena. Ann Arbor, 1960.

———. *Treatise on Grace.* 1865. Reprint, edited by Paul Helm. Cambridge, 1971.

———. *The Works of Jonathan Edwards.* Edited by John E. Smith. New Haven [Yale University Press], 1957–. This edition is not yet complete. The following volumes were used in this book.

    Vol. 1, *Freedom of the Will,* edited by Paul Ramsey. 1957.

    Vol. 2, *Religious Affections,* edited by John E. Smith. 1959.

    Vol. 3, *Original Sin,* edited by Clyde A. Holbrook. 1970.

Vol. 4, *The Great Awakening*, edited by C. C. Goen. 1972.

Vol. 5, *Apocalyptic Writings*, edited by Stephen J. Stein. 1977.

Vol. 6, *Scientific and Philosophical Writings*, edited by Wallace E. Anderson. 1980.

Vol. 7, *The Life of David Brainerd*, edited by Norman Pettit. 1985.

Vol. 8, *Ethical Writings*, edited by Paul Ramsey. 1989.

Vol. 9, *A History of the Work of Redemption*, edited by John F. Wilson. 1989.

————. *The Works of President Edwards.* 2 vols. Edited by Edward Hickman. London, 1834. Reprint. Edinburgh, 1974.

————. *The Works of President Edwards in Eight Volumes.* Edited by Edward Williams and Edward Parsons. Leeds, 1806–11.

————. *The Works of President Edwards: With a Memoir of His Life, In Ten Volumes.* Edited by Sereno E. Dwight. New York, 1829–30.

Eels, Nathanael. "Religion is the Life of God's People." Boston, 1743.

Faust, Clarence H., and Thomas H. Johnson, eds. *Jonathan Edwards: Representative Selections.* New York, 1962.

Finney, Charles G. *Lectures on Revivals of Religion.* New York, 1835.

————. *Lectures on Systematic Theology.* Grand Rapids, Mich., 1878.

————. *Memoirs.* New York, 1876.

Foxe, John. *An Abridgement of the Book of Acts and Monuments of the Church Written by that Reverend Father, Master John Foxe, and now abridged by Timothy Bright.* London, 1589.

Gardiner, H. Norman, ed. *Selected Sermons of Jonathan Edwards.* New York, 1904.

Heimert, Alan, and Andrew Delbanco, eds. *The Puritans in America: A Narrative Anthology.* Cambridge, Mass., 1985.

Heimert, Alan, and Perry Miller, eds. *The Great Awakening: Documents Illustrating The Crisis and Its Consequences.* Indianapolis, 1967.

Higginson, John. "The Cause of God." Cambridge, Mass., 1663.

Hooke, George William. "New Englands Teares for Old Englands Feares." London, 1641.

Howe, John. *The Whole Works of the Rev. John Howe, M.A.* 8 vols. London, 1822.

Johnson, Edward. *The "Wonder-Working Providence" of Sion's Saviour in New England.* London, 1654. Reprinted as *A History of New England.* New York, 1910.

Mather, Cotton. *Magnalia Christi Americana.* Edited by Frederick Ungar. New York, 1970.

————. *Magnalia Christi Americana, Books I and II.* Edited by Kenneth B. Murdock. Cambridge, Mass., 1977.

Mather, Increase. "The 'Day of Trouble' is Near." Cambridge, Mass., 1674.

———. "A 'Discourse' Concerning the Danger of Apostacy." Boston, 1685.

Mayhew, Jonathan. *Practical Discourses Delivered on Occasion of the Earthquakes in November, 1755.* Boston, 1760.

———. *Sermons Upon the Following Subjects.* Boston, 1755.

———. *Seven Sermons Upon the Following Subjects.* Boston, 1749.

———. *Two Discourses Delivered November 23, 1758.* Boston, 1758.

Miller, Perry, ed. *The American Puritans: Their Prose and Poetry.* Garden City, N.Y., 1956.

Miller, Perry, and Thomas H. Johnson, eds. *The Puritans.* 2 vols. New York, 1938.

Morgan, Edmund S., ed. *Puritan Political Ideas: 1558–1794.* Indianapolis, 1965.

Norton, John. "Sion the Outcast Healed of Her Wounds." Cambridge, 1664.

Oakes, Urian. "New England Pleaded With." Cambridge, Mass., 1673.

———. "A Seasonable Discourse." Boston, 1682.

Oxenbridge, John. "New England Freemen." Boston, 1673.

Perkins, William. *A Golden Chaine; or, The Description of Theologie.* London, 1635.

Plumstead, A. W., ed. *"The Wall and the Garden": Selected Massachusetts Election Sermons 1670–1775.* Minneapolis, 1978.

Prince, Thomas. "The Natural and Moral Government." Boston, 1749.

———. "The Salvation of God in 1746." Boston, 1746.

Ridgley, Thomas. *A Body of Divinity.* 4 vols. London, 1731. First American edition, 1814–15.

Sewall, Joseph. "Repentance." Boston, 1727.

Slotkin, Richard, and James K. Folsom, eds. *So Dreadful a Judgement: Puritan Responses to King Philip's War, 1676–1677.* Middletown, Conn., 1978.

Stoddard, Solomon. "An Appeal to the Learned." Boston, 1709.

Tocqueville, Alexis de. *Democracy in America.* Translated by George Lawrence. Edited by J. P. Mayer. New York, 1969.

Townsend, Harvey G., ed. *The Philosophy of Jonathan Edwards from His Private Notebooks.* [Excerpts from the *Miscellanies.*] Eugene, Ore., 1955.

Trumbull, James R. *History of Northampton, Massachusetts, From Its Settlement in 1654,* 2 vols. Northampton, 1898.

Turretin, François. *Institutio Theologiae Elencticae.* 1679–85. Handwritten translation by George Musgrave Giger at Princeton Theological Seminary.

Willard, Samuel. "The Checkered State of the Gospel Church." Boston, 1701.

———. *A Compleat Body of Divinity.* Boston, 1726.

———. "Israel's True Safety." Boston, 1704.

Williams, George H., et al., eds. *Thomas Hooker: Writings in England and Holland, 1626–1633.* Cambridge, Mass., 1975.

Secondary Sources

Books

Albanese, Catherine. *Sons of the Fathers: The Civil Religion of the American Revolution.* Philadelphia, 1976.

Althaus, Paul. *The Theology of Martin Luther.* Translated by Robert Schultz. Philadelphia, 1966.

Augustine. *The City of God.* Translated by Marcus Dods. New York, 1950.

Bailyn, Bernard. *The Ideological Origins of the American Revolution.* Cambridge, Mass., 1967.

Barth, Karl. *Protestant Theology in the Nineteenth Century.* Valley Forge, Pa., 1972.

Bauckham, Richard. *Tudor Apocalypse.* Oxford, 1978.

Bellah, Robert. *The Broken Covenant: American Civil Religion in Time of Trial.* New York, 1975.

————. *Habits of the Heart: Individualism and Commitment in American Life.* Berkeley and Los Angeles, 1985.

Bellah, Robert, and Philip Hammond. *Varieties of Civil Religion.* New York, 1975.

Benne, Robert, and Philip Hefner. *Defining America: A Christian Critique of the American Dream.* Philadelphia, 1974.

Bercovitch, Sacvan. *The American Jeremiad.* Cambridge, Mass., 1978.

————. *The Puritan Origins of the American Self.* New Haven, 1975.

Berger, Peter L. *The Sacred Canopy: Elements of a Sociological Theory of Religion.* Garden City, N.Y., 1969.

Bloch, Ruth H. *Visionary Republic: Millennial Themes in American Thought, 1756–1800.* Cambridge, Mass., 1985.

Bogue, Carl W. *Jonathan Edwards and the Covenant of Grace.* Cherry Hill, N.J., 1975.

Bonomi, Patricia U. *Under the Cope of Heaven: Religion, Society, and Politics in Colonial America.* New York, 1986.

Bouwsma, William J. *John Calvin: A Sixteenth-Century Portrait.* New York, 1988.

Bozeman, T. Dwight. *To Live Ancient Lives: The Primitivist Dimension in Puritanism.* Chapel Hill, N.C., 1988.

Breen, Timothy H. *The Character of a Good Ruler: A Study of Puritan Political Ideas in New England, 1630–1730.* New Haven, 1970.

Bremer, Francis J. *The Puritan Experiment.* New York, 1976.

Bushman, Richard L. *From Puritan to Yankee: Character and the Social Order in Connecticut, 1690–1765.* Cambridge, Mass., 1967.

Campbell, Dennis M. *Authority and the Renewal of American Theology.* Philadelphia, 1976.

Carse, James. *Jonathan Edwards and the Visibility of God*. New York, 1967.

Cherry, Conrad. *Nature and Religious Imagination: From Edwards to Bushnell*. Philadelphia, 1980.

―――. *The Theology of Jonathan Edwards: A Reappraisal*. Garden City, N.Y., 1966.

Cherry, Conrad, ed. *God's New Israel: Religious Interpretations of American Destiny*. Englewood Cliffs, N.J., 1971.

Cohn, Norman. *Pursuit of the Millennium*. Oxford, 1961.

Conforti, Joseph A. *Samuel Hopkins and the New Divinity Movement: Calvinism, the Congregational Ministry, and Reform in New England Between the Great Awakenings*. Grand Rapids, Mich., 1981.

Cooey, Paula M. *Jonathan Edwards on Nature and Destiny: A Systematic Analysis*. Lewiston, Maine, 1985.

Corrigan, John. *The Hidden Balance: Religion and the Social Theories of Charles Chauncy and Jonathan Mayhew*. Cambridge, Mass., 1987.

Cremin, Lawrence. *American Education: The National Experience 1783–1876*. New York, 1980.

Crowley, J. E. *This Sheba, Self: The Conceptualization of Economic Life in Eighteenth-Century America*. Baltimore, 1974.

Davidson, James West. *The Logic of Millennial Thought: Eighteenth-Century New England*. New Haven, 1977.

DeJong, Johan Anthony. *As the Waters Cover the Sea: Millennial Expectations in the Rise of Anglo-American Missions, 1640–1810*. Kampen, 1970.

Delattre, Roland A. *Beauty and Sensibility in the Thought of Jonathan Edwards: An Essay in Aesthetics and Theological Ethics*. New Haven, 1968.

Delbanco, Andrew. *The Puritan Ordeal*. Cambridge, Mass., 1989.

Elwood, Douglas J. *The Philosophical Theology of Jonathan Edwards*. New York, 1960.

Fiering, Norman. *Jonathan Edwards's Moral Thought and Its British Context*. Chapel Hill, N.C., 1981.

Fliegelman, Jay. *Prodigals and Pilgrims: The American Revolution against Patriarchal Authority, 1750–1800*. Cambridge, 1982.

Foster, Stephen. *Their Solitary Way: The Puritan Social Ethic in the First Century of Settlement in New England*. New Haven, 1971.

Gaustad, Edwin Scott. *The Great Awakening in New England*. Gloucester, Mass., 1965.

Gay, Peter. *A Loss of Mastery: Puritan Historians in Colonial America*. Berkeley and Los Angeles, 1966.

Geissler, Suzanne. *Jonathan Edwards to Aaron Burr, Jr.: From the Great Awakening to Democratic Politics*. New York, 1981.

Gerstner, John H. *Jonathan Edwards: A Mini-Theology*. Wheaton, Ill., 1987.

Goen, C. C. *Revivalism and Separatism in New England, 1740–1800.* New Haven, 1962.

Greaves, Richard L. *Theology and Revolution in the Scottish Reformation.* Grand Rapids, Mich., 1980.

Greven, Philip. *The Protestant Temperament: Patterns of Child-Rearing, Religious Experience, and the Self in Early America.* New York, 1980.

Haller, William. *Foxe's Book of Martyrs and the Elect Nation.* London, 1963.

Handy, Robert T. *A Christian America: Protestant Hopes and Historical Realities.* 2d ed. New York, 1984.

Haroutunian, Joseph. *Piety Versus Moralism: The Passing of the New England Theology.* New York, 1932.

Hatch, Nathan. *The Sacred Cause of Liberty: Republican Thought and the Millennium in Revolutionary New England.* New Haven, 1977.

Hatch, Nathan, and Harry S. Stout, eds. *Jonathan Edwards and the American Experience.* New York, 1988.

Heimert, Alan. *Religion and the American Mind: From the Great Awakening to the Revolution.* Cambridge, Mass., 1966.

Herberg, Will. *Protestant, Catholic, Jew: An Essay in American Religious Sociology.* Garden City, N.Y., 1955.

Holbrook, Clyde A. *The Ethics of Jonathan Edwards: Morality and Aesthetics.* Ann Arbor, 1973.

———. *Jonathan Edwards, the Valley, and Nature.* Lewisburg, Pa., 1988.

Holstun, James. *A Rational Millennium: Puritan Utopias of Seventeenth-Century England and America.* New York, 1987.

Hudson, Winthrop S., ed. *Nationalism and Religion in America: Concepts of American Identity and Mission.* New York, 1970.

Hughey, Michael W. *Civil Religion and Moral Order: Theoretical and Historical Dimensions.* Westport, Conn., 1983.

Jenson, Robert W. *America's Theologian: A Recommendation of Jonathan Edwards.* New York, 1988.

Jewett, Robert. *The Captain America Complex: The Dilemma of Zealous Nationalism.* Philadelphia, 1973.

Johnson, James Turner, ed. *The Bible in American Law, Politics, and Political Rhetoric.* Philadelphia, 1985.

Jones, James W. *The Shattered Synthesis: New England Puritanism before the Great Awakening.* New Haven, 1973.

Jordan, Winthrop D. *White Over Black: American Attitudes Toward the Negro, 1550–1812.* Chapel Hill, N.C., 1968.

Kuklick, Bruce. *Churchmen and Philosophers from Jonathan Edwards to John Dewey.* New Haven, 1985.

Lamb, Matthew. *Solidarity with Victims.* New York, 1982.

Leach, Douglas Edward. *Arms for Empire: A Military History of the British Colonies in North America, 1607–1763.* New York, 1973.

Lee, Sang Hyun. *The Philosophical Theology of Jonathan Edwards.* Princeton, 1988.

Leff, Gordon. *Medieval Thought: St. Augustine to Ockham.* Middlesex, 1970.

Lesser, M. X. *Jonathan Edwards.* Boston, 1988.

———. *Jonathan Edwards: A Reference Guide.* Boston, 1981.

Love, W. DeLoss, Jr. *The Fast and Thanksgiving Days of New England.* Boston, 1895.

Lovejoy, Arthur O. *The Great Chain of Being: A Study of the History of an Idea.* Cambridge, Mass., 1964.

Lowance, Mason I., Jr. *The Language of Canaan: Metaphor and Symbol in New England from the Puritans to the Transcendentalists.* Cambridge, Mass., 1980.

McLaughlin, William G. *Revivals, Awakenings, and Reform: An Essay on Religion and Social Change in America, 1607–1977.* Chicago, 1978.

Manuel, Frank E., and Fritzie P. Manuel. *Utopian Thought in the Western World.* Cambridge, Mass., 1979.

Martin, James P. *The Last Judgment in Protestant Theology from Orthodoxy to Ritschl.* Edinburgh, 1963.

May, Henry F. *The Enlightenment in America.* Oxford, 1976.

Mead, Sidney. *The Old Religion in the Brave New World: Reflections on the Relations between Christendom and the Republic.* Berkeley and Los Angeles, 1977.

Middlekauf, Robert. *The Mathers: Three Generations of Puritan Intellectuals, 1596–1728.* New York, 1971.

Miller, Perry. *Errand into the Wilderness.* New York, 1956.

———. *Jonathan Edwards.* 2d ed. New York, 1959.

———. *The New England Mind: From Colony to Province.* Cambridge, Mass., 1953.

———. *The New England Mind: The Seventeenth Century.* Boston, 1939.

Moltmann, Jürgen, et al., eds. *Religion and Political Society.* New York, 1974.

Morgan, Edmund S. *Roger Williams: The Church and the State.* New York, 1967.

Morison, Samuel Eliot, and Henry Steele Commager. *The Growth of the American Republic,* vol. 1. New York, 1942.

Muller, Richard A. *Post-Reformation Reformed Dogmatics.* Vol. 1: *Prolegomena to Theology.* Grand Rapids, Mich., 1987.

Murray, Iain H. *Jonathan Edwards: A New Biography.* Edinburgh, 1987.

Neuhaus, Richard John. *The Naked Public Square: Religion and Democracy in America.* Grand Rapids, Mich., 1984.

Niebuhr, H. Richard. *Christ and Culture.* New York, 1951.

———. *The Kingdom of God in America.* Chicago, 1937.

———. *The Meaning of Revelation*. New York, 1941.

———. *Radical Monotheism and Western Culture*. New York, 1943.

———. *The Responsible Self: An Essay in Christian Moral Philosophy*. New York, 1963.

Niebuhr, Reinhold. *The Irony of American History*. New York, 1952.

Nobles, Gregory H. *Divisions Throughout the Whole: Politics and Society in Hampshire County, Massachusetts, 1740–1775*. Cambridge, Mass., 1983.

Noll, Mark. *Christians in the American Revolution*. Washington, D.C., 1977.

———. *One Nation under God: Christian Faith and Political Action in America*. San Francisco, 1988.

Noll, Mark, ed. *The Princeton Theology*. Grand Rapids, Mich., 1983.

Noll, Mark, and Nathan Hatch, eds. *The Bible in America: Essays in Cultural History*. New York, 1982.

Noll, Mark, and Roger Lundin, eds. *Voices from the Heart: Four Centuries of American Piety*. Grand Rapids, Mich., 1987.

Oberman, Heiko. *The Harvest of Medieval Theology: Gabriel Biel and Late Medieval Nominalism*. 2d ed. Grand Rapids, Mich., 1967.

Oppenheim, Frank M., S.J. *The Reasoning Heart: Toward a North American Theology*. Washington, D.C., 1986.

Pannenberg, Wolfhart. *Human Nature, Election, and History*. Philadelphia, 1977.

Peckham, Howard H. *The Colonial Wars 1689–1762*. Chicago, 1964.

Perkins, Edwin J. *The Economy of Colonial America*. New York, 1980.

Petrie, Charles. *The Jacobite Movement*. London, 1932.

Richey, Russell E., and Donald G. Jones. *American Civil Religion*. New York, 1974.

Robbins, Caroline. *The Eighteenth-Century Commonwealth Men: Studies in the Transmission, Development, and Circumstances of English Liberal Thought from the Restoration of Charles II until the War with the Thirteen Colonies*. Cambridge, Mass., 1961.

Rouner, Leroy S., ed. *Civil Religion and Political Theology*. Notre Dame, 1986.

Ruether, Rosemary R., and Rosemary S. Keller, eds. *Women and Religion in America*. Vol. 2, *The Colonial and Revolutionary Periods*. San Francisco, 1983.

Saum, Lewis O. *The Popular Mood of Pre–Civil War America*. Westport, Conn., 1980.

Scheick, William J., ed. *Critical Essays on Jonathan Edwards*. Boston, 1980.

Schneider, Herbert Wallace. *The Puritan Mind*. New York, 1930.

Simonson, Harold P. *Jonathan Edwards: Theologian of the Heart*. Grand Rapids, Mich., 1974.

Skinner, Quentin. *The Foundations of Modern Political Thought*. Vol. 2 of *The Age of Reformation*. London, 1978.

Smith, Elwyn, ed. *The Religion of the Republic*. Philadelphia, 1971.

Stokes, Anson P. *Church and State in the United States.* New York, 1950.

Stout, Harry S. *The New England Soul: Preaching and Religious Culture in Colonial New England.* New York, 1986.

Strout, Cushing. *The New Heavens and the New Earth: Political Religion in America.* New York, 1974.

Toon, Peter, ed. *Puritans, the Millennium, and the Future of Israel: Puritan Eschatology 1600 to 1660.* Cambridge, 1970.

Tracy, Patricia J. *Jonathan Edwards, Pastor: Religion and Society in Eighteenth-Century Northampton.* New York, 1980.

Trinterud, Leonard J. *The Forming of an American Tradition: A Re-examination of Colonial Presbyterianism.* Philadelphia, 1949.

Tuveson, Ernest Lee. *Redeemer Nation: The Idea of America's Millennial Role.* Chicago, 1968.

Van Dyken, Seymour. *Samuel Willard, 1640–1707: Preacher of Orthodoxy in an Era of Change.* Grand Rapids, Mich., 1972.

Walzer, Michael. *The Revolution of the Saints: A Study in the Origins of Radical Politics.* New York, 1973.

Weber, Donald. *Rhetoric and History in Revolutionary New England.* New York, 1988.

Wilson, John. *Public Religion in American Culture.* Philadelphia, 1979.

———. *Pulpit in Parliament.* Princeton, 1969.

Wilson, Robert J., III. *The Benevolent Deity: Ebenezer Gay and the Rise of Rational Religion in New England, 1696–1787.* Philadelphia, 1984.

Wilson-Kastner, Patricia. *Coherence in a Fragmented World: Jonathan Edwards' Theology of the Holy Spirit.* Washington, D.C., 1978.

Winslow, Ola Elizabeth. *Jonathan Edwards 1703–1758: A Biography.* New York, 1940.

Woody, Thomas. *A History of Women's Education in the United States.* New York, 1929.

Wright, Conrad. *The Beginnings of Unitarianism in America.* Boston, 1955.

Articles and Essays

Albanese, Catherine. "Civil Religion." In *America: Religions and Religion,* 283–308. Belmont, Calif., 1981.

Alexis, Gerhard. "Jonathan Edwards and the Theocratic Ideal." *Church History* 35 (1966): 328–43.

Bellah, Robert. "Civil Religion in America." *Daedalus* 96, no. 1 (1967): 1–21.

———. "The Revolution and the Civil Religion." In *Religion and the American Revolution,* ed. Jerald Brauer, 55–73. Philadelphia, 1976.

Bercovitch, Sacvan. "Horologicals to Chronometricals: The Rhetoric of the

Jeremiad." In *Literary Monographs* 3, ed. Eric Rothstein, 1–124. Madison, Wis., 1970.

Bozeman, T. Dwight. "The Puritans' 'Errand into the Wilderness' Reconsidered." *New England Quarterly* 59, no. 2 (1986): 231–51.

Brauer, Jerald. "Puritanism, Revivalism, and the Revolution." In *Religion and the American Revolution*, ed. Jerald Brauer, 18–27. Philadelphia, 1976.

Bryant, M. Darrol. "America as God's Kingdom." In *Religion and Political Society*, ed. Jürgen Moltmann et al., 49–94. New York, 1974.

———. "From Edwards to Hopkins: A Millennialist Critique of Political Culture." In *The Coming Kingdom*, ed. M. Darrol Bryant and Donald W. Dayton, 45–70. Barrytown, N.Y., 1983.

Buchanan, John G. "Puritan Philosophy of History from Restoration to Revolution." *Essex Institute Historical Collections* 104 (1968): 329–48.

Buffinton, Arthur H. "The Puritan View of War." *Publications of the Colonial Society of Massachusetts* 28 (1935): 67–86.

Carpenter, Frederic I. "The Radicalism of Jonathan Edwards." *New England Quarterly* 4 (1931): 629–44.

Conforti, Joseph A. "Samuel Hopkins and the New Divinity: Theology, Ethics, and Social Reform in Eighteenth-Century New England." *William and Mary Quarterly*, 3d. ser., 34 (1977): 572–89.

Cowing, Cedric. "Sex and Preaching in the Great Awakening." *American Quarterly* 20 (1968): 624–44.

Delattre, Roland. "Beauty and Politics: A Problematic Legacy of Jonathan Edwards." In *American Philosophy from Edwards to Quine*, ed. Robert W. Shahan and Kenneth R. Merrill, 20–48. Norman, Okla., 1977.

———. "Beauty and Theology: A Reappraisal of Jonathan Edwards." In *Critical Essays on Jonathan Edwards*, ed. William J. Scheick, 136–49. Boston, 1980.

Dunn, John. "The Politics of Locke in England and America in the Eighteenth Century." In *John Locke: Problems and Perspectives*, ed. John W. Yolton, 45–80. Cambridge, 1969.

Gerrish, Brian. "The Mirror of God's Goodness: A Key Metaphor in Calvin's View of Man." In *Readings in Calvin's Theology*, ed. Donald K. McKim, 107–22. Grand Rapids, Mich., 1984.

Goen, C. C. "Jonathan Edwards: A New Departure in Eschatology." *Church History* 28 (March 1959): 25–40.

Gohdes, Clarence. "Aspects of Idealism in Early New England." *Philosophical Review* 39 (1930): 537–55.

Hudson, Winthrop. "Fast Days and Civil Religion." In *Theology in Sixteenth and Seventeenth Century England*, ed. Winthrop Hudson and Leonard J. Trinterud, 1–24.

Johnson, Thomas H. "Jonathan Edwards's Background of Reading." *Publications of the Colonial Society of Massachusetts* 28 (1930–33): 193–222.

Kirby, John B. "Early American Politics—The Search for Ideology: An Historiographical Analysis and Critique of the Concept of Deference." *Journal of Politics* 32 (1970): 808–38.

McDermott, Gerald R. "Civil Religion in the American Revolutionary Period: An Historiographic Analysis." *Christian Scholar's Review* 18, no. 4 (June 1989): 346–62.

McGiffert, Michael. "Covenant, Crown, and Commons in Elizabethan Puritanism." *Journal of British Studies* 20, no. 1 (1980): 32–52.

———. "Puritan Studies in the 1960s." *William and Mary Quarterly*, 3d ser., 27 (1970): 36–67.

Maclear, James F. "The Republic and the Millennium." In *The Religion of the Republic*, ed. Elwyn Smith, 183–216. Philadelphia, 1971.

Marsden, George. "The American Revolution: Partisanship, Just Wars and Crusades." In *Wars of America: Christian Views*, ed. Robald A. Wells, 18–24. Grand Rapids, Mich., 1981.

Mead, Sidney. "Christendom, Enlightenment, and the Revolution." In *Religion and the American Revolution*, ed. Jerald Brauer, 30–52. Philadelphia, 1976.

Miller, Perry. "From the Covenant to the Revival." In *The Shaping of American Religion*, ed. James Ward Smith and A. Leland Jamison, 322–68. Princeton, 1961.

———. "Jonathan Edwards's Sociology of the Great Awakening." *New England Quarterly* 21 (1948): 50–77.

Morgan, Edmund. "The Puritan Ethic and the American Revolution." *William and Mary Quarterly*, 3d ser., 24 (1967): 3–43.

Murphey, Murray. "Jonathan Edwards." In *A History of Philosophy in America*, vol. 1, ed. Murray Murphey and Elizabeth Flower, 137–99. New York, 1977.

Niebuhr, H. Richard. "The Idea of the Covenant and American Democracy." In *Puritanism and the American Experience*, ed. Michael McGiffert, 219–25. Reading, Mass., 1969.

Pocock, J.G.A. "Machiavelli, Harrington, and English Political Ideologies in the Eighteenth Century." *William and Mary Quarterly*, 3d ser., 22 (1965): 549–83.

Rice, Howard C., Jr. "Jonathan Edwards at Princeton: With a Survey of Edwards Materials in the Princeton University Library." *Princeton University Library Chronicle* 15 (1953–54): 68–89.

Schafer, Thomas A. "Jonathan Edwards and Justification by Faith." *Church History* 20 (1951): 55–67.

———. "Jonathan Edwards' Conception of the Church." *Church History* 23–24 (1954–55): 51–66.

Spalding, James C. "Restitution as a Normative Factor for Puritan Dissent." *Journal of the American Academy of Religion* 44 (1976): 47–64.

Stein, Stephen J. "Providence and the Apocalypse in the Early Writings of Jonathan Edwards." *Early American Literature* 13 (1978): 250–67.

Stout, Harry S. "Religion, Communications, and the Ideological Origins of the American Revolution." *William and Mary Quarterly,* 3d ser., 34 (1977): 519–41.

Valeri, Mark. "The Economic Thought of Jonathan Edwards." *Church History* 60, no. 1 (1991): 37–54.

Weddle, David L. "The Democracy of Grace: Political Reflections on the Evangelical Theology of Jonathan Edwards." *Dialog: A Journal of Theology* 15 (1976): 248–52.

Westbrook, Robert B. "Social Criticism and the Heavenly City of Jonathan Edwards." *Soundings* 59 (1976): 396–412.

Dissertations

Valeri, Mark R. "Joseph Bellamy: Conversion, Social Ethics, and Politics in the Thought of an Eighteenth-Century Calvinist." Princeton University, 1985.

Weber, Donald. "The Image of Jonathan Edwards in American Culture." Columbia University, 1978.

Index